RAVE REVIEWS

"The gripping combat memoir of a highly decorated American helicopter pilot's Vietnam service. Accounts of the Vietnam War often relegate the stories of U.S. soldiers to the periphery and concentrate instead on political discourse. This may be understandable in light of the ambivalence with which most Americans viewed the conflict, but it has resulted in a somewhat sterile and Olympian history of the events. Alexander, a helicopter pilot repeatedly decorated for valor in Vietnam, desanitizes discussion about the war by sharing his candid memories of the jungle-carpeted battlefield . . . . A rousing tale, full of sharp details and told in the harsh language of soldiers baptized in fire."
— *Kirkus Reviews*

"Combat-heavy . . . . [Alexander and Sasser] succeed quite well in evoking the Vietnam War from the point of view of a helicopter pilot who served bravely and with distinction."
— *Publishers Weekly*

"The reader shares Alexander's own amazement as the lackadaisical recruit is transformed into a highly skilled and thoroughly professional combat officer . . . . An honest and exciting narrative of the stress of war." — *Library Journal*

"*Taking Fire* is filled, page by page, chapter upon chapter, with vivid illustrations of combat . . . . He makes us feel like we are flying in the seat next to him. He takes us with him on some of his most dangerous missions. Whether he's flying combat missions, lying in his bunk, or drinking beer with his crew, our hero is quick to offer his opinions on the war and share his emotions with the reader. This is, without a doubt, an honest and sincere account of a chopper pilot's tour of duty in Vietnam. If you like action, you will like this book."
— *The Roanoke Times*
MORE . . .

"With wry humor and gut-knotting, [Alexander] recounts his experiences in one of the fiercest theaters of the war.... One of the best accounts of that war in print .... The writing is taut, terse and rocks like a roller coaster. *Taking Fire* is that rare book that you have to put down once in a while just to catch your breath."

—*The Flint Journal*

TAKING FIRE

THE TRUE STORY OF A DECORATED CHOPPER PILOT

RON ALEXANDER
AND
CHARLES W. SASSER

St. Martin's Paperbacks

TAKING FIRE

Copyright © 2001 Ron Alexander and Charles W. Sasser.

Cover photograph © Photri

All rights reserved. No part of this book may be used or reproduced in any manner whatsoever without written permission except in the case of brief quotations embodied in critical articles or reviews. For information address St. Martin's Press, 175 Fifth Avenue, New York, NY 10010.

Library of Congress Catalog Card Number: 2001019159

ISBN: 0-312-98017-5

Printed in the United States of America

St. Martin's Press hardcover edition / July 2001
St. Martin's Paperbacks edition / April 2002

St. Martin's Paperbacks are published by St. Martin's Press, 175 Fifth Avenue, New York, NY 10010.

10 9 8 7 6 5 4 3 2 1

This book is dedicated to my wife, Sandy, who lived through much of this with me, and to my daughters, April and Angela.

— RON ALEXANDER

And to Commander Roy Boehm, U.S. Navy SEALs (retired), and to Sergeant Major Galen Kittleson, U.S. Army Special Forces (retired), heroes and friends.

— CHARLES W. SASSER

AUTHOR'S NOTE

This is a personal narrative of the helicopter war in Vietnam.* Actual names are used throughout this book except in those instances where names could not be recalled or where public identification would serve no useful purpose. Dialogue and scenes have by necessity been re-created in various instances. Where those occur, we have tried to match personalities with the situation and action while maintaining factual content. The recounting of some events may not correspond precisely with the memories of all individuals. Much time has passed since the events in this book occurred. Time has a tendency to erode memory in some areas and selectively enhance it in others. Where errors in recollection occur, the authors accept full responsibility and ask to be forgiven.

The authors apologize to anyone who has been omitted, neglected, or slighted in the preparation of this book. While some interpretational mistakes are bound to have occurred, we are certain that the content of this book is true to the spirit and the reality of the pilots and aircrews who served in the Vietnam War with the Air Cavalry. To that end, we are confident that we have neglected no one.

Captain Ron Alexander was one of the most highly decorated helicopter pilots of the Vietnam War. Among his awards are two Distinguished Flying Crosses; Bronze Star with "V" device for valor and one oak leaf cluster; Army Commendation Medal with "V" device and two oak leaf clusters; and twenty-six Air Medals, each with a "V" for valor.

PROLOGUE

Firefights, I was always surprised to discover, were silent if you flew a helicopter. What you had instead were vibrations and deafening noise. You only heard the bullets when they struck the bird—a *tick!* sound—and you never heard them if they hit *you* inside the bird. I tried not to think about all that. The night snapped and cracked with rifle and machine gun fire. Green tracers streaked silently past as I tapped the Huey's skids on the black forest's leafy roof. Clouds of leaves and small branches blown about by rotor downwash rattled against the ship's belly.

Radios were going ape shit. Three separate channels and they were all going ape shit.

"You got to get us outa here, Mini-Man! *Fuckin' gooks are all over us!"*

Nothing like getting shot at to make you sound like someone was yanking up on your shorts. You got shot at, you got excited. Those were the game rules.

I triggered the radio switch on the cyclic stick between my legs. Trying to sound calm, to get through to our five guys down there in the trees. It required cooperation and concentration—and luck—from everybody if we hoped to jerk their asses out of there before the bad guys overran them.

"Four-One?" I snapped into my helmet mike. "Awright, listen up. I gotta find out exactly where you are down there, understand? I'm down on top of the trees. Gimme a long count and I'll home in on you. Roger that?"

"Roger, Mini-Man. *You're gonna have to hurry, man!"*

"How far away are they, Four-One?"

"I smell fish on their breath. I smell their armpits . . ."

"Okay, start the long count . . ."

Immediately: *"One . . . two . . . three . . . four . . ."*

Chief Warrant Stockton, my copilot in the right seat, kept

an eye on the RDF gauge. When the two bars met, it meant the radio transmission was directly below. He looked stiff and tense in the faint red glow from the instrument panel. He looked like a giant insect, with his helmet and face bubble reflecting back the instruments like burning eyes. His hands rested lightly on his controls, in case one of us got it and the other had to take over.

"Seven . . . eight . . . nine . . ."

A helicopter was not like a truck. It was never designed for close-in maneuvers, but we did whatever we had to do to get our guys out. They would have done the same for us.

I looked out over the black ledge of the instrument panel or peered intently down through the chin bubble at my feet where foliage swirled dimly violent in the glow of my position lights. I floated the Huey slowly forward, concentrating. Feet on pedals, left hand squeezing the collective and throttle, right on the cyclic. Steady . . . steady . . . One fuckup and the chopper became a jungle weed eater.

Inside on the cargo deck, my gunner and crew chief, O'Brien and Renko, each took an open doorway and dropped down on his belly to act as observer, helmeted head stuck out into the darkness. Monkey lines led off their bodies like umbilical cords and secured them to the chopper's womb.

Tracers dueled below us in the trees. Green for the North Vietnamese, red for the Americans. Darting back and forth, crisscrossing and leaping about in the night like a bunch of psychedelic supersonic fireflies gone bugfuck. Swarms of the green erupted from off the forward right flank, overwhelming the responding red.

Sweat rolled from underneath my helmet and streamed down my face. I sweated all the way to my crotch. I couldn't tell if it was sweat or if I had pissed my pants. My bone joints felt fused together. Whereas most pilots flew with their heels braced against the floor, I was too short. I had to fly with my legs stuck straight out. Same for my arms, which were likewise too short. It had always been a handicap not to be able to steady my elbows on my thighs. Other pilots ribbed me about looking like a little kid trying to reach the pedals to drive his dad's Chevy. Lieutenant Ron Alexander, call sign *Mini-Man*. Shortest helicopter pilot in Vietnam and the U.S. Army. A quarter-inch *shorter* than regs allowed. And getting too short in Vietnam for this shit.

The two bars on the RDF met. I hovered.

"Four-One?" I said into my keyed mike. "I'm directly above. Can you see me?"

"*Negative. I can hear you, but I can't see you. They're getting closer,* Mini-Man."

Rifle fire snapped and chattered through his mike.

"Stand by," I directed, then switched to VHF to talk to the Cobra gunships.

"Apache Red, can you see me?" I asked the Cobra leader.

"*Affirmative,* Mini-Man."

"Look to my right. Almost all the tracers are coming from one side. You should be able to see the flashes. Can you keep their heads down while I get these guys out?"

"*Roger Roger. We're coming hot,* Mini-Man."

The two Snakes rolled into racetrack mode, one behind the other. Their miniguns sparkled and laid streams of red eating into the trees as they immediately dived to the attack. They bounced in, bounced out. Their running lights blinked and smeared across the stars as they rose swiftly on their track and came back for a second pass.

At the same time, the bad guys started homing in on me. They probably couldn't see me through the foliage, but that didn't keep them from reconning by fire. Tracer bullets were much brighter at night. Especially when they came close. Greenish-white balls of fire, each appearing about the size of a basketball, rushed up out of the darkness of the forest and past the helicopter like a string of UFOs in a hurry. Quiet, relentless, almost pretty. First a short string of them, then a larger burst leapt up from the dark. They glowed bigger and looked closer than during the day. Just being in the same sky with them was enough to make you nervous.

I instructed my crew chief, O'Brien, to drop the McGuire rigs, lines 110 feet long with harnesses on the ends to which men strapped themselves preparatory to being yanked up through the jungle canopy and spirited away across the sky.

"Four-One, the lines are down," I reported to the ground patrol leader. "Get on."

"We can't!" The voice was strident, accusing, desperate, threatening, and terror-stricken. All at the same time. *"They're too short! The ropes are about ten feet above us. You gotta get lower!"*

Lower? How? I already had the chopper nesting in leaves and limbs. Frantic thoughts raced through my mind. Options, Plan B . . .

There was only one way. One chance. Maybe . . .

"I'm coming down and under the trees," I radioed. "Throw a trip flare out in front of me so I can see."

"Mini-Man, *that'll pinpoint our location!"*

"You have to give me some light if you want me to get your butts out of there. I have to be able to see my rotor tip path plane."

Radio traffic went into momentary seizure as the impact of what I proposed struck home. A prayerful, *"Jesus,* Mini-Man!" over the air broke the hush.

If I intended to risk flying a helicopter into jungle, where choppers were never meant to fly, the least the LRRPs could do was light the way. Below, a flare suddenly went off like an exploding miniature sun, illuminating in black silhouette a latticework of tree branches all being whipped violently about, clawing and rattling at the Huey's metal underside.

"Be ready!" I said. "I'm coming down!"

1

The way I ended up in Vietnam as a helicopter pilot was by looking for a way *out* of Vietnam. I was a smartass kid a little brighter and a little more cunning than the average turkey off the turnip wagon. At least that was how I figured it. My old granny always said when you weighed 125 pounds soaking wet with a squirrel in your pocket and stood all of five-three and three-quarters, it wasn't brawn that put you on top of the ant hill. Brains was the only thing that kept you from going around armpit high to the rest of the world.

Actually, I might not have been that bright after all. It was my idea to join the U.S. Army in the first place.

"Tell you what," I said to my high school buddy, Randy Huntzberry.

"What?" Randy said, biting.

"Let's join the army."

"I thought you were brighter than that, Ronnie Alexander."

Randy and I had graduated from South Hagerstown High, Hagerstown, Maryland, in the spring of 1963 and started at a local junior college that fall. After the first semester, we were both eager to get out of Maryland and see how the other parts of the world lived. We might not have been so anxious if we had listened to the low and steady storm rumble of Vietnam over the horizon. But when you were eighteen years old, you never listened anyhow. The dark clouds had not yet appeared. Besides, I couldn't have picked Vietnam out on the map if it were the *only* country on the map. For all I knew, Vietnam was a town in Texas or New Mexico.

"Hey," I said to Randy, sensing his hesitation, "joining the army is better than hanging around this one-horse burg and watching them roll up the street every night."

It took him a few days to make up his mind. "Let's do it," he finally agreed.

"We're *out* of here, partner."

We trotted down to the local induction center and enlisted on the buddy plan as ground-pounding infantry soldiers. E-1 grunts—first pay grade enlisted, earning about seventy-something dollars a month. By the time we were halfway through boot camp, I had already decided double-timing in the rain and sun, digging foxholes, and getting smelly in the woods was for suckers. I looked around for a way out.

"Randy, let's volunteer for the airborne," I suggested.

"What?"

"At least we *fly* to wherever we're going instead of having to walk," I argued.

"But we have to *parachute!*"

We both volunteered for airborne training after basic training. Turned out Randy was colorblind. Couldn't tell his reds from his greens. Airborne rejected him. I ended up alone in front of the gate at Fort Benning, Georgia. THROUGH THESE PORTALS PASS THE FINEST AIRBORNE SOLDIERS IN THE WORLD. A column of sweating troops jogged by chanting a Jodie call.

> *"Two old ladies lying in bed;*
> *One looks over to the other and said:*
> *'I wanna be an Airborne Ranger,*
> *I wanna live a life of danger . . .*
> *Airborne! Airborne! All the way!"*

It began to seem the more I tried to get *out* of things, the deeper I got *in*.

Soldiers called summertime Fort Benning "The Frying Pan." Appropriately. Damn, it was hot. Black Hats—parachute instructors—ran us through outdoor sprinklers six or seven times a day, clothes and all, to keep us cooled off. In between showers, it was balls to the wall starting at five A.M. every day. *Double time! Hut!* Don't let a Black Hat catch you *walking* anywhere, anytime.

"What are you *doing,* Leg?" *Leg,* spoken contemptuously, meant non–airborne personnel. "Get down, Leg! Drop! Drop! Give me fifty!"

"Yes, Sergeant!" Bellowing it out.

"Are you stupid? Don't you know my first name? It's *Airborne*! Got that, Leg?"

"Airborne Sergeant! All the way!"

Assholes and elbows in the front leaning rest position. My company's Black Hats were "Smoky" Jackson, so dubbed because he brought down smoke on everybody, indiscriminately, and "Drop-Drop" Estelle. It was obvious where he got his name.

"Drop, Leg! Drop! Drop! Give me fifty push-ups."

Drop-Drop was one of the original Rangers and a Korean combat vet. He wore the scrolled Ranger patch on his left shoulder rather than the new Ranger tab. We held the guy in total awe. He had been there, done that, collected the medals. In Korea, the bones in his left forearm had been shattered by a bullet and replaced with steel. When he scowled down at me in formation, I felt like a Shetland pony confronted by a Budweiser Clydesdale.

"This ain't kindergarten. How old *are* you, Leg?"

"Nineteen, Airborne Sergeant."

"Huh! Jesus, they get younger and smaller every year. We'll have to strap a ton of lead to your ass to get you to fall out of the sky."

"Airborne Sergeant! All the way!"

When it came time for our first parachute jump, we were more scared of Drop-Drop than we were of the jump. Better to bail out and crash on the drop zone than to turn chickenshit and face the man mountain's contempt. Because everything was done according to the alphabetical order of our last names, *Alexander* was one of the first jumpers in the stick. Adrenaline pumped through my veins like water through a fire hose.

We shuffled belly button to asshole out the open door of the C-119 Flying Boxcar, stamping our boots and shouting to build up courage. Out that terrible door into nothingness. The roar of slipstream in my ears. The "positive opening" of the T-10 parachute that turned baritones into tenors if the harness wasn't tight enough.

As expected, I was the last man out of the air although I had been one of the first into the air. I hung suspended in a thermal and watched in exasperation as heavier jumpers passed me and landed on the DZ, their 'chutes collapsing. They formed in ranks and looked up at me with amusement. Drop-Drop stomped back and forth. He pointed his finger up at me and shouted in make-believe rage.

"Get down here, Alexander! Do you hear me, trooper? Get your bantam-ass down here right now!"

That was the first time he called me *trooper* instead of *Leg*. He grinned when I finally did my PLF on the ground and trotted up. I was now a member of the elite airborne forces. I had leaped—*fell*—out of a perfectly good airplane and lived to bullshit about it.

We graduated after making four more jumps that same weekend. Drop-Drop and Smoky pounded blood-wings into our puffed-out chests.

"I've been dropping you guys for three weeks," Drop-Drop said. "It's your turn to drop me."

"Awright!" somebody shouted. "Drop! Drop! Give me fifty!"

"Which hand?"

"Your left." The arm with the steel in it.

He did fifty push-ups so fast he was a blur. Then he bounced and switched hands and did another fifty with his right hand.

2

Arrival of the U.S. escort carrier *Card* in Saigon had received little fanfare. A war was on, and America was in it—but only in a small way. So far, the only role the U.S. military played was in advising and training the Army of the Republic of Vietnam (ARVN) in its struggle against Communist insurgents from North Vietnam. After the defeat of the French at Dien Bien Phu in 1954, the country had been divided by treaty along the seventeenth parallel into two separate nations: the Communist People's Republic of North Vietnam, with its capital at Hanoi, and the Republic of South Vietnam, a democracy with its capital at Saigon. Wily old Ho Chi Minh vowed not to rest until Vietnam became a single nation ruled under communism. His National Liberation Front (NLF), whose guerrillas became known as Viet Cong, began infiltrating South Vietnam to foment its overthrow.

The appearance of the *Card* in Saigon that December morning heralded a significant reshaping of America's low profile in Indochina. Strapped to the carrier's deck were thirty-two U.S. Army CH-1 Shawnee helicopters—big, dual-rotor craft well suited to carrying troops into battle. They would be piloted by Americans, demonstrating a newfound American willingness to aid South Vietnam in combat operations, particularly with aviation support.

In the space of a few years, however, this first modest inclination would explode into an enormous national commitment that would bring about nine million U.S. soldiers to this tropical land and claim 58,000 American lives. It would be a war unlike any other ever fought by the United States, lacking conventional battle lines and waged mostly by small actions against an elusive enemy. At times, it would encompass an almost phan-

tasmagoric fluidity, characterized by rapid shifting of men and
weapons across sodden lowlands, jungle-clad mountains, and
lush valleys, insertions and extractions of troops in response to
a jack-in-the-box enemy. The prime agent of all that movement
would be rotary-wing aircraft, helicopters, the first of which
clung to the deck of the *Card*.

Vietnam would become known as the Helicopter War, a concept of *airmobility* that was just taking shape in 1961. Some
military planners saw the helicopter as catalyzing a revolution;
others believed these relatively slow-flying aircraft would fare
poorly in the rigors of war. The fighting in Vietnam would be
the acid test.

3

I drew orders out of parachute school to the 82d Airborne Division at Fort Bragg, North Carolina. Clerks checked my GT aptitude scores. You had to have a minimum GT of 115 to become a parachute rigger while 110 got you into Officer Candidate School. Riggers had to be smarter than officers. My GT was 122.

"Alexander, Ronald? You want to go to rigger school and learn how to pack parachutes?"

I hesitated. "What are my options?"

The clerk shrugged. It was no hair off his balls either way. "You can stay with the company and walk in the woods, mud and rain and eat C-rats. Or you can be a parachute rigger and work normal hours in an air-conditioned building. You get a chow break and two coffee breaks a day. Come four o'clock, you're off-duty."

What a deal. Sign me up. I had this man's army dicked.

By the time I returned to the 82d as an honor graduate rigger, the rumble and black clouds of Vietnam on the horizon were drawing nearer. LBJ had not yet sent combat troops, but a lot of rumors were floating around. Since the 82d was a reaction force, trained to drop our socks, grab our cocks and be ready to *go* when the balloon went up, we expected to be the first on line. By April 1965 I could at least pick out Vietnam on the map.

The 82d was *always* on alert. You were either IRF or RRF. The IRF, Immediate Reaction Force, had to be ready to go immediately, your shit already packed in one rucksack. The RRF, Ready Reaction Force, had two or three days to get ready. On a warm spring evening in April, a bunch of the guys and I were hanging around the barracks bullshitting in our skivvies just before taps and lights out. We were on IRF and confined to quarters. The NCO on duty at HQ burst in like somebody had stuck a rocket up his butt.

"This is an alert!" he shouted. "This ain't no drill!"

War? We were going to *war*? Where were we going to war *at*?

"How the hell should I know?" the NCO snapped.

"Vietnam? Is it Vietnam?"

"All I know is this is the *real thing*. Grab your cocks and socks and draw your M16s. Transportation is waiting outside. Double time, troopers!"

Nothing like a little *This is the real thing!* to poke a stick down your anthill.

In the event of an action, parachute riggers bailed out with the assault force to recover 'chutes and equipment. Ten IRF riggers with Staff Sergeant Johnston in charge drew our M16 rifles and were helmeted, rucked-up and climbing into the back of a truck within a few minutes. Although it was near the middle of the night, Smoke Bomb Hill at Fort Bragg blazed with enough energy, electrical and otherwise, to power the entire state of North Carolina. Soldiers and vehicles filled with soldiers rushed madly about. Trucks loaded with artillery, ammunition, and other supplies rumbled toward Pope Airfield, the martialing area. A single question rocketed back and forth. It became a standard inquiry. *Where are we going?*

Damn. I didn't know war happened *this* fast. But, damn, wasn't it exciting for a nineteen-year-old American boy to be part of something like this? Getting out of it never even occurred to me. I wanted *in*.

The airfield was lit up from one end to the other. C-130 Hercules aircraft parked noses to tails lined the ramps, APUs already hooked up to them and ready to start cranking their engines. Pallets laden with materiel formed mazes, down which blunt-nosed forklifts scurried like cockroaches, moving stuff here and there and poking other stuff up the open rear ramps of the C-130s.

If you were nothing but a lowly grunt, one of the privates, you never saw the Big Picture of what was going on. You simply followed orders. Go there, do this, get that. . . . You bitched about it, naturally, because as an enlisted man you doubted the colonels and generals knew what they were doing. You still did what you were ordered to do. That this was *the real thing* took some of the edge off the chickenshit. That it *was* the real thing became even more clear when trucks drove up and issued parachutes and live ammo and grenades. It was a little sobering, what with the initial excitement wearing off.

"What do you think, Shorty?" a buddy asked.

"I think we're gonna win combat jump wings."

"It can't be Vietnam. They wouldn't be issuing us ammo and parachutes now. Maybe it's a race riot."

"They wouldn't send out a whole brigade for a riot."

Sergeants with their jaws stuck out and their shoulders hunched stalked around shouting, like they were afraid of being shouted at by officers unless they shouted at us first.

"Okay, people. Get a move on. Draw your 'chutes and gear. Goddamnit, people. This ain't no fucking tea party, ladies. Get your asses moving. Formation in front of the big hangar in ten minutes."

Somehow, even though the colonels and generals didn't know what they were doing, the entire brigade formed up in battalions and companies on the ramp in front of the hangar. Every swinging dick was helmeted and rucked and loaded down with weapons and ammo and parachutes still in kit bags. Everyone went silent. Silent and so tense you couldn't have driven a hat pin up an asshole with a sledgehammer.

The brigade commander climbed up on a forklift to address the troops. The scuffing of his boots echoed against the front of the hangar. Floodlights behind chased his shadow across the formation. Out on the ramps, APUs shot juice to the C-130s. Props started to turn.

"Men," roared the commander in his best leader's voice, "our destination is Santo Domingo in the Dominican Republic—"

"Where the hell is Santo Domingo?" the trooper next to me whispered.

"Weren't you listening?" I shot back. "It's in the Dominican Republic."

"At ease!" sergeants yelled to quell the muttering in ranks. "At ease!"

The commander stared directly at us as he continued.

"Rebel forces supported by Communists have captured strongholds in the city and are attempting to overthrow the duly constituted government. The Eighty-second Airborne, the All American Division, is tasked with taking them out of there—and, men, that's what we're going to do. We start right now. We're skying-up immediately. You can rig parachutes en route. We will combat jump onto the Santo Domingo Airport, which we believe is being held by rebels. You'll receive your briefings and combat orders from your subordinate leaders. Okay, men. We have a job to do. *Let's go do it . . . !*"

4

Troopers packed into the C-130s like fish from a cannery. Four long rows of us in each aircraft, two on each side of the airplane facing each other, so close together that our knees banged. Roar of engines and aircraft vibration made talking difficult. Some of the guys soon nodded off with chins bouncing on the tops of their reserve 'chutes. Others, withdrawn and reflective, stared down between their boots. Glances flitted around like ricochets, eyes refusing to meet for fear of revealing the creepy little worms crawling around inside our intestines. You couldn't let your buddies see that you were afraid.

If I twisted around in the web seating, jostling awake the soldier napping on either side of me, I managed to look out the airplane's round porthole behind me. It was dark out. All e the stars and a sliver of moon and the ocean below with a moon streak leading away across it into infinity. My mouth felt dry and I couldn't sleep, but I wouldn't admit it was because I was afraid. I pictured myself strutting around at the NCO club wearing a combat jump star on my silver parachute wings. I was still a teenager; I turned twenty at the end of the month. At that age, you were immortal, invincible, and stupid.

From what I recalled from high school geography refreshed by talk among the troops as we on-loaded the planes, the Dominican Republic was a big island half of which was Haiti. When daybreak filtered weak and watery through the C-130's small portholes, I twisted in my seat to see if I could see it yet. The sea still stretched away unmarred by land. It was a beautiful cobalt color made translucent in reflection of a cloudless sky. Other dark-green C-130s flew in formation off our flank. I wondered how many aircraft there were in our flight, and how many flights there were. It was an impressive sight when the 82d Airborne and America went to war.

Word came down. "Make sure your weapons are loaded. Keep them on *Safe* until you hit the DZ."

The DZ, we had been told after donning parachutes by squads inside the aircraft, was a large cane field next to the airport. I felt for the magazine in the M16 secured butt up over my left shoulder and fingered the selector switch for the *Safe* position. I readjusted my reserve 'chute pack. Because of my small size, it covered most of my chest. It occurred to me unexpectedly that a combat jump was conducted from eight hundred feet AGL. Why were we issued reserves then? Even if your main malfunctioned, you didn't have time to activate a reserve before you creamed in.

Maybe the reserve was just to make us feel better.

Another thought occurred to me. What if they started shooting at us while we were still in the air? The Nazis had done it in World War II. I glanced at the guy across from me. His eyes were round and very wide. Maybe he was thinking the same thing.

"Thirty minutes!" came the word. I looked out the window, but still saw no land.

I was sweating. Judging by the odor, we were all sweating. I told myself I would feel better after the jump doors opened and we got some fresh Caribbean air.

Watch out, commies. The mighty Airborne is gonna kick some ass.

Sergeants started pumping us up for it, shouting and slapping our helmets. We stamped our feet and bobbed in our seats. We fisted each other on the shoulders and grinned to show that, hey, the AA, the *All Americans,* feared no fuckin' commies. I would have to call on ol' Drop-Drop Estelle and show him my medals when we got back.

Just when we were *really* pumped up, more word came back. The aircraft crew chief passed it on to the jumpmaster first. He frowned and climbed up on the webbing above the troops so he could shout and be heard above the engine noise.

"The jump is scrubbed," he bawled out. "The Marines have landed and secured the airfield. We'll be air-landing."

Although we naturally felt obligated to boo the Marines, I saw more relief than disappointment in the faces around me. I felt actually let down, however. I had really been counting on that combat star for my wings.

"Take off your 'chutes and stack 'em. It'll be a hot landing. Get off the airplane as fast as you can get down the ramp when we land. The plane will be taking off again immediately."

I had been looking out the window all the way for a first sighting of the Dominican Republic. I was never to see it from the air. As we bled off altitude on the final approach to the airport at Santo Domingo, the crew chief suddenly bellowed, "Get down! Everybody get down on the deck! We're taking fire!"

Paratroopers tumbled to the floor like a bunch of startled puppies. The belly of a C-130 was armor-plated whereas the sides were only thin metal. I discovered myself crushed against the cool metal floor underneath other bodies. I could hardly breathe.

I heard what sounded like dull thuds striking the airplane. Something like isolated hail stones thumping the roof of your Ford Fairlane. I later learned we took sixteen hits from a .30-cal machine gun on our way in. Rebel snipers hiding in the swamps around the airport's approach shot at everything that flew by. That was the first time it occurred to me that, in an aircraft, the only thing you heard of gunfire was when the bullets hit.

C-130s set down with screaming of rubber on asphalt. They slowed but never fully stopped. Ramps lowered and troopers spilled out onto the tarmac. I scrambled for cover. Everything was brought to a halt when someone shouted in surprise, *"What the fuck, over?"*

A U.S. Air Force tech sergeant stood at the edge of the runway with his arms crossed, laughing at us. Other Air Force guys and some Marines walked casually about in the morning sunshine, for all the world like guys back in garrison out for a Sunday morning stroll. Some of them had coffee cups hooked on their fingers.

"Glad you fellas could make it," the tech sergeant jeered. "Come on in. Have some coffee, courtesy of the U.S. Air Force and the U.S. Marines."

5

Ironic, I thought later, considering the way things turned out, how it was in an aircraft that I received my baptism under fire. So it was only a few rounds and they weren't exactly aimed at *me*. But even one bullet coming anywhere near you in the air was enough to get you court-martialed for destroying government property by putting skid marks in your skivvies. It wasn't like you could jump in a hole or hide behind a rock. Up there, you were *exposed*.

The Dominican Republic wasn't much of a war, as wars go. A few of our guys got hit, but the only people I knew to get killed were rebels. The division commander, General Palmer, issued a directive that the 82d would search and secure three square blocks a day from the rebels in the city. When GIs took twelve square blocks one day, he made them give back nine of them. I suppose orders were orders and fair was fair.

"I'd go anyplace with the Eighty-second," he reportedly exhorted. "They're born killers."

My duties as rigger were almost nil. What there were kept me largely confined to the airport at first. Occasionally, I heard gunfire banging in the city as paratroopers flushed bad guys out of hiding, but nobody was shooting at me. It was a good war, as Bill Mauldin, the World War II cartoonist, said through his characters Willie and Joe, as long as nobody was shooting at you. I was bored. If this was war, then it was highly overrated as an activity.

Later, when most of the fighting moved to the southeast quadrant of the city, we riggers were appointed as guards to the labor buses. Each morning a bus drove the twenty miles from the airport to downtown Santo Domingo to pick up indigenous civilian laborers to do the menial work of the 82d's buildup of supplies and forces. They dug holes, unloaded aircraft, moved boxes, cooked. . . .They were returned downtown by the same bus at the end of the workday.

Three guards were assigned to the bus for each trip. One soldier rode on the roof while the other two took front and back inside. The bus was a rickety "chicken bus" painted in fading psychedelic colors with a plastic Jesus on the dash, a crucifix hanging from the rearview mirror and a portable radio blaring Spanish music. The buses were never shot at when they were loaded, but they became prime targets on the trip into town in the morning and the trip back to the base in the evening. The driver, a local, floored the gas pedal and the vehicle careened and screamed and knocked and complained at full speed along the macadam road through the countryside between the airport and the city.

None of us rigger guards were combat vets. We didn't know to look for muzzle flashes. When the bus took a sniper hit, that was how we knew the direction of the shooter. We opened up on bushes and trees with full automatic, returning two hundred rounds for every eight or ten we received. The driver scrunched down behind the wheel and just kept going hell-for-breakfast while we guards rocked 'n' rolled with our M16s. It was good sport since none of us was ever hit and we never knew if we hit them or not.

One afternoon we had just dropped off the laborers downtown when a .50-caliber machine gun opened up from a nearby intersection on a sandbagged GI emplacement. A sniper with the .50 was hiding in a top floor of the building diagonally across the intersection and pinging at our guys. The other two guards and I maneuvered into a safe position to watch the action. We saw our GIs returning fire, but couldn't see the sniper's position because of the angle of the street.

A troop driving a quarter-ton jeep with a mounted 106mm recoilless rifle came roaring up the street in response to a radio request. He talked to the sergeant at the emplacement, who pointed and gestured and informed him of the situation. Then he cranked down the barrel of his gun to about the right level, turned the jeep backward and snaked around the corner into the intersection behind the sandbags, gun already pointed.

He shot off a spotter round, followed immediately by the *Bang! Whoosh!* and *Crump!* of a high-explosive shell that wiped out the entire corner of the building in which the sniper was concealed.

All of us cheered mightily.

Santo Domingo was my introduction to war, a rather sanitized version of it. None of my buddies was wiped out or mangled. I saw no blood and guts and eyeballs. Mostly, for me, it was just hanging out for about six months. I received my overseas ribbon and returned to Fort Bragg and garrison duty where a couple of older hands showed me the ropes on how to get out of KP and guard mount. There was always a way out if you looked for it.

I bought a special helmet liner and new poncho, pistol belt, and ammo pouches. I put aside one uniform on which I measured every single patch according to regulations. I kept it starched so stiff it would stand on its own. My jump boots were so spit-shined you could see to shave in their reflection. I was one short little *strac* trooper.

I made battalion Soldier of the Month, which carried an automatic promotion from private E-3 to specialist fourth class, or Spec 4. Two months later, I made battalion Soldier of the Year. That gave me E-5 buck sergeant rank. I went from E-3 to E-5 in two months. No more KP, no more guard mount. A different world opened up once I became an NCO. It wasn't bad bucks for a single guy, and being a rigger on an eight-to-five work schedule wasn't bad duty. I thought about reenlisting for my E-6 stripe and a big re-up bonus.

By this time, of course, Vietnam was becoming a consideration. I even knew where to find it on the map. Guys were filtering back from tours there and telling their "no shit, there I was" stories. LBJ had sent in 3,500 Marines in March 1965, followed by the 173d Airborne Division, the 101st Airborne, and the 1st Air Cavalry. The "big build-up" of U.S. forces in

Vietnam was on. On December 31, 1965, there were 184,300
U.S. servicemen in-country; that figure rose to 385,300 twelve
months later. It was a real war this time, no Santo Domingo
with a few rounds popped into the belly of a C-130 or the sides
of an old laborers' bus.

I figured the odds. I had watched all these young second
lieutenants running around giving orders. Most of them, in my
opinion, were dumber than dirt. I was as smart as they were,
probably smarter. I could do what they did. I could be an officer
and a gentleman by act of Congress.

The way I figured it, Officer Candidate School and branch
training would eat up almost a year. The war should be over
by the time I finished training and received my commission.
There I'd be—a first lieutenant, an officer and a gentleman
drawing the big bucks, hanging out at some posh stateside post
chasing skirts and sipping suds at the O Club. Talk about
having it made.

I reenlisted for six years, received my bonus, bought a new
car, went home on leave to Maryland and applied for OCS
when I got back to Bragg. There were only a couple of things
I hadn't figured on. One was a blonde. The other was how
long this war was really going to last in Vietnam.

6

Senator Mike Monroney of Oklahoma spoke for a sizeable faction of the military in viewing the helicopter as too complex and too vulnerable to rate a major role in combat, "other than hovering behind the line and doing a fine job of directing artillery fire or other jobs that could be done with a Piper Cub . . . I get kind of nervous when I read of a UN helicopter over Africa being shot down by a bow and arrow."

General James Gavin disagreed. Gavin had commanded the 82d Airborne Division during World War II and served in the Pentagon as army chief of operations afterward. In several articles he published on helicopter mobility, he suggested that the low-level airspace over a presumed combat zone was the very place for helicopters. They could operate well forward of friendly lines to identify and pinpoint targets for artillery and air strikes, airlift troops quickly to key defensive points and provide logistical support. He cited the potency of the cavalry of Alexander the Great, Roman legions marching along the strategic roads of the empire, and the German blitzkrieg in World War II—all strikingly innovative blends of force and mobility. He believed helicopters held similar promise.

The Soviets were already experimenting with helicopters and had been for some time. On June 24, 1956, during a celebration of Soviet Air Force Day at Tushimo Airport, a horde of low-flying helicopters burst into view and disgorged an assault force of troops, vehicles, and support weapons. While the troops carried out a mock attack, the helicopters roared away, then returned in waves carrying additional vehicles, ammunition, and fuel. The Soviets were practicing what General Gavin had been preaching for years.

On April 19, 1962, Secretary of Defense Robert McNamara

sent an important memo to the secretary of the army. Although helicopters had been in Vietnam since the previous December when CH-1 Shawnees were delivered by the escort carrier *Card,* McNamara proposed the formation of a group to study tactical mobility and the further use of helicopters—"new organizational and operational concepts, possibly including completely airmobile infantry, artillery, antitank, and reconnaissance units." He appointed Lieutenant General Hamilton Howze, commander of XVIII Airborne Corps at Fort Bragg, as chairman of what became known as the Howze Board.

Howze's report, submitted four months later, called for a thorough overhaul of the army. The Howze board recommended that a third of the infantry divisions be airmobile. Each such division should replace about half of its 3,000 vehicles— trucks, tanks, self-propelled artillery and so on—with about 330 helicopters. The report spelled out a vision of airmobile operations that included reconnaissance, calling in artillery fire, air assaults in which troops arrived by helicopter to attack the enemy, and aerial supply lines.

"In the air just above the treetops," the Howze report stressed, "lies one of the greatest hopes for victory on the ground."

7

A soldier named Butch Ferguson completed a year's combat tour in Vietnam, then returned to Fort Bragg where he promptly got himself and another kid killed in an auto accident in December 1966. Talk about irony. Butch and I weren't close, but I knew him. The company first sergeant asked me to escort the body home since I was an NCO and known to be *strac*. Sounded like good duty for ten days at fifteen dollars a day per diem extra. All I had to do was catch a commercial flight with the casket to Tulsa, Oklahoma, make sure the body was transported feet first according to protocol, attend the funeral and present the flag off the coffin to the next of kin, which in this case was the mother.

I packed my bag, put on dress greens with scarf and blouse, spit-shined jump boots, and flew to Tulsa. A hearse from Moore's Funeral Home met me at the airport. I rode to the funeral home in the hearse with Butch and stayed in the viewing room with the body as military escort.

About eight o'clock that evening, mother, father, and little sister came in. I snapped to attention like a well-drilled toy soldier and introduced myself with a little canned speech.

"I'm Sergeant Ron Alexander. I accompanied Butch home. If you need any assistance with paperwork or anything else, that's what I'm here for. I'll be here as long as you need me."

I bowed politely and formally. Little sister Sandy was tiny. I doubt if she weighed one hundred pounds dunked and soaked in the Arkansas River. I towered over her by nearly two inches. She was blond and as cute as any guy's baby sister ought to be. Crying for the past two or three days had reddened her eyes and puffed them, making her look even younger. She had little to say when her father invited me to their home for dinner. I was alone in the city and had nowhere else to go except to my motel room.

Dinner at the Fergusons' turned into rather a strained, quiet affair. The house felt heavy with grief. Afterward, her father asked, "Will you ride in the family car with us tomorrow during the funeral? You can be Sandy's escort, since she isn't married."

I blinked while I tried to cover my double-take. What was with these Okies? The little girl couldn't be more than twelve years old, thirteen at the most. Why *would* she be married?

Sandy surprised me even further by offering to drive me back to my motel. She laughed. Apparently, she was used to it.

"I have a driver's license," she said. "Do you want to see it?"

I cleared my throat tactfully. "Uh ... How old do you have to be in Oklahoma to get a license?"

She laughed her amused laugh. "I'm twenty years old," she explained. "I'll bet you're no older than that yourself." Her blue eyes looked me up and down, appraising me. "And you're certainly not much bigger," she added.

I felt my face turn red. Right on both counts. I liked her direct manner, even though it left me slightly nonplussed. I suspected she could tell you off faster than an Oklahoma dust devil could whip through a pile of leaves.

She picked me up again the next morning at the motel in time for the funeral. After the ceremonies, she sprung yet another surprise on me.

"Would you like to ride with me to Okmulgee to pick up my daughter?" she offered. "I'll give you the Blue Ribbon special tour of Tulsa when we get back."

"You have a driver's license *and* a daughter?"

"Her name's April. She's three. She's with her father's folks."

"I didn't think you were married."

"If I were still married, do you think I'd be picking up soldiers?"

She was better at the snappy comeback than I. We were old friends by the time the afternoon was half over. We word-dueled, wise-guyed, and laughed, totally at ease and comfortable with each other. Her baby daughter April was as blond as her mother and every bit as delightful. I found myself thinking, *Why can't they live closer to Bragg?*

"Do you have a girlfriend?" Sandy asked.

"Not so you'd notice. Why?"

"Just asking."

"How about you?"

"I have lots of girlfriends."

We had dinner together and ended up in a redneck bar shooting pool and listening to shit-kicking country music on the jukebox. She had her hair pulled back in a long ponytail and wore jeans, a shirt and sneakers. I noticed how blue her eyes were when she looked me directly in the eye. The girl was completely without pretense or guile, as open and direct as a military regulation. She also shot a mean cue stick.

She ran the table on me a couple of games. We had a beer or two and I started winning.

"You're too drunk to see the balls," I laughingly accused, although neither of us drank much.

"You think so, short stuff?"

"How about a little bet on the next game?"

"What do you have in mind, Minnesota Fats?"

"I don't know. A kiss?"

She stood straight at her end of the table, outside the dim hooded illumination of the light, hands on her girlish hips, pretty head cocked to one side in a challenging manner.

"I'll go you one better," she said.

Was I going to get lucky or what?

"If you beat me," she proposed, throwing it out offhandedly, "you'll have to marry me."

I took it as a joke. "You're on, girl." I laughed.

I beat her. We were married at a justice of the peace in Nowata, Oklahoma, the next day at four P.M., less than seventy-two hours after I met the little blond girl with tear-reddened eyes in a Tulsa funeral parlor.

When I returned to Fort Bragg, I learned that the escort for the other crash victim had gone to a bar, picked a fight and got the shit kicked out of him. I ended up married. The first sergeant exploded. "*Nobody* from this outfit goes out on escort duty again, *ever!*"

In January 1967, I went before the OCS board, passed, and received orders to report to artillery OCS at, of all places, Fort Sill, Oklahoma. I was going to be an artillery officer.

"This is great!" I exhorted. "It's not far from Tulsa."

Sandy was more cautious. We were only married a month. "What about Vietnam?" she worried.

I brushed her fears away with a dismissive gesture. "Don't worry, honey. I can get out of it. By the time I graduate from OCS in five or six months, most people won't even remember where Vietnam is."

8

The U.S. military did things back-asswards. The British army sent out a full major with five or six years' experience in artillery to locate enemy positions and direct accurate fire on them. The American army sent out a second lieutenant so green he could barely read a map and couldn't find his behind with both hands, who had only directed artillery fire five or six times *in practice* and who, consequently, sprayed the whole countryside. Although we officer candidates at Fort Sill were kept mostly in the dark about what was going on in the outside world, busy as we were JARKing up MB-4 Mountain to atone for demerits, marching each other around, standing inspections and practicing our "leadership," we still heard enough to know that the reason for the big buildup in OCS classes was because we were losing so many lieutenants in Vietnam. You had to keep the fodder coming to keep the machine running.

The classes were enough to chill your blood. The different ways men devised to blow up, rip apart, tear asunder, and bring death and destruction on each other. Big bullets, little bullets, shells, grenades, rockets . . . Booby traps, punji stakes, Bouncing Betties, snares, tiger traps . . . Ambushes, search and destroy, recon by fire, body count . . . An entirely new lexicon of war. The phrase "In Vietnam" preceded almost every lesson.

"Now, in Vietnam," TAC instructors began, "if the dinks capture you, you'll be tortured in the most devious ways imaginable outside the fires of hell. . . ."

I shuddered.

"They'll hang you upside down by the tendons in your heels and skin you alive. . . . They'll cut off your dick and stuff it in your throat and let you suffocate on it. . . . They'll dump you in pits of *human shit*. . . ."

Damn. *Damn!*

During E&E, Escape and Evasion training, we found our-

selves dunked gagging into pits full of pig shit, a reasonable
substitute. For somebody like Acree, the tall, skinny redhead
from Tennessee, it wasn't as big a deal as it was for men like
Mike Cohen and me. The level of pig shit only came up to
Acree's chest, which gave him a foot or two of breathing room.
Cohen and I found yet one more drawback in being vertically
challenged. Cohen was an inch shorter than I and had to tiptoe
to keep his mouth and nose out of deep shit. I didn't have to
tiptoe, but the fragrance was still right there at chin level.

"Now I understand why good Jewish boys don't eat pork,"
Cohen said.

"At least it's *pig* shit and not from the enlisted barracks," I
rationalized. "I wonder when they start hanging us up by our
heels and cutting off our dicks."

"Don't tempt them."

It became increasingly apparent that the war wasn't about to
end as quickly as I initially anticipated. Quite the opposite; the
war was escalating. It also became apparent that we officer
candidates were being groomed to have our butts packed off
to Vietnam as soon as we graduated OCS. The thought was
enough to give you nightmares. All these green second lieutenants with maps stuck out in the jungle to direct artillery fire.

"I heard directly from the clerk in the commandant's office,"
Candidate Oldham relayed with all the authority the source
demanded, "that every swinging dick in the class ahead of us
was shipped over—and that the same thing is going to happen
to us. Alexander, I hope you like rice and slanted pussy."

By this time the war was regular TV dinner fare: *Six U.S.
Marines died today in a firefight near Cu Chi, Vietnam. . . . And,
oh, by the way, would you please pass the scalloped potatoes?* Campus protesters were already learning how to chant, "Ho, Ho,
Ho. Ho Chi Minh is going to win!"

Even Sandy, who knew little about the military and assumed
on faith that I knew what I was doing, grew a bit anxious. I
only got to see her on the weekends and then for only a few
minutes at a time on the parking apron. Discipline required

that I stand stiffly at parade rest and not touch her while we talked. I lost even the privilege of seeing her if we touched.

"Are you going to Vietnam?" she asked in her direct, no-nonsense manner.

I brushed it off. "Leave it to me. I'm working on not going."

"You'd better not go, you little short shit. I love you and don't want to lose you."

Marriage presented me with an entirely different outlook on going to war. Santo Domingo had been an adventure; I looked upon Vietnam as an intrusion. It occurred to me that there was one sure way to make war obsolete. All you had to do was pass a law that required all young men to get married and stay home to work.

If nothing else, I learned one thing as an enlisted man: There was always a way out if you wanted out. An old officers' saying went something like, "The enlisted are deceitful and cunning and not to be trusted." I was still an enlisted man until I graduated from OCS.

I commandeered every ounce of deceit and cunning I possessed trying to honorably avoid going to Vietnam, but things weren't looking good. I could almost see myself all alone with a map in a foreign and exotic place where little bitty guys like myself tried to kill me. It wasn't until I reached Happy Battery, however, which was the last week of OCS before graduation, that an out unexpectedly presented itself. From out of the blue, so to speak. TAC officers showed up one afternoon.

"The army needs helicopter pilots," they announced. Apparently more than it needed artillery forward observers. I also thought most chopper pilots were warrant officers. "The army needs commissioned pilots to command units as well as to fly. If you want to go to flight school, raise your hand."

I did some quick math in my head. Say I hung around a couple of months waiting for flight school, then pissed off another nine months learning to fly. That was almost a year. Vietnam would surely be over by then.

Otherwise, I was out of here in a couple of weeks with my

ticket punched *Destination Vietnam.* Just me and an RTO—radioman—alone out there in the middle of the jungle calling in fire missions. You could get shot! Or snakebit! Even on the long shot that the war lasted longer than expected, I had much rather go over as a helicopter pilot up above the jungle than an FO—forward observer—for artillery *inside* the jungle.

My hand shot up.

9

About twenty volunteers from my company showed up at the flight surgeon's office for acceptance physicals. We lined up in alphabetical order according to last names. Acree ... Alexander ... Cohen ... Acree on my one side was six-feet-two while Cohen on the other was five-two. Acree's height served to further diminish Cohen's and my stature and call attention to it. Minimum required height for acceptance was five-four. No waivers. No exceptions. Acree slouched against the wall, waiting. Cohen and I, looking like a pair of scrawny plucked bantam roosters in our skivvies, stood as tall as possible.

A Spec5 medic strolled out with a clipboard and looked us over. I stretched my spine. Cohen quivered from the strain of tiptoeing while trying to hide it.

"How tall are you?" the medic asked, directing the question at both of us.

"Five-four!" we responded in eager unison.

One or both of us were obviously lying. Both couldn't be five-four. I was an inch and three-quarters taller than Cohen.

"You two come with me," the medic snapped.

He led us directly to the height chart on the wall—and flunked both of us on the spot. My face blazed with humiliation as I slunk out past all the tall guys. I felt smaller than ever.

What I lacked in the category of stature, I made up for in perseverance. I went through the chain of command all the way to the Fort Sill commandant seeking a height waiver. It was only a quarter of an inch, I argued. General Charlie Brown—that was his real name—looked me over. Cartoons were always being stuck up around base lampooning his name. A pregnant Lucy: *Damn you, Charlie Brown.*

"Candidate Alexander," the general said, "you must live by regulations like everyone else. There are absolutely no waivers for flight school."

I left this court of last resort in a pissy mood, determined to flak General Brown myself with a new barrage of cartoons. My ass was bound for the jungle. Move over, snakes.

I was walking by the post dispensary in this mood, so low the bill of my cap shaded my boot laces, when I heard my name called. "Hey, Alexander!"

I looked up. Staff Sergeant Smith, a medic I knew from the 82d at Fort Bragg, ran out of the dispensary. He had been transferred to Sill. We got to talking about old times in the Airborne. I told him how I had failed my physical for flight school.

"Do you really want to go?" he asked.

"I think I do."

"Chopper pilots don't live long in Vietnam," he cautioned.

"Do they live longer than FOs?"

"Yes."

"Then I think I want to be a pilot."

He thought about it a minute. "Come on in and let me make a phone call to a buddy over at the flight surgeon's office."

I overheard only Smith's side of the conversation: "Yeah, an old friend from Bragg . . . Yeah, he really wants to go. . . . He's already been over and flunked 'cause they said he's a quarter-inch too short . . . Yeah, he's a really good guy and he really wants to go. . . . Okay, I'll send him over tomorrow. . . ."

He hung up and turned to me. "Go over in the morning at nine o'clock and take your physical."

The same Spec5 medic who turned me down before now had all my paperwork filled out when I reported to him. My height was already listed on the chart as five-feet-four. He didn't even measure me.

I passed the physical. My application for flight school was approved. I was going to be a helicopter pilot after all. The shortest one in the entire U.S. Army. Saved at the last minute from Vietnam.

Officers were right about enlisted being deceitful and cunning. I had to remember that when I became an officer myself.

10

JANUARY 18, 1963

General Earle Wheeler, army chief of staff, summoned to his office Brigadier General Harry Kinnard, assistant division commander of the 101st Airborne.

"Harry," Wheeler said, "I want you to determine how far and how fast the army can go and should go in embracing the airmobile concept."

To accomplish this, Kinnard was to create an airmobile division at Fort Benning, Georgia—the 11th Air Assault Division (Test)—and use it to explore the issues and problems posed by the Howze Board recommendations.

A West Point graduate, Kinnard had parachuted into both Normandy and Holland during World War II as a battalion commander with the 101st Airborne. He earned the Distinguished Service Cross, the nation's second-highest medal for valor, and was promoted to full colonel at age twenty nine. He developed a strong interest in the helicopter and its potential the first time he saw one.

He began building his airmobility test unit from a base of three thousand soldiers, one-fifth the strength of a combat-ready division, and 125 helicopters. Some of the men had never even seen a helicopter. Training texts did not exist and there was no SOP, standard operating procedure. The division had to work out methods of communications, modes of formation flying, and countless other basics—how to lash down cargo, how to disperse troops onto a landing zone, how to rappel from a helicopter by rope, how to achieve surprise, how to deal with antiaircraft fire, how to refuel in the field.

The standard drill he and his subordinates worked out aimed for maximum shock effect. It began with artillery and air strikes softening up the LZ—landing zone—prior to the insertion of troops. As troopships headed into the LZ, artillery stopped firing and rocket-firing gunships took over in air support of the landing. Other helicopters picked up and shifted artillery as needed to more advantageous positions. Still other choppers resupplied troops, evacuated wounded, brought in replacements, and extracted the force when it finished its work. The airmobile commander directed all these activities from a control helicopter flying three thousand feet above the fray.

A new generation of rotor-winged aircraft began to arrive even as the test division worked out tactics. The twin-rotor CH-47 Chinook supplied an unprecedented degree of heft. It could haul forty-four battle-ready soldiers or carry a 105mm howitzer, plus ammunition, slung underneath its belly. The UH-1 Iroquois helicopter, soon to be known simply as "Huey," provided the bulk of the unit's capability. A smaller, more nimble, more versatile bird, it carried eight combat-equipped soldiers along with a crew of four airmen, hauled equipment and supplies, and could be rigged into a gunship to support ground forces.

Kinnard conducted a long series of field tests throughout 1963 and 1964. They climaxed in one of the largest post–World War II "war games" maneuvers ever staged in the United States. The thirty-day trial, held during October and November 1964 in the Carolinas, pitted the 11th Air Assault against the 82d Airborne, reinforced. It began with some initial sparring, followed by both offensive and defensive phases. On deep penetration raids, helicopters roared in just above the treetops, hit the opposition guerrilla-style, then withdrew just as quickly, only to strike again and again. On the defense against heavily armed ground troops, airmobile forces melted back while counterpunching with gunships.

Referees were impressed. Regardless of the tactical situation, the airmobile division proved it could seek out an enemy over a large area and then rapidly bring together the necessary firepower and troops to defeat him. While the division's ground mobility was not particularly good and its vulnerability to armor was something of a problem, Kinnard's "Sky Soldiers," as they called themselves, could simultaneously fight in several directions, could react quickly, and could carry out operations at an amazingly high tempo.

Army recommended that the test division be moved to the active list. On June 28, 1965, the 11th Air Assault Division (Test) was deactivated; men and equipment were transferred to the 1st Division, now to be known as the 1st Air Cavalry Division.

Mere weeks before this transaction, General William Westmoreland, commander in Vietnam, reported that the enemy's spring offensive had been devastating. South Vietnam, he said, could not on its own "stand up successfully to this kind of pressure." President Lyndon Johnson responded by deploying 200,000 combat troops to Southeast Asia. General Kinnard received orders to prepare his 16,000-soldier force for deployment. The 1st Air Cav, whose four hundred helicopters exceeded the total number of aircraft possessed by South Vietnam at the time, would be the first full-strength army division to go to Vietnam.

11

Typical army. I graduated from OCS in October 1967, received my commission, then hung around Fort Sill until April the next year. The target acquisitions battalion was stuffed with 323 second lieutenants when TO&E tables called for only 10. At the annual St. Barber's Day dinner—St. Barber being the patron saint of artillery—the battalion commander was given a joke DX card allowing him to trade a dozen second lieutenants for one private.

Trade me! Trade me! The more time I killed around here, the better chance I had of not being killed in Vietnam.

In April 1968, I reported to U.S. Army Primary Helicopter School at Fort Wolters, Texas, located at Mineral Wells between Dallas and Fort Worth. Flight school was nine months long— five months at Wolters in ground and primary flight training, another four months of advance flight training at either Fort Rucker, Alabama, or Savannah Beach, Georgia. As I drove through the main gate, I watched helicopters swarming about overhead and flitting over the nearby flats. I grinned. I must admit that I had had no driving ambition to be a pilot, not until threatened by Vietnam and its jungles and snakes. But now, once I was here and it was a reality, I felt excitement beginning to build. I was going to be out there soon, *flying*, provided no one double-checked and discovered I had arrived on a fraud of a quarter-inch too short in height.

Because of a shortage of officers' quarters, students were paid per diem and allowed to seek off-post housing. Sandy, little April, and I moved into a two-bedroom, 12 × 60–foot mobile home. The rent was outrageous, as the local economy knew we were drawing big per diem and intended to feed off us before we shipped out to Vietnam. Single guys moved two or three strong into trailer houses and launched a poker game that shifted from place to place but seemed to continue forever. A lot of money went across the table. I won as much as $3,000 in a single night.

Flight candidates were issued gray flight suits that were like lightweight coveralls with neck-to-crotch zippers and a dozen pockets all over; flight helmets; flight gloves; aviator's sunglasses; Jeppsen course plotters; wind-face computers; bags full of textbooks; and blue baseball caps. Since five or six classes were being conducted at the same time, the different colors of baseball caps distinguished classes from each other. Everyone knew the color of the new guys' hats.

Trainees were marched to a low building next to the main heliport and divided into groups of four students to each gray table. *Everybody* attended flight school here—army, navy, air force, and marines as well as Vietnamese, Iranians, Italians, and a half-dozen other nationalities. We were given a brief orientation talk about what to expect. Then the IPs—instructor pilots—came into the room and were introduced. Like the Black Hats at paratrooper training, the IPs were almost mythical human beings. We had already heard horror stories about how their entire aim in life was to wash out as many student pilots as they could.

The IP assigned to my four-man group, all four of whom coincidentally were Americans and army, was a granite block of a man with jet black, short-cropped hair and a swarthy Latin complexion. Captain Morales. He stood at the end of the table and looked us over with contempt barely concealed in his dark eyes.

"Today is your only 'free ride,' " he growled in a voice as rough as gravel washed downstream. "You had better enjoy it, because I'm not here to be nice. I'm here to teach you to fly helicopters—after which you'll go to Vietnam. We're not going to be friends, we're not going to be buddies. I expect a lot from you. I expect you to deliver."

My group immediately dubbed him "Captain Nice."

Flying began from day one. Captain Nice escorted us one at a time out to the flight line for our orientation ride. The training helicopter, a Hughes 300, was such a comical-looking little machine that but for the scowl on the IP's face I would have laughed out loud. It was nothing but an oval-shaped plastic bubble out of which stuck the tail boom. I thought it looked like an Easter egg with a hard-on.

The blades had to be phased in by hand before starting the engine. Captain Nice indicated I should buckle into the right pilot's seat while he took the other seat. Unlike fixed-wing air-craft in which a pilot flew left seat, helicopters were normally flown from the right. That was not the case in Vietnam, as I was to find out. Pilots flew Hueys there from the left because that side was less cluttered with instrumentation and permitted an unobstructed view downward through the Plexiglas chin bubble.

"Can you reach the pedals?" Captain Nice asked. He shook his head in a mixture of amusement and scorn at how my arms and legs stuck straight out in order to manipulate the controls. He tossed me a flotation cushion. "Put this in the seat behind your back."

He gently lifted the Easter egg off the helipad and flew it to one thousand feet altitude while he explained the purposes of the various controls. There were four main ones: the collective in the left hand by your side (if you flew left seat), which controlled up and down movements; the throttle in a hand grip on the end of the collective stick, which increased or decreased power and had to be coordinated with all other maneuvers; the cyclic stick between your legs for forward, backward, or side flight; and the rudder pedals, which changed flight direction and controlled torque caused by the spinning rotor blade.

Halfway through some explanation about the instruments, Captain Nice unexpectedly chopped the throttle. The engine cut to idle in a sudden heart-stopping silence. The bird seemed to float for a moment through the sound of wind rush and the pounding of blood in my ears. Then it nosed down and the earth rushed up kaleidoscopically into my face. I felt like a panicked cat stuck to a screen door.

A terror-filled glance at Captain Nice showed him to be remarkably unperturbed. His gravelly voice smirked into my earphones.

"Even if the engine quits," he explained smoothly, "you can still land it. It's the safest thing in the world—"

Yeah. Right. Convince me of *that*.

"It's called autorotation. You immediately push in full right pedal to compensate for lack of torque and push the collective full down to neutralize pitch angle of the blade. The weight of the helicopter will keep the blade spinning once the pitch is flat, providing lift. It's like the little whirligigs you get at carnivals."

All this time we were dropping like a greased anvil. I could taste what I had for breakfast.

"If you tried to keep flying it level without power, the rotor blades would slow and stop—and you would fall out of the sky. It's fatal not to push down collective and right rudder. Remember that."

I couldn't even remember my name. He pointed to a field about a mile away.

"We're going to land over there. We have enough altitude to make it. As long as we don't put too much lift on the blades, we'll continue to glide. If your rotor speed bleeds off, you can increase it again by making a few slow S-turns."

He demonstrated. I held on.

"Just don't increase the rotor speed too much or you'll spin off the rotor."

What? *What?*

"Now, on top of all this," he said coolly, "imagine that you have about four hundred mean little bastards down there shooting up at you and waiting for you to crash in the middle of them."

I couldn't even remember why I wanted out of artillery. I swallowed what tasted like my asshole a half-dozen times during the descent. Captain Nice could have been sitting at home watching *The Tonight Show* on TV for all the excitement he displayed. He calmly explained step by step how at the last moment you flared to bleed off speed—and then you landed.

It was a bit of a jolt, but we were safely on the ground without damage other than to my suddenly fragile ego. Captain Nice shot me a twisted, humorless grin. I managed to grin back rather than let him know how unnerved I had been. The demonstration was intended to be a confidence-building maneuver.

"How did you like that?" the IP asked.

I feigned nonchalance as much as a pale-faced man could. "Can we do it again?"

We would do it many times in the days ahead. IPs taught us to fly the machine as though the engine were temperamental and might quit at any moment. All through training, whether taking off, landing, hovering, or cruising at altitude, the instructors would suddenly cut power to see how we reacted. You didn't solo until they felt confident you could survive a real emergency.

12

Students spent an hour or so each day in the cockpit and the rest of the day either in the bleachers watching classmates fly or attending classes in aerodynamics, weather, navigation, and maintenance. We lived and breathed flying. Allen Borden, an OCS classmate and now in flight school with me, contended we were in an accelerated program designed to get us to Vietnam as quickly as possible. I still thought the war would end soon, but I wasn't nearly as convinced of it as before.

We started by learning the controls, one at a time. Sitting in the bleachers watching, you could always tell whenever a student took over the helicopter. The Hughes went from a perfect steady hover to a penduluming Easter egg hopping around all over the airfield. The more advanced classes jeered at the efforts of the newest blue hats.

"Hey, newbies! Have you found the hover button yet?"

What the hell was a hover button? I had a feeling our chains were being jerked, but I discreetly looked for it in the cockpit anyhow.

The first control we learned was the pedals. I practiced using all four controls in a chair at home and therefore thought just one of them would be a breeze. Captain Nice took me out and held the bird in a low hover above a large practice field. Each field had its own color marked with painted auto tires. White tires meant a large beginners' area; yellow signified intermediate; and red, as Captain Nice put it, was a "Vietnam LZ" barely large enough to set a helicopter down in and get it out again. Any student who landed a helicopter in a red area without an IP in the cockpit with him automatically washed out, never mind that his landing there meant he had to be a pretty good pilot in the first place.

"See that hill out there?" Captain Nice said, pointing.

"Yes, sir," I replied through the intercom.

"All I want you to do is take the pedals and keep the helicopter pointed in the direction of that hill. I'll take the rest of the controls. Think you can do it?"

"Yes, sir."

The harder I concentrated, the more the helicopter wanted to go its own way. It oscillated around its axis, sweeping back and forth across the horizon. Blades whirled madly overhead, spinning relentlessly while the engine roared and growled at me. Sweat poured down my face. I felt overwhelmed by the bird's bouncing, vibrations, and clamor.

"Okay, I got it," Captain Nice said.

"You got it."

That exchange always preceded turning over controls from one pilot to the other. Captain Nice settled the helicopter down.

"Alexander, you *do* see the hill I mean, don't you?"

I acknowledged I did.

"Well, try to at least keep it pointed in that general direction, if you don't mind."

"*I* don't mind. But it seems this helicopter has a mind of its own."

"You're supposed to be smarter than it, Alexander."

I began to understand why there was a minimum height requirement for flight school. Everyone else had legs long enough to reach the pedals while resting their heels on the deck and arms of sufficient length to brace their elbows on their thighs while flying. I pulled the seat all the way forward, let out the pedals to their maximum extension and used a flotation cushion in the seat with me, but my legs and arms still stuck straight out with nothing on which to rest and steady them.

Captain Nice next added the collective and throttle. That meant coordination between pedals and the collective and throttle. Then came pedals, collective and throttle, *and* cyclic. Cyclic was the main control. I felt like a little old lady trying to sweep out the cockpit with the cyclic stick as I fought valiantly with the bird to at least keep it within a fifty-acre field. Everyone else in the class learned to hover while I continued to bounce the Hughes around like an Easter egg on a bungee cord. I was so frustrated I felt like crying. So was Captain Nice.

"Damnit, Alexander," he fumed. "I can teach a monkey to fly this thing if you give me enough bananas and a bottle of Compose. Now why can't you learn?"

Just what I needed for self-confidence—a monkey to take my place in flight school. I knew I was in danger of flunking out. I'd be back in artillery tomorrow and in Vietnam next week.

The next morning during my regularly scheduled flight time, Captain Nice appeared especially surly. He didn't speak to me as we cranked up the Hughes and buckled in. He flew out and landed in the middle of a white practice field. Still without speaking, he screwed everything down so the chopper would squat there on its own while the engine continued to run. He removed his hands from the controls, unbuckled his seat belt and turned toward me.

"Alexander, you either learn to hover this sonofabitch or I'm gonna leave this chopper like it is, take you out there in the field and whip your puny ass. Have I made myself clear, Lieutenant?"

He had at that. That was all he said. He let me stew on it while he took off and silently flew directly back to the airfield.

"Tomorrow, Alexander, you'd better hover this thing," he said in parting. "Think artillery, Lieutenant. Think FO, 'cause that's where your butt is headed if you don't hover this bird."

I don't know which motivated me the most—the threat of Captain Nice whipping my ass or the prospect of going to Vietnam to muck around in the jungle with snakes. Whichever, the very next day I discovered the hover button. I did nothing differently from before, but suddenly everything seemed to click. I looked out to a reference point some two hundred meters away, which cured overcompensating for every little drift, and instead of sweeping out the cockpit with the cyclic to cause the chopper to do all kinds of crazy things, I *hovered*.

Captain Nice grinned. He meant it. "I *told* you you could do this," he almost chortled, as though it were as much a personal triumph for him as for me.

13

"I think it's time," Sandy said, shaking me awake.

"Time for what?" I grumped.

"To go to the hospital."

"Have you timed the pains?"

"No."

"You time them. When they're a minute apart, we'll go."

We had gone through a number of similar false alarms during Sandy's pregnancy. The baby had been due in July. Here it was August and still no baby.

About midnight Sandy woke me again while crashing and banging around the house. I knew she was provoked by the way she was stuffing things in a bag with one hand, clutching her belly with the other and glaring miserably at me. She was about the size of one of the Easter eggs I flew, only with stick arms and legs instead of that other protrusion.

"What are you doing?" I asked her.

"I'm going to the hospital whether you take me or not," she snapped.

"I'll take you," I capitulated. "But if you get me up again in the middle of the night for nothing when I have to fly tomorrow, then you're fired."

I deposited her at the hospital while I drove April to stay with friends who promised to watch her. A nurse ran up and hustled me to delivery as soon as I returned.

"She's gonna shoot you," the nurse warned. "She's in there having the baby right now."

I walked in at 2:00 A.M. Angela was born at 2:14. I was a family man with a wife, a stepdaughter, and now a new daughter. All reasons to keep my scrawny little undersized ass out of Vietnam.

14

Learning to hover was, at least for me, a major training milestone. I advanced rapidly after that. I was among the first to solo. I felt more than a little cocky when Captain Nice got out and told me to take it. I made a smooth hovering takeoff, pushing the cyclic slightly forward, pulling up on the collective and twisting the grip throttle to keep my rpm. The helicopter accelerated across the tarmac until the rotor system moved into undisturbed air and reached the speed of transitional lift. It immediately jumped into a climb.

A pilot on his solo flight kept his landing lights blazing, sort of like a "Student Driver" sign. I made three trips around the traffic pattern, came in and landed. Damn, was I hot or not? I went through the traditional ritual of sewing solo wings on my blue cap and getting dunked in the pool of the local Holiday Inn above the entrance to which the management had erected a huge portal sign made of helicopter rotor blades: THROUGH THESE ROTOR BLADES PASS SOME OF THE FINEST AVIATORS IN THE WORLD.

Advanced maneuvers followed—takeoffs and landings in the confined areas of the red tires; eights around pinnacles; night flying; day and night cross-country navigation; and, always, emergency drills and autorotation procedures. I received a strong jolt of reality during our first night cross-country exercises. This, I realized, was more than a game. It had life-or-death consequences which grew more acute as the reality of Vietnam inevitably approached.

The cross-country navigation course consisted of an hour-long flight during which nine different checkpoints had to be recorded. Two students went up together. They took turns either flying or navigating and watching for checkpoints that were particularly hard to see after dark. We were all a little nervous about it.

Those of us not presently in the cockpit waited on the flight line for our turns around the course. Yawning, sipping strong coffee, having last cigarettes and attempting to look professionally bored. Suddenly, word came down that there had been a crash. Tension crackled through our ranks like lightning trapped in a bag. No more self-imposed torpor. Students and IPs alike stood craning our necks at the Texas stars. None of us was sure what we were looking for since the bird was already down; we were simply looking to keep from feeling so helpless.

All further flights were scrubbed for the night, but no one left the flight line. Details continued to filter in throughout the evening. Tension turned to gloom as cold as a winter's fog. By this time, most in the class were old buddies. We counted faces to see who was missing. It came down to two Iranians, Abdul and Rashish.

A few of our guys, would-be hotshots, had already been busted out of class for pulling stupid stunts like chasing cows or flying underneath bridges. One pair of feckless students got lost and ended up in the traffic pattern of the Dallas–Fort Worth airport. Neither Abdul nor Rashish was feckless, reckless, careless, or stupid. We learned they had had a genuine in-flight emergency for which they were not equipped to cope.

The engine flamed out. Daytime autorotation had become second nature, routine. Autorotation at night was trickier when landmarks were hard to see and distances difficult to judge. The two Iranians apparently became rattled and fought over the controls. IPs heard them on the radio quarreling over which of them had the helicopter. They rolled the Hughes into a mangled ball on the ground. Both were dead by the time Rescue reached the site.

IPs took their small groups of four aside.

"In Vietnam," Captain Nice said in a softer tone than normal, "you'll find pilots will be somewhat distant. They don't make friends, they only have acquaintances. They know you might be the next one to go. Staying aloof is their way of dealing with it."

He hesitated, glancing away. The look on his face said he had been there, that he had personally experienced loss of comrades. His dark eyes hardened and his voice returned to its former gruffness. While I had first thought him insensitive and callous, I soon understood that he was merely being realistic.

"Get used to it," he said, "because things like this are going to happen when you get to Vietnam."

15

President Johnson announced on television: "We will stand in Vietnam. I have today ordered to Vietnam the Air Mobile Division."

It took four aircraft carriers, six troop transports, and eleven cargo ships to move the more than 15,000 soldiers, 3,100 vehicles, 470 aircraft, and 19,000 long tons of cargo of the 1st Air Cavalry Division to the other side of the world. A 1,030-man advance element went first, airlifted from Robbins Air Force Base, Georgia, to Cam Ranh Bay. They were then flown by C-130 aircraft to the Special Forces camp airstrip at An Khe. Brigadier General Jack Norton, assistant division commander under Harry Kinnard, did not want heavy earth-moving equipment clearing the airfield site, since the scraped ground would cause severe dust problems. Instead, he set his men to work with machetes.

"If each of us swings a machete enough times, and if we cleared enough of those twenty-to twenty-five-foot circles, then they would all finally fit together, and we would have a rectangle two kilometers by three kilometers where there would be nothing but this beautiful green grass—like a fine golf course."

The 1st Air Cav Division headquarters at An Khe thus became known as the "Golf Course."

On September 18, 1965, ninety-five days after the reorganization of the 11th Air Assault Division (Test) into the 1st Air Cav, the division was engaged in combat. By the end of the war, 926 helicopter pilots and 2,005 aircrew would be killed under hostile fire.

16

Graduates among the top 10 percent of the class from Primary Helicopter School at Fort Wolters were provided the option of choosing the site of their advance training—either Fort Rucker, Alabama, or Savannah Beach, Georgia. I was included in that 10 percent in spite of a rather undistinguished beginning. I chose Savannah Beach primarily because fixed-wing training was also conducted there. I was still looking for ways to avoid Vietnam. If I could wangle my way into fixed-wing cross-training after I finished with helicopters, it meant at least an additional six months stateside. After all, I had a wife and two daughters now.

Damn! It seemed this war would never end.

I knew a little about the UH-1 Iroquois utility helicopter, the "Huey," dating back to my Fort Bragg days when helicopters and the "airmobile" concept were still in their developmental stages. Other parachute riggers and I used to go out on a Saturday for a few recreational hops-and-pops in a Huey. They were easy, fun jumps. You sat rigged in the door with your legs hanging outside. When you reached altitude, you simply pushed yourself out hard enough to miss the skids. By the time you hit the DZ, the chopper was waiting to take you right back up. I must have gone up in a Huey twenty or thirty times at least, but when I reached Savannah Beach I had yet to come back *down* in one.

The Huey was the army's primary utility helicopter and the one most of us would be flying. First off, we incoming students were hustled into a dark room and treated to a training film. The army was damned proud of the UH series.

"The UH-1 Iroquois is the army's latest utility helicopter," narrated the voice-over while the film showed Hueys taking off and landing, hovering and flying in formation. None of them were getting shot at, however. "The T53-L-11 gas-turbine engine weighs only five hundred pounds, yet develops eleven hundred horsepower. The turbine is basically a jet engine with a fan placed in the exhaust. The fan is connected by a shaft that runs through the engine to the transmission. The pressure of gases pushing through the fan generates enough force to turn the forty-eight-foot rotor system and the eight-foot tail-rotor assembly and lift the five-thousand-pound machine and a maximum load of forty-five hundred pounds into the air. The Huey's streamlined design allows for a maximum cruise speed of one hundred twenty knots with a VNE, Velocity Never Exceed, of one hundred forty knots. . . ."

Hughes trainers at Fort Wolters flew at about eighty knots.

"Though not recommended, the Huey is capable of hovering vertically up to an altitude of ten thousand feet on a standard day. It is fast, it is efficient, it is dependable. It also comes in several configurations."

The film showed each of these configurations: a gunship, or "hog," as it was called, bristling with pilot-directed machine guns, rockets, and grenade launchers; a troop carrier or "slick" with room for eight combat-equipped soldiers plus two pilots, a crew chief, and a door gunner; and an air ambulance or "medevac" carrying six litters. It had also been adapted as a flying command center and as a light cargo ship.

I could hardly wait to get a shot at flying it. My first impression was that *this* must be the Cadillac of helicopters. When on my orientation flight the IP squeezed the starter trigger, he received a shrill responding whine as the high-speed starter motor began to move the blades. That was a startling contrast to the hacking cough of the Hughes 300. The IP indicated that I was to do the takeoff.

"You got it," he said.

"I got it."

I pulled collective. The big rotor thudded a little with increased pitch. Then the bird *leapt* into the air like it had been goosed. This machine had *power*.

I did the "Huey shuffle," the characteristic wagging of the

tail back and forth by neophytes overcontrolling the sensitive pedals. I grinned at the IP as I flew the bird above Georgia. The heavy thudding sound of the main rotor, that distinctive *wop-wop-wop-wop!* that was becoming so familiar over Vietnam, was more than compensated for by the smooth whine of the engine. All helicopters were noisy, but there was no excessive roaring, vibrating, or shaking with the Huey.

The IP landed the bird on the helipad with the engine running at a normal 330 rpm. He looked at me, then cut power completely. He immediately pulled collective—and to my astonishment the machine lifted itself off the pad and did a 360-degree turn before the blade lost its inertia and lift and the helicopter sank back to the ground. Only a Huey had that kind of power. Ballast weights on each of the two main rotor blade tips gave the system tremendous inertia. I was much impressed.

Training at Savannah was what we had received at Wolters, except more of it, more advanced, and all of it in the UH-1. We did a lot of instrument training under the hood when all you saw were needles and bubbles on the instrument panel while your body told you you were flying on your side or upside down. Traditionally, helicopter pilots maintained visual contact with the ground. VFR and IFR were the same thing. Visual Flight Rule, VFR, stood for "visually follow roads"; Instrument Flight Rule, IFR, meant "I follow roads." If weather came in and you couldn't fly lower and slower, you set down in a field and waited. That wouldn't work in Vietnam, we were told. Monsoon season produced a lot of rain and fog. You had to really fly IFR in it, because if you set your ship down you might be nesting in the middle of a bunch of pissed-off commies.

All training was geared toward a single goal: Vietnam. Combat flying techniques generally meant "contour flying" low to the earth to keep down exposure to enemy ground fire. Skimming along only feet above the treetops at one hundred knots per hour with the world passing by underneath in a green blur. As part of a "confidence course," we sailed choppers under power lines and made low turns so steep the blade tips almost chopped into the ground. It was thrilling, it was exciting, and, we were told, we would find it practical and useful when we got to Vietnam.

Every lesson started with the preface *In Vietnam* . . . In Vietnam, because of terrain and enemy presence, flights of helicopters had to land in small LZs in the forest. They had to get in quickly, do their business whether that meant depositing troops or picking them up, then get out again just as quickly. On the ground itself was a helicopter's most dangerous zone. The other danger zone lay in that belt of air below 1,500 feet altitude and above contour flight. Safety lay either in flying high or flying low and fast.

We practiced formation flying and formation landing on LZs. Distances between ships were measured in rotor diameters. Three diameters' distance between birds was normal formation flight, but we often flew at one diameter or less. Some of the IPs who had been to Vietnam actually flew with their whirling blades *overlapped*. It took some getting used to. Visions of splintering rotor blades and helicopters tumbling out of the sky haunted my dreams.

"Honey! Wake up!" Sandy poked me with her elbow. "What were you shouting about in your sleep?"

"Promise me you won't turn into the Wicked Witch of the East?" I said.

"You're such a little smart-ass."

Even our mistakes and accidents served as examples of what we might expect in Vietnam. One day a student in a Huey caught his skid under a refueling hose. The hose flipped the helicopter when he started to lift off. The bird beat itself to death like a chicken with its neck wrung. By some miracle, both pilots got out safely. In his desperation to escape, the student pilot ripped the door handle completely off and still had it gripped in his hand.

"In Vietnam," the instructor explained, "you'll all find out that these kinds of things happen when the adrenaline starts pumping."

In Vietnam. My options for avoiding *in Vietnam* were steadily running out. The army needed *helicopter* pilots, I was told when my request for fixed-wing cross-training was rejected. It was no classified secret, it was common sense, that 99 percent of us were heading for Vietnam as soon as we graduated. Choppers were getting shot down over there, pilots killed. Replacements were needed.

"At least flying choppers is safer than being in artillery," I tried to reassure Sandy.

I wasn't so sure about that anymore.

It seemed that in attempting to circumvent Vietnam, I had got myself caught up in a whirlwind that was bearing down upon that which I most wanted to avoid. I resigned myself to the fact that I *was* going. I saw no way out. All doors had been closed to me except the one opening into southeast Asia. I cast around looking for an outfit in the war zone that might give me the best survival chance, wondering how I could get myself assigned to it.

It was common knowledge that of all the American units fighting in Vietnam, the 1st Air Cavalry Division was seeing the most action. Pilot survivors of the 1st filled us in on the situation.

"Within the First Cav," they explained, "the most dangerous place to be is in the First Squadron of the Ninth Brigade. Apache Troop of the One-Nine is always in deep shit. You don't want to go there."

How could I avoid it? I was still pondering that question in January 1969, looking for an out, when I graduated from advanced flight training. It was the beginning of the bloodiest year of the war. The entire graduating class assembled in formation in front of the TAC office to receive our orders. The training commander called us forward in alphabetical order. Abraham . . . Akins . . . Alexander . . .

I frantically scanned my orders. There it was: *Report to 307th Transportation Company, Vung Tau, South Vietnam.* Where the hell was Vung Tau?

"Have you ever lucked out, Lieutenant!" an IP exclaimed.

Vung Tau, he explained, was a coastal in-country rest and recreation center on the seacoast. No guns were allowed inside city limits. Even the Viet Cong there played by the rules. It was a place where warriors from both sides went to drink beer, chase pussy and bask in the sun.

Had I *ever* lucked out! And I hadn't done a thing to engineer it. *Luck*. That was all it was. If I *had* to go to war, this was the way to go. Lt. Ron Alexander was going to lie around on white sand beaches, haul ass and trash, and fly steaks to generals in safe rear areas. I had this war *dicked*.

17

New meat was flown to Vietnam in commercial airliners, a load at a time, complete with pretty stewardesses, airliner meals, and free drinks. Just like you were going on vacation to Hawaii or Miami Beach, except everybody was in uniform, there were no women other than the stews, and everybody was a little tense. There were two types of men on board: loudmouths bragging about how they were going to kick ass and win the war single-handedly; and the silent, scared, introspective types, which were the majority.

Vietnam had two primary debarkation points for incoming replacements. Loads intended for assignments to units fighting in the Central Highlands and north to the DMZ were offloaded at Cam Ranh Bay; replacements for the southern peninsula down through the Mekong Delta were landed at Bien Hoa. Bien Hoa was our destination. It was a major airfield and supply point located about twenty miles northeast of Saigon and forty miles northwest of Vung Tau.

After what seemed an eternity of flying over water and brief landings at Anchorage, Alaska, and Tokyo, Japan, we newbies received our first glimpse of Vietnam, a thick finger of emerald green in a cobalt sea. The loudmouths got louder and the silent types got quieter. Funny, I thought, it didn't *look* like a war was going on down there.

"Gentlemen," came a sweet stew's voice over the cabin intercom. She stood up front, speaking into the mike and smiling at us. "We would like to be the first to welcome you to lovely Vietnam. We hope your tour here will be safe and that we'll be seeing each of you again for your homeward flight. We will be making our landing in Bien Hoa in about twenty minutes."

The plane was crammed shoulder to shoulder with infantry, clerks, artillerymen, officers and enlisted, chopper pilots and APC drivers—a mixture of replacement parts for the military machine. Even the loudmouths went temporarily hushed. I looked around at the strained faces of men all gone inward to contemplate this last step before they were forced to confront the harsh reality of war. It occurred to me that some of these men and boys would never return home, at least not alive. I inspected the faces of those nearest me, as though I might be able to determine their fates. Which ones would be dead next week or next month, in three months or six months?

I am really in Vietnam, I thought. *I've really had it done to me.*

I looked away with a jerk. I didn't want the knowledge of other men's fates. I had my own to contend with. But at least I had a relatively safe pud job with the 307th. So I was going to be an REMF, a rear echelon motherfucker. I never claimed to be a hero.

I was becoming comfortable with the idea of our arrival when the pilot came up on the intercom. "Gentlemen, I'm sorry about this. We have good news and we have bad news."

Always a comedian somewhere.

"The bad news is, there's a mortar attack under way at Bien Hoa, so we can't land there. The good news is, we can land at Cam Ranh Bay, so you won't have to go back home."

"What a deal!" came a sarcastic remark from the back of the plane.

A little worm of uneasiness started crawling around somewhere inside my gut. I had been in the army long enough to know that people got screwed whenever there were sudden changes. I had a sudden bad feeling about this.

"Don't worry about it," said my seatmate, a lieutenant colonel on his way back to Vietnam for a second tour. "They'll process us at Cam Ranh and get us where we're supposed to go."

How far was Cam Ranh Bay from Vung Tau? A long, long, *long* way, as it turned out.

Final approach to Cam Ranh led us in over the water of the South China Sea. Funny, the water was blue; I always imagined it being yellow. I pressed my face against the porthole window to look out. Ahead, growing larger and closer as we approached, loomed docking areas and cargo ships and pallets of crates piled everywhere, all being worked by men and machinery swarming everywhere.

Beyond on bare reddish earth were concrete bunkers, sandbagged gun emplacements, and rows of metal-roofed buildings glinting back the sun. More equipment was stacked and piled about. OD green-colored vehicles darted and nosed through the debris like cockroaches. Revetmented next to the airstrips were C-130s, Caribous, fighter jets, Cobra gunships, and coveys of Hueys.

Around the wire perimeter stood spindly-legged guard towers linked together by sandbagged fighting positions and echelons of barbed and concertina wire. Out from the wire the fields had been cleared of all vegetation. The base was a desolate, bare place with virtually nothing green growing anywhere within its confines. Green was Vietnam, but brown and red and OD and dusty were the American military posts.

When I walked off the airliner, Vietnam struck me like a physical force with its heat and humidity and the stench of open sewers and fish and fumes from the city nearby. My uniform immediately wilted and hung off my frame like damp dish rags. We were herded sweating and irritable into a big hangar where a clerk Spec5 came out and announced that the list of where everybody was supposed to go would be posted the following morning. In the meantime, he said, pointing to a bulletin board, here were the locations of transient quarters, mess halls, showers, latrines, and bunkers in case we were attacked.

"Make yourself at home in Vietnam," he concluded.

"How long are we going to be at Cam Ranh Bay?" I demanded.

He shrugged.

"I'm supposed to report to the 307th Transportation Company at Vung Tau," I protested.

"Check the bulletin board in the morning, sir."

It was the first thing I did. That little worm crawling around inside my gut kept me awake all night. Apparently, I wasn't the only one attacked by worms. Almost the entire planeload of FNGs—fucking new guys—was waiting at the bulletin board when the Spec5 came out with the list and posted it. The list was alphabetical, of course. *Alexander* stood out near the top. My heart pounded at a cadence of about 120 beats per minute as I ran my finger across the page and came to—*1st Cavalry Division*. The cadence jumped to about 150.

"What's this shit?" I demanded of the Spec5 before he could escape. I felt flushed and grim. "I'm supposed to go to the 307th at Vung Tau."

The clerk took a step back. "Let me explain, sir . . ."

"Somebody had better explain."

Or what? Take my toys and go home?

"Orders have been changed," the clerk stammered.

"I can see that. Why have they been changed?"

He took a deep breath. "What happened," he said, "is that each incoming plane is composed of about the same mixture of people. There are so many enlisted men, so many artillery, so many infantry, so many pilots. . . . Occasionally, an incoming plane is diverted for one reason or another from its intended debarkation point. When that happens, we just switch everything over. We keep the incoming load and reissue orders."

I stared at him, stunned.

"You mean . . . *somebody else* will get *my* orders to Vung Tau?"

He looked at my orders. I thought I detected a smirk. Enlisted men could be devious and cunning; I used to be one. "Yes, sir. It says you've been reassigned to the First Cavalry Division headquartered at An Khe."

The 1st Air Cav, the most active combat unit in Vietnam.

My hands trembled, rattling the paper. *Where* in 1st Cav? Maybe I was being sent to division headquarters.

Oh, shit. There it was—*9th Brigade*.

Okay, okay, okay. Maybe to brigade headquarters. Anywhere except 1st Squadron.

1st Squadron, the 1/9.

Oh, Jesus. My heart was going to pound its way out of my chest. Not Apache Troop. Anywhere except Apache.

A/1/9—Apache Troop, 1st Squadron, 9th Brigade, 1st Air Cavalry Division.

Warnings from flight school drummed in my head: "... *always in deep shit. You don't want to go there.*" The enemy shot down an average of one helicopter every seven days.

I stood in the busy hangar gripping my orders, too shook to move. I had never particularly believed in fate and the laws of fate and all that. But now it seemed ol' Murphy was taking revenge for my disbelief. His law stated that anything that could go wrong, would. Ol' Murphy was pointing his fickle finger directly at me. Yeah, you boy. I am going to fuck you over.

Why the hell hadn't I stayed in artillery?

Oh shit Oh shit Oh shit Oh shit . . .

18

Barely three weeks after the 1st Cav hacked out a base for itself at An Khe, there occurred in the plateau country southwest of Pleiku City a series of skirmishes and larger actions that became known as the Battle of the Ia Drang Valley. Airmobile tactics developed piecemeal at Fort Benning were now to be tested in war.

Three regiments of the North Vietnamese Army (NVA) had filtered out of Cambodia along the Ho Chi Minh network of trails into South Vietnam. Together, they constituted an entire division under the command of Brigadier General Chu Huy Man. It was the largest massing of North Vietnamese strength since the fall of Dien Bien Phu to the Viet Minh in 1954, which ended French rule of its Indochina colony.

Chu positioned his force along the eastern slopes of the Chu Pong Massif, a formation of mountains rising above the Ia Drang Valley, about halfway between the South China Sea and Cambodia. The highlands were wild and desolate, a ravine-slashed region of scrub and huge termite hills, virtually empty except for tigers, elephants, and scattered Montagnard tribesmen. His goal was to capture Pleiku, a provincial capital, and then drive eastward to the port city of Qui Nhon, cutting South Vietnam in half.

He started his campaign an hour before midnight on October 19, 1965, by attacking the Plei Me U.S. Army Special Forces camp. Commanding General Harry Kinnard of the 1st Cav sent a battalion-size task force to reinforce defenses at Pleiku, then conducted the first real airmobile operation of the campaign by choppering in Sky Soldiers ahead of a column of ARVN (Army of the Republic of Vietnam) on their way to relieve the besieged Special Forces camp. General Chu, taken aback by the helicopters' injection of heavy firepower into the fray, withdrew to the Ia Drang Valley, a VC stronghold so remote and so infested with enemy troops that the South Vietnamese army had never dared enter it. Chu had suffered his first defeat.

General Westmoreland gave Kinnard his head.

"I think the Cav is ready," he said, defining the mission in starkly simple terms: "Find, fix and destroy the enemy forces threatening Plei Me, Pleiku, and the Central Highlands."

One by one over the next month, Kinnard put all three brigades of his division into the fight and let them use their newly forged skills. This was a war that demanded mobility of the most supple and quick-reflexed kind—a war without clearly delineated front lines and rear support areas, a war of attrition rather than territorial gains, a hide-and-seek war fought on terrain almost designed to frustrate ground vehicles.

Kinnard's assault units used a three-team organization for search-and-destroy. Each company-size outfit encompassed a "White Team," a "Red Team," and a "Blue Team." The White Team flew bubble-nosed OH-13 Sioux helicopters and were charged with finding the enemy through reconnaissance. Red Teams flew Huey "hog" gunships armed with rockets and machine guns. They cleared landing zones and provided supporting fire; later, Huey gunships were replaced with the more deadly AH-1 Cobras specifically designed and equipped as attack choppers. Blue Teams consisted of Huey troop carriers, called slicks because, unlike gunships, they had no externally mounted guns or rockets to increase their aerodynamic drag. Blues inserted troops after Whites located the enemy and Reds cleared a landing zone.

During the last week of October, reconnaissance helicopters probed every corner of the tumbled and tangled region, nosing right down to treetop level for a look at trails or other signs of activity, constantly harassing Chu's withdrawing forces. The choppers repeatedly drew enemy fire, but the North Vietnamese found both the OH-13s and the bigger Hueys difficult to bring down. Few were lost, partly because of NVA inexperience in dealing with them and partly because of the 1st Cav's fast-moving, low-flying tactics.

On October 29, a Blue Team force landed in the middle of an enemy cache of weapons and food, killing sixteen NVA soldiers, capturing eight and wounding twelve. Three days later, a rifle platoon commanded by Captain John Oliver surprised a regimental aid station along the Tae River and killed fifteen NVA.

When the enemy counterattacked with a battalion, Oliver formed a tight defensive perimeter around a small clearing uphill from the aid station. Over the next two and a half hours, two companies of reinforcements—about two hundred men—were fed into the fight to assist Oliver. They arrived one bird at a time in his tiny clearing above the streambed while gunships hammered at surrounding NVA soldiers to keep them pinned down. Eight helicopters were hit, but all of them continued flying.

That was the first major action of the Pleiku campaign. The Sky Soldiers stopped the NVA counterattack cold and quickly regained the offensive. When the NVA 33d Regiment withdrew in defeat the next morning, they left ninety-nine dead soldiers on the field. The 1st Cav casualties were eleven dead and fifty-one wounded.

General Chu sent his fresh 66th Regiment into the fight against Kinnard's Sky Soldiers, giving the North Vietnamese a substantial edge in numbers. But the helicopter proved to be what military planners called a force multiplier—a technological advantage that changed the odds.

On the afternoon of November 3, four platoons of the 1st Cav established a patrol base on a hilltop clearing north of the Chu Pong Massif and sent three platoon-size ambush forces into the enemy stronghold of the Ia Drang Valley. One of the forces ambushed a heavy-weapons company of NVA and then beat a hasty retreat back to the patrol base.

Barely had the platoon reached the base than the NVA

attacked in battalion strength. Night-flying skills practiced back in the United States now came into play. A company of reinforcements landed in the clearing in six-helicopter lots. The first lift, escorted by a Red Team of armed helicopters, swept in under the light of flares. Subsequent runs used only the light of the full moon. A platoon leader dubbed the landing zone "LZ Spiderweb" because the sky was crisscrossed by a brilliant pyrotechnical webbing of red tracers fired by the Americans and bluish-green tracers from NVA weapons.

General Chu once again lost what should have been an easy victory against outnumbered U.S. forces. He suffered seventy-two dead to two Americans killed.

By November 7, when Kinnard began to withdraw the 1st Brigade and replace it with Colonel Thomas Brown's 3d Brigade, the 33d NVA Regiment alone had lost, by U.S. intelligence estimates, about 900 of its 2,200 men. American losses so far were 59 dead, 196 wounded.

The decisive battle of the campaign, the ultimate test of airmobility against ground infantry, occurred around an opening in the trees, no more than one hundred meters long, that nestled near the foot of one of the mountains of the Chu Pong Massif. When White Team helicopters, dipping below treetop level, spotted well-used trails and communications wire nearby, no one suspected the size of the force in the vicinity. As it happened, the clearing that would gain fame as LZ X-Ray was located almost on top of the headquarters and staging area for Chu's regiments.

On November 14, the First Battalion of the 1st Cav's 7th Regiment commanded by Lieutenant Colonel Harold Moore was inserted onto the LZ as the starting point for search-and-destroy missions. At 12:30 P.M., platoons of B Company spread out to explore the ground toward the Chu Pong heights. One of the platoons led by Lieutenant Henry Herrick ran head-on into about 150 NVA soldiers. Herrick was killed immediately and his platoon pinned down.

While survivors of the surrounded platoon fought for their

lives, A Company of LZ X-Ray battled waves of khaki-clad NVA regulars in pith helmets. Through the rest of the day and night, enemy troops attempted to break the Americans' perimeter.

Meanwhile at the Brigade Operations Center, Kinnard orchestrated his airmobile resources. Chinooks lifted two batteries of 105mm howitzers—twelve guns in all—to LZ Falcon, a clearing about five miles east of the battle. During the two nights during which the battle raged, artillery at LZ Falcon pumped more than 4,400 rounds of high explosives into the fight. Many fell within fifty meters of the X-Ray perimeter in an effort to prevent NVA troops from getting "into a bear hug with us," as Moore put it. Between artillery barrages came flights of navy, marine, and air force fighter-bombers to bomb, strafe, and napalm enemy positions.

Huey transports, escorted by gunships pouring 7.62mm machine gun fire and 2.75-inch rockets into the trees, continued to bring in reinforcements and supplies and to carry out the wounded.

X-Ray was a scene of mayhem. Choppers rose and descended through dust and smoke; exploding artillery shells and rockets hammered at the air; and staccato bursts of machine and rifle fire mixed with the screams and shouts of the combatants.

By the second nightfall, the Americans were well dug in all around the clearing. Mortars and artillery were calibrated to drop shells within twenty-five yards of their lines. Helicopters stopped shuttling in and out of the LZ at ten o'clock. Some of the pilots had been flying for sixteen hours straight. "When I tried to get out of the aircraft," said slick pilot Major Bruce Crandall, "it caught up with me. My legs gave out, and I fell to the ground vomiting and shaking." The inside of his helicopter was awash with the blood of the wounded.

Having slackened their efforts during the night, the NVA struck hard at first light on November 15, sending a force estimated at one thousand against the X-Ray perimeter. Fighting was so furious—including violent hand-to-hand combat in some places—that midmorning arrived before the battle waned sufficiently for helicopters to begin landing a company of reinforcements from An Khe. A larger, battalion-size unit landed at a clearing two miles away and started a forced march to flank the enemy and relieve X-Ray. By noon, they reached the battlefield. One soldier said, "My God, there's enemy bodies all over this valley. For the last thirty minutes, we've been walking around and over and through bodies."

The North Vietnamese continued to attack until ten in the morning, when they withdrew under fire. Scores of corpses and weapons were left to litter the battleground. Shortly after three that afternoon, a rescue force from X-Ray fought its way to the position of the trapped Second Platoon. By half past four, the survivors and the dead were back on X-Ray.

The NVA returned to the fight that night and continued it into the next day. By that time, Moore had been reinforced in battalion strength and amply resupplied with ammunition. In the end, American firepower, climaxed by the bombing of the Chu Pong heights by B-52s based on Guam, proved too much for the North Vietnamese. General Chu's command was all but destroyed. The body count of NVA dead was 634; additional dead and wounded were estimated at more than 1,200. American casualties were listed as 79 killed, 121 wounded.

General Kinnard's 1st Cav had more than lived up to the expectations of airmobility advocates such as Gavin and Howze. From October 19 to November 28, 1965, the 1st Cavalry Division had played a pivotal role in rescuing the Plei Me Special Forces camp; Sky Soldiers had applied new airmobile tactics to chase the enemy back to its stronghold in the Ia Drang Valley, and then, outnumbered seven to one, had won a huge victory. In doing so, the 1st Cav moved complete infantry companies 193 times, conducted 6,000 sorties, logged 27,000 hours of flying time, airlifted 13,000 tons of supplies, moved entire artillery batteries 67 times, provided close air support, conducted reconnaissance missions—and virtually obliterated two of North Vietnam's best infantry regiments. Only four cavalry helicopters were shot down during that period, and three of them were recovered to fly again.

Vietnam became the Helicopter War. By the late 1960s, more than 2,000 Hueys would be in the air over Vietnam on any given day. Inevitably, the VC and NVA adjusted to the new challenge. They learned how to fire at choppers flying overhead, how to mine likely landing zones, how to lure Sky Soldiers into ambushes. During the course of the war, a total of 4,112 helicopters would be downed. Five of the eight generals who were killed in Vietnam died in helicopters.

19

Sayonara to flying steaks and grits to generals in safe rear areas. After the initial shock of having my orders changed wore off, however, I experienced an awakening sense of curiosity about war accompanied by a faint stirring of excitement and expectation. Deep inside all young men lurked a thirst for adventure. Just because I was married and had two daughters didn't change that. I was only twenty-three years old. Of course, I would *rather* have gone to Vung Tau, but now that I wasn't it surprised me to find that I wasn't nearly as pissed off as I should have been. I couldn't figure it, what with all the energy I had invested in attempting to avoid Vietnam combat. It must be something genetic in males.

I boarded a Caribou airplane along with a bunch of other FNGs, both officers and enlisted, and flew from Cam Ranh Bay to 1st Cav division headquarters at An Khe for a week of in-processing and orientation. There I was issued jungle fatigues, boots, socks, poncho liners, and mosquito netting. Immunization records were updated, physicals given, malaria pill regimes started (I would take the big pills for the rest of the time I was in Vietnam), and we were all indoctrinated into the organization and work of the 1st Cavalry as well as in how sneaky, underhanded, cunning, and vicious "Charlie" could be.

"Charlie?" I asked.

"Charlie," it was explained, was short for "Victor Charles," the phonetic alphabet pronunciation for VC, Viet Cong. "Charlie" and "Mister Charles" were common terms applied to the enemy, along with other more disparaging labels such as "dink," "gook," "slope," and "shithead." The Vietnamese called us "big nose" or "cat eyes." I was sure they also used their own less-complimentary terms for us as we did for them.

General George Forsythe was now commanding officer of the division. I learned that the 1st Cavalry Division, with

approximately fifteen thousand men, consisted of three major
subordinate units—the 1st, 2d, and 3d Brigades—along with
Division Artillery, a Support Command, and an Aviation
Group. Within this structure were nine battalions of infantry,
five battalions of artillery, three assault helicopter battalions,
four support-type battalions, an aerial reconnaissance squadron,
one engineer battalion, one signal battalion, and a number of
independent specialized companies and detachments.

The outfit I was joining, the aerial reconnaissance squadron
in the Aviation Group, was a division asset employed wherever
it was needed. The 1st Squadron of the 9th Cavalry, the 1/9,
consisted of fewer than one thousand men and some one hundred helicopters divided into three troops, "A" through "C."
Each troop in turn, such as Apache Troop, was organized into
an aero scout "White" platoon, which now flew OH6A LOHs
(light observation helicopters) called "Loaches"; an aero weapons "Red" gunship platoon, whose Huey "hogs" had been exchanged for deadly AH-1G Cobra attack helicopters; and an
aero rifle "Blue" platoon made up of UH-1H Huey "slicks"
and squads of "Sky Soldier" infantry.

The U.S. military had divided South Vietnam into four separate Areas of Operations called "corps," beginning with I
Corps located in the northernmost area along the DMZ and
ending with IV Corps in the southern Mekong Delta. Apache
Troop was now located at Tay Ninh base camp in War Zone
C, III Corps. Tay Ninh lay about fifty miles northwest of Saigon in a dog head's protrusion of Vietnam into Cambodia.
Cambodia wrapped around the Dog's Head both to the north,
the so-called Fishhook, and to the south, the Parrot's Beak. The
base camp was about ten miles from the Cambodian border.

The area had been a hot spot since at least 1965, leading to
the reputation of Apache Troop of the 1/9 being the most dangerous outfit in Vietnam in which to serve. NVA and VC units
filtering across the Cambodian border had tried repeatedly to
reach the South Vietnam capital at Saigon and capture it.
Northeast of Tay Ninh lay the Iron Triangle, in which a num-

ber of ops had been waged against enemy entrenched in an amazing miles-long series of underground tunnels, the so-called Tunnels of Cu Chi. It was being assumed from activity along the Cambodian border that the enemy had not given up on Saigon. It was a constant expectation that when a new offensive was launched, it would originate in War Zone C.

Apache Troop's mission was to locate the enemy through aerial reconnaissance and sweeping patrols along the border. "White" Loaches sniffed around at treetop level looking for trails, bunkers, base camps, and other signs of activity; "Red" Cobra gunships provided fire support and air cover; "Blue" slicks, to which I was being assigned as a pilot, picked up and inserted troops as required. Blues also rescued downed aviators and extracted infantry under pressure.

Horror stories about enemy atrocities circulated among the FNGs, relayed to us by the "old timers." One soldier had been chopped up into little pieces and stuffed into a water urn; a VC woman tied up American prisoners, put baskets over their heads and filled the baskets with rats; captured soldiers were sometimes tortured at night within sound of a U.S. unit so that the GIs had to listen to their screaming.

The moral of the stories: *Don't get caught.* Some of the guys, it was said, always saved their last bullet for themselves. I shuddered at the thought of getting shot down out there in the middle of such *uncivilized* people. Damn! Maybe I should have tried to retrieve my orders to Vung Tau.

About thirty chopper jocks were undergoing the in-country indoctrination. I half-expected some of my flight school classmates to be there, but apparently they had preceded me, would come later, or had been assigned elsewhere. It was during an outdoors bleacher session that we encountered our first "enemy."

A major was explaining more about what we should expect. Like diarrhea, until we got used to things; about how Charlie dipped his punji stakes in his own feces in order to increase infection in whoever stepped on them. We should expect mortar and rocket attacks against whichever post we were assigned, along with occasional sapper penetrations. Sappers were particularly devious and skillful. They were shadows, ghosts who slipped through defensive wire carrying satchels filled with explosives.

As he talked, the major paced slowly back and forth between his audience in the bleachers and a berm of mounded earth. Beyond the berm stretched rows of concertina and barbed wire, part of the perimeter at An Khe. He was nearing the end of his spiel when a scrawny little Asian wearing only khaki shorts popped up from behind the berm. He yelled something and at the same time hurled a heavy canvas bag at the bleachers. All eyes fastened horrified on its slow-motion progress as it arced high into the air.

The major screamed a warning. *"Satchel charge!"*

We damn near killed ourselves diving, leaping, scrambling, stampeding and falling off the bleachers. I ended up on the ground with my face buried in the dirt. I couldn't get any lower, my buttons were in the way. I could have crawled underneath a pebble. I braced myself against the expected explosion.

After a few moments when nothing happened, I heard a nervous titter and cautiously opened one eye. The major stood at parade rest displaying a shit-eating grin. The Asian "sapper" stood soberly at his side. The guy next to me got up off the ground wearing a sheepish look and dusted himself off. I got up and looked around. The "explosives" still lay in the bleachers, undetonated.

As the class slowly and suspiciously reassembled, the major asked, "Gentlemen, do you understand? Did anyone here see Minh slip through the wire right in front of your eyes and get close enough to wipe us all out?"

No one had.

"Remember what happened here today when you reach your assignments," he cautioned in a funereal voice. "Minh is a *chieu hoi,* a former VC who has come over to our side and serves as a Kit Carson scout. Lack of vigilance is exactly what will get you killed. This is a war in which you never know where the enemy is, how he will appear, or even *who* he is. Trust nobody except your own."

I looked Minh over closely. So this skinny little fella, no taller than I, was what the bad guys looked like?

"I'll sleep in a flak jacket," I murmured.

20

Another Caribou flew replacements from An Khe to Phuoc Vinh, which was where the 1st Cav was in the process of moving its headquarters. We remained overnight and flew in a Huey to Tay Ninh the next morning. A veteran pilot returning from an admin trip to Cav headquarters sprawled in the canvas next to me as the chopper prepared to take off. In Vietnam, anyone in-country over a month or six weeks was considered a "veteran." I was tense and introspective as were the four other FNGs bound for the combat base camp. The veteran stuck out his hand.

"Name's Norm Bilby," he said. "Everybody calls me Snake Eye. Nobody uses first names around here. It's either last names, aircraft numbers, nicknames, or 'Red,' 'White,' or 'Blue' if you're a platoon leader. You just flying in?"

New fatigues, new jungle boots, new frozen look on the face. It should have been obvious. I introduced myself.

"Alexander?" he mused. "As in Alexander the Great?"

"More like Alexander the Small," I muttered.

Bilby chuckled. "We all feel like that when we first get here," he said.

I had little clue as to what the hell I was doing, where exactly I was going except to some place called Tay Ninh, or what to expect once I got there. As if all the probing, prodding, and herding around I had endured over the past couple of weeks weren't enough to diminish my ego.

"What outfit are you assigned to, Lieutenant?" Snake Eye asked.

I told him. "You?" I asked.

"I'm with the Blue Max platoon down the road from you Apaches. We fly Cobras." He hesitated, as though unsure if he should bring it up. He looked at me, sucked his teeth reflectively. He said, "The Apaches have taken a lot of losses."

That certainly made me feel better.

The flight lasted about a half-hour, during which time Snake Eye kept up a running commentary on the terrain, the Cav, Vietnam, and how fucked up the world was in general. We flew over green jungle so thick you couldn't see down through it. Once in a while I glimpsed a sun flash of reflection off a stream or pond hidden in the forest, but then it was gone. The terrain was as flat as a table with few wrinkles in the green that covered it. Here and there were a few scattered hooches, little grass-or tin-roofed shacks surrounded by rice paddies. There were few villages and almost no roads connecting them. Simply foot trails and bicycle paths. Snake Eye explained that civilians had been evacuating the area for years, abandoning it to the NVA and VC.

"That's the Michelin rubber plantation over there to the northeast," Snake Eye said, pointing out the Huey's open door. "Gooks are always hiding in there. The rubber trees are so thick you can't see down through the foliage."

One readily identifiable feature jutted up out of all that flat land—a single mountain peak, like a gigantic anthill crusted with vegetation. It was about five miles north of the base and protruded to about three thousand feet in height. It appeared about a quarter-mile in diameter at its base.

"That's Nui Ba Den, the Black Virgin Mountain," Snake Eye said. "That's your principal checkpoint, because you can see it from anywhere in the AO. We have a radio relay station on top. We own the top and the bottom. Charlie owns everything in between. The whole damned mountain is hollowed out with VC tunnels. Charlie can sit over there and see the entire base at Tay Ninh to direct in mortar and rocket fire when he has a few rounds to spare. He must have a surplus lately because we've been taking a lot of incoming."

"Why doesn't someone go over there and run the enemy out?" I asked naively.

"You think that hasn't already been tried? We lost a lot of men. Finally, I guess, we decided to let them keep their share of it if they want it that bad. Coexist."

A small brown river ran between the large military base at Tay Ninh and the city of Tay Ninh. Most posts were named after the nearest burg. Other than size, I saw little difference between this base camp and the larger ones at An Khe and Phuoc Vinh.

The base was about a mile long and ran from north to south. Irregular in shape, the perimeter ranged from about a half-mile wide on the north end and narrowed to about one hundred yards in width on the south end. The small end pointed toward Tay Ninh the city and the river about five miles away. A long runway ran from north to south for the landing of conventional aircraft and warplanes. There were two shorter runways to one side and a number of helipads, aircraft parking ramps, and sandbagged revetments. C-130s, Caribous, and helicopters were secured here and there, while other choppers were taking off as we approached. Three flight control towers stuck up above a shack city of tin-roofed buildings with screened-in sides. Artillery emplacements, guard towers, and sandbagged fighting positions ringed the perimeter.

The base camp seemed as cluttered and as devoid of vegetation as Cam Ranh Bay. A depressed-looking ghetto of red and brown clay, brown or gray unpainted buildings, and drab OD green vehicles and aircraft.

The Huey landed near the center of the base, where a three-quarter-ton truck waited to transport the five newbies to our assignments. Coming down from cooler rarefied air at altitude, my jungle fatigues immediately soaked with sweat. As if the heat and humidity weren't bad enough, a breeze blowing off the city smelled as bad as a stale anchovy-and-onion pizza left out too long in the sun.

"I'll be seeing you around," Snake Eye said. "Do you know how to spell my name?"

I looked at him, puzzled.

"It's Bilby," he said with a grin. "B-I-L-B-Y. I hope you remember that so you don't forget me in your will."

21

The truck dropped me and two grunt troopers off at the end of a red-clay street. The troopers were as green as I, greener actually since they had probably only been in the army six months at the most. The truck driver pointed to a building at the end of the street.

"Troop headquarters," he said. "Report there."

We hoisted gear on our shoulders and walked between rows of the tin-roof buildings. Some were smaller, some larger, all with open screened-in half-sides. Overhanging awnings protected the screens from sun and rain. All the buildings sat on concrete blocks to raise them up from the ground.

Off to one side, behind some barracks, was a short helicopter landing strip with Huey slicks parked in L-shaped concrete and sandbagged revetments on one side and mean-looking Cobra gunships in revetments on the other. Farther down were the Loaches. All the helicopters were marked with yellow triangles on the doors to identify them as Apache Troop. As nose art, the Cobras looked predatory with red-and-white sharks' jaws, while the Hueys bore crossed sabers above the bold proclamation *Headhunters*.

The idea of hunting heads was a bit disconcerting. Stones painted white lined the walkway leading up to the door of the sergeant major's hooch at Troop headquarters. I half-expected to find a shrunken skull hanging on the wall of his office.

Sergeant Major Rogers was a big bluff man with reddish-gray hair cropped so short his skull looked sunburned. He stood up behind his desk. There were no shrunken heads or strings of ears; I looked.

"Welcome to beautiful Tay Ninh and the First Cav," the sergeant major growled. He sounded a little sarcastic. I understood why. I had already seen part of the post. "The old man is expecting you. He's right through that door. When you've finished, we'll do your paperwork, show you around and get you settled in."

I knocked on the wall outside the open door and said, "Sir, First Lieutenant Alexander reporting for duty, sir."

"Come in, Alexander."

He looked me over. I expected him to comment on my height, but he didn't. The two enlisted men reported and we all stood at attention.

"At ease, men. I'm Major Calhoun, troop commander."

We had a short briefing, which amounted to telling us where the mess hall was located and assuring us we would thrive and prosper at Tay Ninh if we kept our noses clean and did our jobs.

"We'll attend to formalities later," he said. "First, let's get you comfortable. We're a crazy bunch up here, but some pretty good people. We look after each other."

The two enlisted cherries were herded off to their respective outfits while I was introduced to my platoon leader, Captain William Cody Beatty, a tall, whip-thin man whose face and head were so sun-weathered that his brown hair looked brittle. Like Major Calhoun and the sergeant major and several other pilots I saw walking around, he wore a waxed handlebar Snidely Whiplash mustache. He stared at my hairless lip.

"This is the cavalry, Lieutenant," he said, like it was something I didn't know but should. "The cavalry wears mustaches, *real* mustaches. Have you got your cavalry hat yet? Don't worry about it. Fork over a hundred bucks to S-three and he'll get you squared away. Come on. Grab your bag. By the way, you *can* grow a mustache, can't you?"

I felt my face burning. "Of course I can grow a mustache. I'm not as young as I look."

"I was wondering," Captain Beatty said, nonplussed.

He led me to one of the long wooden buildings. The top half was screened in while piled-up sandbags covered the bottom half. A Huey took off from the short landing strip and blew sand and dust through the screens.

"We have to build everything off the ground to keep from being flooded during the monsoon season," Captain Beatty explained. "And because of snakes."

"Snakes?" I repeated.

"Watch out for the little green ones. Ol' Two Step. He bites you and you take two steps and keel over."

"Reassuring."

"He's not as bad as Charlie. We don't have much trouble with snakes. I'll show you why in a minute."

Apache Troop compound, I couldn't help noticing, was situated right next to the "Green Line," the post perimeter. From the porch of my barracks, I could look out to a guard shack crouched next to a spread of barbed wire and concertina wire. A field of fire about two hundred yards wide had been cleared all around the outside of the post. There were more rolls of wire spaced across it. Bases were also surrounded by trip wire flares, land mines, Claymores, and foo gas. The green of the untamed VC jungle still appeared uncomfortably close. I recalled how Minh the Kit Carson scout had slipped through all that wire and mines at An Khe to hurl a satchel charge at us. What prevented a *real* VC from doing that to us here?

"Our quarters are right next to the flight line," Beatty said. "You won't have any trouble waking up when the first choppers light up. We call it 'Apache Sunrise.' It comes before regular sunrise."

"How do you see the enemy in the dark?" I asked.

"About the only thing that flies around here after dark are incoming mortar rounds unless we have to put in troops or extract them. We usually don't start work until the low birds can see down through the trees. The dinks come across the border as soon as it gets dark, hit one of our fire support bases out in the bush, then try to shag it back across the border into Cambodia before the sun comes up. When we're lucky, we catch their yellow asses trying to cross just as the sun comes up."

There were six sets of bunks and wooden wall lockers inside

the barracks, three on each side. Mosquito nets were draped over each bunk, isolating it and offering a degree of privacy. One guy was sleeping. Otherwise, the barracks was empty. One of the bunks was stripped and its mattress folded back. Captain Beatty pulled a chain above it and an electric light went on. I assumed fuel-burning generators supplied the power.

"Take that one," Beatty invited. "It belonged to your predecessor."

"What happened to him?"

Beatty shrugged. "He went down. *Out there.*"

I asked no more questions. I didn't want to know.

"The showers and the ash can crappers are outside," Beatty continued. "Toss your gear and I'll show you the rest. There's a bunker right around the corner from the barracks where you can run to when the gooks get frisky and the incoming siren goes off."

It was a piece of steel culvert pipe about five feet in diameter and twenty feet long, open at both ends and covered between with soil and piled sandbags.

On the way to the mess hall, Beatty showed me a small pen surrounded by sandbags. Inside was a pair of small brownish animals that resembled ferrets.

"Mongooses. Or is it mongeese?" Beatty grinned. "That's why we aren't bothered with snakes. Yosemite Sam and Pepe LePhew are little snake and rat getters. They have the run of the place. Sometimes one of the Blues catches a cobra out there and we really have a show."

The way I felt about snakes, Sam and Pepe were going to be my best friends.

When we walked through the door to the mess hall, I noticed a kitchen area to my right and two large dining areas studded with wooden tables to my left. One area was for enlisted, the other for officers and warrants. We had coffee while Captain Beatty explained my duties as a slick pilot.

Apache Troop was made up of five platoons plus a small headquarters platoon: Maintenance; "White Team" Scouts;

"Red Team" Cobra gunships; "Blue Team" lift ships; and a Blue infantry platoon of about thirty ground soldiers. My Blue platoon currently had eight Hueys, sixteen pilots, twelve door gunners, and eight crew chiefs. Captain Beatty said we were always short of aircraft because of normal maintenance, combat attrition, and lack of spare parts.

Basically, the Headhunters' mission was to find the enemy, gather intelligence, act as artillery spotters, secure crashed aircraft, rescue downed pilots, insert and extract infantry and LRRPs (long-range reconnaissance patrols, pronounced "Lurps"), search and rescue, reconnoiter, support ground troops, provide air cover and air surveillance, haul ass and trash and whatever other duties the CO tasked us with.

"Most of the guys are out on missions now," Beatty said. "Some of them are probably down at the volleyball court. All the pilots are warrants except you and me. Even though you're a commissioned officer, you'll still fly second seat to a warrant. He's the aircraft commander. We want you to have at least three months in-country before you become AC. Understand that?"

"Clear, sir."

"Can the 'sir' shit, Alexander. Call me Bill or call me 'Blue.' "

"Blue" was the radio call sign for the Blue Team platoon leader.

The TOC, tactical operations center, was Apache Troop's nerve center. All info and intel from units operating in the AO or from brigade or division headquarters funneled through the TOC. Maps and charts cluttered a wall in front of soldiers monitoring a bank of radios. The TOC was usually a busy place to be and was manned twenty-four hours a day.

On one wall hung a large poster headlined CHARLIE KILLS. It was my first look at a body count chart. Tick marks in squares denoted the number of kills for each day of the month. I added them up. So far in February it seemed Apache Troop had killed, wiped out, greased, exterminated, or otherwise got rid of more than sixty enemy soldiers. Gooks, dinks, slopes.

Someone with a ghoulish sense of humor had drawn two cartoonish vultures above the board. One vulture was saying to the other, "Patience, hell. Let's go out and kill something."

"The objective," Beatty commented, "is to kill more of them than they kill of us. People's lives depend on how well we keep our cool when everything is turning to shit. I'm not *asking* you not to let me down, Alexander; I'm *ordering* you not to let me down."

Put that way . . . I felt a knot tightening inside my gut. How *would* I react when the proverbial feces hit the oscillator? I suddenly didn't feel much the wiseass anymore. This was serious business. The Vulture Board told me that. I hoped I had it in me, the right stuff.

What surprised me most that evening when Captain Beatty introduced me to the rest of the platoon pilots was that none of them appeared scared or tense. They were all young, these combat pilots, as young as or younger than I. Some of them couldn't have been out of high school all that long; one or two grew cavalry mustaches that resembled mangy caterpillars. They seemed to be a happy-go-lucky bunch of nutcases, real jokers. Watching them in the barracks, listening to them, I saw no indication that they were experiencing the doubts and fears that were making my guts roil. Shooting and being shot at weren't discussed in somber tones. Quite the contrary. The talk was more on the level of college students returning from panty raids. They were like a fraternity of fighting brothers, members of a winning football team. I sensed the team spirit. I wondered if I would ever become a part of it.

Shortly after dark, eight-inch guns and 175s on the perimeter began firing H&I, harassment and interdiction. The entire hooch vibrated from the air concussions of the initial barrages. I dropped to the floor and was halfway underneath my bunk before I noticed the other guys watching me, grinning.

"They start banging almost every night about this time," a warrant officer called Mighty Morris explained. He was a wiry kid with a blond mustache, short-cropped yellow hair and freckles. "You'll get used to it."

"I suppose you can get used to crotch rot too," I cracked, attempting to salvage some dignity.

"Come on, little man," Mighty Morris said, grabbing his guitar. "It's after work hours. Let's head over to the O Club and I'll buy you your first beer in-country."

The Officers Club was another hooch similar to the barracks. The interior decorators—previous pilots—had used a lot of rocket boxes. They were easy to come by, as the Cobras went through at least four boxes of rockets a day in normal operations. The bar was built of rocket boxes, scorched with fire around the edges for atmosphere. The walls were also adorned with scorched rocket boxes. A long piece of linoleum covered the top of the bar, with a bamboo rail around the edges.

Someone had gone to Tay Ninh and bought bar stools and wicker tables and chairs for playing poker. There was a radio and a TV with a single channel broadcast from the Armed Forces Network. On the bar next to the refrigerator stocked with beer and sodas was a cigar box, which served as an honor system bartender.

The mongooses Yosemite Sam and Pepe LePhew were already sniffing around and begging for treats. The club always smelled like a soured bar rag. Morris popped suds for the two of us and raised his in a toast.

"*Salud!*" he said.

"*Salud!*" the others roared. "To the Headhunters!"

Morris strummed his guitar and sang in a rich baritone voice pleasing to the ear. I felt a twinge of loneliness, of homesickness as the haunting melody of "Folsom Prison Blues" filled the club. Only the words were different.

> "*If I had my druthers, and that Freedom Bird were mine,*
> *I think I'd move my DEROS a little further up the line.*
> *Just to piss in potable water, that'd make my day;*
> *And to sit on cool hard comfort, and shit my blues away....*"

22

The 1st Air Cavalry remained in constant action following the Battle of Ia Drang Valley. The aerial reconnaissance squadron, the 1/9, with its current 88 helicopters and 770 personnel, was the only army unit of its type, a unique combination of scouts, gunships, and troop lifts that was proving deadly effective on the battlefield. Practically every fight started with a first contact by 1/9 helicopters. The 1/9 thrived on speed in the hunt and quick reaction after contact.

Operation Pershing, which began in June 1967 and lasted into 1968, was a typical result of helicopters and airmobile troops working together to develop a first contact. It began at the village of An Quang near a lake tidewater basin connected to the South China Sea. A pair of 1/9 Loaches buzzing An Quang spotted fresh diggings and field work in surrounding farms but saw no farmers. Slicks inserted a Blue rifle team to investigate. The cavalrymen found a large whitewashed boulder containing a notation in Vietnamese: WELCOME TO THE VC AND NVA. When the team approached the village, it was fired upon.

What began as a scouting report quickly became a brigade action. Gunships rocketed the village while four and a half cavalry battalions were airlifted to the scene, where they surrounded An Quang. An estimated two companies of NVA regulars and a company of VC defended the village.

Artillery, aerial rocket helicopters, gunships, naval and air force tactical air strikes, naval gunfire, medium battle tanks, 40mm self-propelled guns, and Chinooks armed with 7.62 miniguns all were hurled into the battle to soften up the village. Despite this destruction, cavalry troopers were still hit when they entered the smoldering village.

Machine gunners and snipers swept the Americans with accurate close-in fire. VC dashed out of spider holes and hurled grenades. Dead and wounded GIs littered the open ground where they were cut down next to tunnel entrances. Cavalrymen withdrew from the village, dragging their wounded with them while a pair of tanks fired cover with Bee Hive rounds.

The next morning, a battalion of cavalry launched an assault after another barrage of air strikes and artillery. This time the Sky Soldiers successfully secured the hamlet. A total of eighty-nine NVA and VC corpses were counted in the rubble.

Throughout the Pershing coastal campaign that began at An Quang, the 1/9 aerial reconnaissance squadron continued to spark the majority of contacts. Scouts initiated action by sighting activity on the ground; Red Team gunships moved in to strafe and rocket the enemy; Blue slicks inserted infantry to exploit the situation on the ground.

Over the course of the 343-day campaign, the 1/9's forward recon role exacted such a heavy toll that the aircraft were replaced twice over. The squadron came under fire 931 times, resulting in 250 helicopters being hit. Of these, 102 were so badly damaged they never flew again in combat while 14 were shot down and destroyed. The squadron lost 55 killed, 1 MIA, and 264 wounded in aerial and ground combat.

The day after my arrival at Tay Ninh, Captain "Blue" Beatty took me out for a combination check ride and orientation flight. Regulations required all incoming pilots to be checked out and certified. I was a little nervous about it since this was my first time piloting over enemy territory. I cleaned my issued .38 Smith & Wesson revolver and felt like a medieval knight girding for battle as I drew on the rest of my gear—NOMEX fire-resistant flight suit, color OD green; leather fire-resistant boots; fire-resistant flight gloves and OD helmet with adjustable visor; sunglasses that would probably melt in a fire; survival vest equipped with a K-bar sheath knife, a pencil flare gun, a map on oilcloth, a booklet containing key Vietnamese phrases, a portable AM/FM radio; and a bulletproof "chicken vest" that most of the guys, instead of wearing, stuffed into the Plexiglas chin bubble at their feet as added protection.

I reached inside the cockpit and connected my helmet to the radio cord and hung it above the seat on the hook before I stepped back to follow Beatty's preflight check. Most of the time, he said, preflights were conducted when we came in from a mission in order to be ready in case of a scramble. He would go through it now, however. He was a stickler for a good preflight.

"Too many assholes kill themselves by overlooking a good preflight," he lectured. "Two things I want you to do. First is a good preflight. Second, memorize the emergency procedures. I want you to know the location of every damned circuit breaker on this helicopter. Sooner or later something will happen—a malfunction, a bullet through the electrical system or the hydraulics—and you won't have time to decide on which circuit breaker is which or to try to think what to do. It has to be automatic reflex. Is that clear?"

My guts told me everything he said was absolutely right.

I was impressed. He understood the machine thoroughly. I intended to take the same precautions to increase my odds of getting home in one piece.

He checked the crew chief's log book for repairs, concerns, peculiarities, and other notations. After draining the pitcock valve to bleed off moisture condensation from the fuel, we checked the tail rotor and removed the tie-down strap. After that, I followed him climbing onto the roof deck, using concealed foot holes between the pilot's door and the cargo door. We inspected the rotor hub, the mast, transmission mounts and control rods, safety wires, push-pull tubes, stabilizer bars, and the control dampers. He pointed to the top of the mast at the big nut that held the whole works in the air. It was called the "Jesus nut." If it went, the only thing you had left between you and the ground was Jesus.

"But what good does the Jesus nut do if you don't look for hairline cracks in the blade-root laminations at the same time?" he asked rhetorically. "If the blade splits and breaks off, you're coming down like an anvil, Jesus nut or not."

Preflight completed, Beatty tossed me a short weapon that resembled a sawed-off single-barrel shotgun of an incredibly large gauge. "Take this," he said. "Do you know how to use it?"

"I was in the Eighty-second Airborne." I broke open the 40mm M79 grenade launcher and looked down the barrel. It was clean.

"Take it with you from now on, in case we go down and have to fight our way out."

I started to climb into the right seat.

"Take the left," Beatty said. "Over here, most ACs fly left seat so they can see down through the chin bubble."

He was the one conducting the check ride. I stashed the M79 in netting behind the seat where I could reach it quickly. Blue stuffed an M16 standard-issue infantry rifle behind his seat. I climbed in, donned my helmet and switched into the intercom. A crew chief called Shaky, a lanky Texas kid with a hay straw cowlick and a drawl, helped me strap in.

Following Beatty's example, I slid the armor plate across the door. There was also armor behind the seat and underneath it. That left the pilots most unprotected and therefore vulnerable from the front. I detected another drawback to being short when I pulled the seat all the way forward; it left me partially unprotected by the side armor.

"You can help protect your family jewels by sliding that thar pistol around between your legs," Shaky suggested.

I looked at him.

He shrugged. "It's your jewels," he said.

"Anytime today will do," Beatty commented, waiting for me to fire up the bird.

"I gotta be able to reach the pedals first."

I adjusted the pedals to their farthest extension. With the seat forward and the pedals extended, I could fly it all right. Shaky murmured something about making me pedal extenders out of wooden blocks. He grinned and ducked into the cargo bay to tend to his machine gun. From now on, I knew, pilots who flew after me would be cussing me while they tried to let out everything and get their knees out from underneath their chins.

I pressed the starter trigger. The rotor moved slowly until the turbine caught. Then it blurred overhead. Stress patterns spiderwebbed brightly in the plastic windscreen canopy against the morning sun. I eased in power to get the Huey light on its skids. When the nose came up light and shifted, I corrected for drift, then added power and lifted the tail. Nose down, I hovered away from the bird's revetment before climbing out of the base and roaring over the trees east of camp at a steady speed of eighty knots.

Not bad, I thought. I looked to Blue for his endorsement. He stared out the side window, pretending indifference. I was actually flying a helicopter above Vietnam, a war zone.

Once we crossed the brown ribbon of the river that ran through Tay Ninh the city, Beatty directed me up to four thousand feet, well out of most ground fire range. That suited me.

There were no clouds. The sky was a fine cobalt blue. A rare good day for flying.

Blue pointed out the Michelin rubber plantation, the relay station and antenna on top of Black Virgin Mountain, and, in the distance, the cities of Bien Hoa, Saigon, and Cu Chi. I thought of B-I-L-B-Y.

"Where's Vung Tau?" I asked.

He pointed far off to the sparkle of the South China Sea. I sighed.

Our AO was an irregular-shaped thirty kilometers by eighty kilometers. It included more than one hundred miles of border with Cambodia. The border was our primary concern. Flying near it, I studied the trails webbing the other side, part of the Ho Chi Minh Trail network. Beatty said Cambodia was full of NVA troop staging areas and camps teeming with military activity. The NVA engaged in maybe a week or two of fighting each month. They would come across the border, attack our FSBs and conduct a few ambushes, then hightail it to safety to recuperate for the next round. Not being able to cross the border and strike the NVA in their backyard was a real source of frustration for pilots at Tay Ninh, but we had strict orders forbidding it. The rear echelon pukes issued lots of such orders regarding "rules of engagement." For example, said Beatty, if you were shot at, the "source must be positively ascertained before the target can be attacked." You got your tail in a wringer if you didn't.

Blue ran me through a series of movements, emergency procedures, and an autorotation. Then he relaxed in his seat, hands in his lap, and sighed.

"I've had enough for one day," he said.

"I take it I passed my check ride?"

He looked at me.

"What if I had failed?"

He shrugged. "You'd still be flying until you went down. We're always short of pilots. Now see if you can find your way home."

How could you get lost? Black Virgin Mountain stuck up out of the flats like an ol' girl I once heard of at Bragg who had only one tit and that a D-cup in the middle of her chest.

"Sometimes during the monsoon season when there's fog and rain, you can't see the mountain," Beatty cautioned.

I found my way back to base. I thought I did all right for my first mission over a hostile zone. But, of course, I hadn't been shot at yet.

24

The zone was going through some kind of quiet, relaxed period. Beatty said it was because Charlie was taking a breather between operations. Two months before I arrived, one of our infantry companies had been all but decimated on LZ Eleanor. After that, for the rest of December and into January 1969, the 1st Cav had busily kicked ass in interdiction ops in the Angel's Wing area. Charlie broke up into platoons and squads the better to evade and hide and pulled back into Cambodia.

"They'll be back, though," Captain Beatty predicted. "They always come back."

The guys bitched about it every night at the O Club.

"They sit over there giving us the finger and waiting until we're not looking to slip over and kick us in the balls," Mighty Morris fussed.

"We could cut the activity in War Zone C to zilch if they'd let us raid Charlie's camps in Cambodia," said a warrant named W. B. Farmer. He was a big rawboned farmer from Alabama with speech so slow you almost went to sleep before he finished a sentence. Everybody called him Farmer Farmer. "If y'all fly along the border you can actually see them bringing arms and supplies down the trails from North Vietnam—and there ain't a cotton-picking thing we can do about it."

Some of the Cobra jocks had a crafty way of dealing with it. Rather than return to base with unexpended firepower, they pointed their sharks' jaws toward Cambodia and all of a sudden they experienced an electrical short or malfunction that released all their rockets in that direction.

Oh, hell. It was an accident. We don't know what happened. Them rockets just took off on their own.

Vietnam wasn't so bad. I had seen more action riding shotgun on buses in Santo Domingo. We still patrolled *out there,* searching for enemy activity, but no one was getting shot at and no one saw anything. Blue complained that it was almost too quiet. Some of the guys were getting jittery about it. Mighty Morris said he could almost hear Van Heflin or Victor Mature in some jungle movie muttering after the native drums stopped beating, "Quiet. Yeah, *too* quiet." One of the problems with being a snuffy in war was that you rarely saw the "Big Picture." You knew only what was happening in your immediate vicinity. As far as you were concerned, there wasn't even a war if you weren't personally being shot at, while a few miles away other guys might be fighting for their lives on isolated FSBs.

The days were hot and muggy and dirty. I got diarrhea because of the malaria pills and had to be grounded to the ash can crappers for a few days. Chow wasn't too bad. Mostly it was D-rations heated up in the mess hall. Ds were like Cs, only more of them in bigger cans. Now and then somebody made a supply run to Vung Tau or Cu Chi and returned with steaks.

The volleyball game was the cultural center of Apache Troop. It continued day after day. The same game, it seemed, as though it had started at the beginning of time and would still be playing when Gabriel blew his horn. Much like the poker games at Fort Wolters. Somebody had built a private bunker next to the court out of sandbags and construction steel. A Cobra jock presently lived in it. He often brought a chair out, leaned it against the side of his little residence and sipped coffee contentedly while he watched the game.

Blue explained that the bunker was for short-timers, guys who were nearing the ends of their tours. They got nervous when they got short, afraid something freakish might happen to them, like a mortar round in the bed when they only had a few weeks to go. Each guy in turn when he got ready to DEROS back to the United States auctioned the bunker off to the next paranoid short-timer with the highest bid.

On the volleyball court was where guys got acquainted. Fortunately, I had learned long ago as the shortest kid in high school not to be sensitive about my size. The guys were going to be on you about *something,* even if you had a harelip. That was the way it was. All the old "short" jokes were brought out, dusted off and spiked into my hip pocket. My radio call sign was "Blue Apache Three-Seven." The others changed that to "Squatty Body Three-Seven."

Mighty Morris wrote his songs and played them in the O Club.

> *"He stood in the steeple,*
> *and pissed on the people;*
> *But the people*
> *couldn't piss on him. . . ."*

Beer cans flew in the O Club like mortar rounds. In the middle of a session, Mighty Morris stood up and lamented, "I'm so damned bored. If I knew I was going to be killed before I got out of this shitbag country, I'd just as soon it be now to get it over with rather than put up with all the bullshit and waiting."

I had no complaints. I liked it boring. I kept busy hauling ass and trash, conducting low-risk troop and LRRP insertions and extractions, and growing a mustache. I flew mostly with Blue Beatty, but sometimes with Warrants Mighty Morris or the lumbering Alabaman Farmer Farmer, who flew almost as clumsily as he walked. Our most exciting mission was flying two Hueys full of boisterous pilots to Phuoc Vinh, where 1st Cav had moved its division headquarters, for a squadron hail-and-farewell party. Hail to new arrivals like me, farewell to departing vets.

I wore my new expensive black Stetson cavalry hat with the gold braid and my new mustache. The mustache was a pitiful, mangy thing compared to some of the others, whose waxed ends were perfectly capable of stabbing you to death if you got too close. Everybody got drunk except the "designated drivers." It was a singing, laughing, boisterous, quarrelsome bunch of chopper jocks and crews who returned to Tay Ninh late at night. The chopper cargo doors were closed to keep us from falling out. Major Calhoun demanded to know who left a booby-trapped bottle of piss at the entrance to the mess hall. Nobody confessed.

"That's all right," he said. "You had what piss was left in the bottle with your breakfast oatmeal."

Alexander, I told myself, *you are one lucky little bastard, all in all.* Flying over Vietnam, I looked down and saw that it looked very big and glowed very green with its thick covering of jungle, spotted darker here and there from clouds passing by. It was a great place for a guerrilla war if you were the guerrilla. But here I was, high and safe in the sky. Nobody was shooting at me, and I was perfectly happy to be up above it all rather than down inside it directing artillery fire missions.

There was a big air horn on top of the TOC at base camp. It sounded whenever there was an emergency that required our services, like a ship going down or a Blue platoon getting caught in deep kimchi. I kept expecting it to go off, but it remained as mute and aloof as a bleached blonde at a bar before midnight.

I *was* one lucky bastard. War wasn't nearly as bad as I expected it to be. At least my war wasn't.

25

VC units penetrated Saigon itself during the Tet offensive of January and February 1968, even attacking the U.S. Embassy. They doubled the political embarrassment to the American government when they invaded Saigon again in May. General Creighton Abrams, who replaced General Westmoreland as commander of Military Assistance Command Vietnam (MACV), learned in October 1968 that at least four North Vietnamese divisions were building up strength in Cambodia along the border of III Corps. It appeared another major attack might be imminent against Saigon. Determined to prevent it, General Abrams ordered the 1st Cavalry Division on October 16, 1968, to be shifted from the Central Highlands and points north into III Corps.

The division would act as a screen to meet the NVA if and when they came across the border. Although Abrams did not expect a single American division spread out over such a large area to stop a multidivisional enemy advance, he knew the cavalry's airmobile infantry and firepower could wreak havoc among the enemy and delay him. He ordered 1st Division CO General George Forsythe to move his cavalry into position along the Cambodian border at once.

"If they come across," he directed, "ride them with your spurs all the way down, down to the point where, if and when they do get to the populated areas, they will be a relatively ineffective fighting force."

Movement began ninety minutes after Forsythe received the order. Code-dubbed Operation Liberty Canyon, it was the largest Allied intratheater deployment of the war. The division withdrew its scattered battalions from one end of the country and moved them more than 550 miles by air, land, and sea in order to commit them against the enemy at the other end of the country. Over a frantic period of sixteen days, the Air Force shuttled 11,550 troops and 3,399 tons of cargo from Quang Tri, An Khe, and Phu Bai to Tay Ninh, Quon Loi, and Phuoc Vinh. At the same time, the U.S. Navy sailed another 4,037 troops and 16,593 tons of cargo from Hue to Saigon.

The 1st Cavalry Division formally occupied new headquarters at Phuoc Vinh, a former 1st Infantry Division brigade base, on November 7, but would not completely move in until March 1969. By November 15, the division was in place to commence operations. Operations began with a screen stretched across 4,800 square miles of the northern frontier with Cambodia, a belt of fire support bases similar to the Indian forts once used on the American frontier. It covered the "Sheridan Sabre" area, the Fishhook, and the northern NVA/VC approach route to the flat rice fields and the marshy Plain of Reeds of the western Saigon corridor facing Angel's Wing and Parrot's Beak. Nine U.S. cavalry battalions on one side of the international boundary were thus squared off against perhaps four *divisions* of North Vietnamese on the other side.

26

I soon developed a particular regard, almost an awe, for the LRRPs, the long range reconnaissance patrols. These guys had balls so big they should have been pushing them around in wheelbarrows. If King Kong had had balls like that, he would have swatted all those helicopters like flies, torn down the Empire State Building, turned it into a parking lot, married the girl and been elected to the Senate out of Texas. While Charlie might have been taking a breather, the LRRPs weren't. They continued their snooping and pooping *out there,* looking for the bad guys. Sooner or later, Charlie was going to get active again and when he did, the LRRPs would probably be the first to know.

Generally, we slick pilots inserted them at night or at dusk on isolated LZs barely big enough to slip in a helicopter and get out again. There were usually five of them, sometimes six, occasionally four. Young, tough-looking kids with their faces mottled with green, black, and loam camouflage paint out of which shone the whites of their eyes. They went in loaded to their eyeballs with Claymores, grenades, C-4 explosives, rifles, shotguns, two pistols each, and about eighty billion rounds of ammo. Like they were prepared to win the war all by themselves, which maybe they were. They could hardly walk for all the weight they were humping.

It was eerie enough just being the pilot and landing them out there. My sphincter drew up around my neck so tight at first that it threatened to suffocate me. All that blackness of jungle. Dropping down out of the darkness into a weed-choked clearing only a shade lighter than the surrounding forest. Although I was only on the ground ten or twenty seconds at most, I was ready to get the hell out of there. I couldn't imagine *staying.*

Skids barely kissed earth before the team was out of the

helicopter, tumbling out and instantly disappearing into the night. Just gone with hardly a sound. Out there in the hairy darkness full of enough terrors to keep paranoids supplied with nightmares for several lifetimes. Sneaking around searching for signs of the enemy. Trailing sneaker and sandal prints, following cart and bicycle tracks to hidden way stations, weapons caches, and secret tunnels. They told nerve-wracking tales of lying so close to VC supply trails that they could have reached out and tied Charlie's shoes for him, of having watched Charlie drop his drawers not ten feet away to relieve himself. So accustomed were they to being out in Indian Country alone that they had a habit of whispering into the radio. If it were true, as everybody said, that the jungle had eyes, some of those eyes were round and belonged to LRRPs.

A LRRP mission lasted anywhere from a single RON, remain overnight, to four or five days, depending upon the mission requirements. The team normally traveled under cover of darkness. Just before dawn they would hole up in thickets near well-used paths or other areas of activity to record traffic and, sometimes, to call in an artillery barrage or summon infantry troops to engage an enemy concentration. They moved during daylight only when it was necessary and always at great risk.

Mighty Morris and I inserted a five-man team led by Sergeant Snider. We returned to base camp and our bunks while Snider and his men struck an azimuth for the Cambodian border a mile or so away. They were shook out of their hide an hour or so after daybreak when a company-sized NVA element filtered into the jungle on two sides of them. VC, the guerrilla irregulars, generally wore black pajamas and straw cone hats. These guys were hard-core North Vietnamese regular soldiers in full khaki uniforms and pith helmets. They seemed to be everywhere in the foliage, as thick as an army of forager ants. Sooner or later, one of them was going to stumble upon the hiding Americans. Snider decided the team should attempt to steal away before the gooks surrounded and trapped them.

He led his men deeper into the jungle along an unguarded

retreat that led toward Cambodia. Around ten in the morning when the LRRPs thought they had escaped and were looking for a new hide, they came upon a tiny clearing. It was a park-like glade where the trees grew large and at spaced intervals. They skirted the opening and continued for a short distance up a slight incline. Sergeant Snider, who had marked the location of the NVA company on his map, huddled with his RTO, radio telephone operator, to call in a SITREP pinpointing the enemy for an artillery fire mission or an air strike.

One of the other boonirats scouted the immediate vicinity. He came upon campfire ashes. He stuck his hand into them. They were still warm. Live coals smoldered in a second bed of ashes. He soon located even more fresh campfires. The surrounding grass was well trampled, as though quite a large army had slept the night here. Hooch poles to support shelters remained stuck in the ground.

Apparently, Charlie was on the move again, preparing for another round with the Americans and their South Vietnamese ARVN allies. Suddenly alarmed and wary, the scout backed out of what had surely been a VC or NVA temporary cantonment. The LRRPs cautiously retreated.

Too late. Charlie had already heard them coming. The enemy opened fire in a withering ambush from the tops of trees and from behind rock piles, anthills, and jungle giants. Two Americans dropped hard, already dead before they hit the ground.

Snider's anguished plea for help filled the airwaves and set off the scramble alarm at Apache headquarters. He was whispering out of habit, but it was a shrieking whisper.

"We need help! We've been ambushed! God! God! Get us out of here! Please . . . ?"

The crackle of rifle fire in his radio background accentuated the urgency of his message.

27

Since I had flown the night before while putting in Sergeant Snider's LRRP team, I was on "five-minute standby" and not scheduled to fly today unless there was an emergency. Five-minute standby meant you had to be in your helicopter and in the air within five minutes after the alarm went off. I was enjoying a leisurely cup of mid-morning coffee and a cigarette at the mess hall when the scrambler horn on top of the TOC suddenly emitted a single long, shrill blast. There were two different signals. A single peal meant troops in contact. Three short barks signified a downed bird.

It damned near froze my blood. Adrenaline started pumping and nerves jumping. This was my first alarm. My feet hit the floor and I was out the screened door, letting it slam behind me, before my breath and ass caught up with my heart and feet.

Chopper drivers were more like grunts than pilots in the classic sense. Grunts who learned to fly. We slept with grunts, drank with grunts, identified with grunts. We raced to our choppers to be first in the air. First in the air meant you were the retriever, the one who went into the shit to get the good guys out. Why the hell would anyone race for *that* honor? Because you knew if you were the one down *out there,* you wanted the other guys to do the same for you. You *expected* it of them, they expected it of *you.* We weren't going to let any of *our* grunts get killed if we could help it.

As I dashed for my duty chopper, I caught a glimpse of Shaky paralleling me from the direction of the enlisted quarters where he had been reading a crotch novel. He was a long-legged south Texas boy, but he wasn't moving like molasses over corn pone this morning. He streaked by me like the Road-runner passing the Coyote. *Beep! Beep! Zoom!* By the time I reached the flight line he already had the tie-down released and was getting his M60 machine gun ready.

Captain Beatty was playing volleyball when the alarm blared. I jumped into the right seat, the copilot's position, while Blue "kicked the tires and lit the fires." This was why preflights were always conducted the night before. I took over while Blue jerked on his helmet, flight suit, and chicken plate. Shaky helped him strap in while I rigged up. I cinched my seat belt.

Helicopters had three different radios—FM for communicating with boonirats and ground bases; a UHF band with other helicopters and airports; and a VHF frequency for talking to each other. All three were going nuts with excitement. Through my helmet headphones I heard automatic rifles firing, crisp and hard and solid in bursts. LRRPs were crying and sobbing over the radio, completely freaked out.

"We're getting hit! We need help! Get your asses out here . . . !"

"Ready?" Captain Beatty asked.

I hit the radio foot switch. "Let's go."

I looked back at Shaky. He was helmeted and hooked into his monkey line. Door gunners and crew chiefs suspended their M60s on rubber bungee cords that allowed them to shoot the guns in any direction. The monkey line safety strap permitted them to move about in the ship while it secured them to it. They could stand out on the skids and shoot underneath the helicopter.

Shaky fed a belt of 7.62 into his gun and slammed the receiver cover. He cranked the handle, chambering the first round, then turned his head to look at me. I saw myself magnified in his sun visor in wraparound Panavision. He gave the thumbs-up.

Blue had the machine light on its skids. He hovered it out of the L-revetment and over the green line. We took off in less than three minutes from when the alarm sounded. Beatty pulled pitch and pressed cyclic toward the firewall. The Huey leaped into the air and soared out over the perimeter wire and across the river. Tay Ninh the city sprawled off to our right with the river running through it. Black Virgin Mountain, Nui Ba Den, stuck up ahead of us.

Farmer Farmer and another warrant named Miles flew wing with us in the second slick. We were out a minute ahead of them. A pair of Cobra "Snakes" with their red-and-white shark-mouth noses bright and fierce in the tropical sunlight overtook us and poured on the coal. They pulled a good lead on the much slower Huey slicks as we strung out across the sky.

"Looks like we're *it*," Beatty commented. We were first slick in the air.

He got on the radios with TOC to obtain grid coordinates and with the LRRPs to reassure them that help was on the way. Excitement vibrated through the airwaves, transmitting itself to us. My heart pounded as I broke out the map, plotted grids quickly and gave Blue a compass heading. It gave me something to do. I was flying into my first combat mission. I was more stunned than scared.

"We'll be on station in ten mikes," Blue promised Sergeant Snider.

"We got two men down! You copy?"

We were really scooting at about 110 knots, high enough at 1,500 feet to avoid most ground fire but low enough not to waste time climbing. In the distance, the Cobras circled over an unseen ground point like a pair of wasps, darting and dodging. Their air chatter merged with that of the frightened and frantic GIs trapped on the ground. White smoke streamed behind the gunships as they got into a racetrack pattern and made their runs. Rockets and miniguns exploded earth and vegetation into the air.

Blue dropped down to 1,000 feet and made a long approach from five miles out. Farmer and Miles trailed in their bird. Everything was new to me. I had never seen tracer tracks before. Bluish-green tracer bullets probing for the Cobras made long, silent, lazy-looking flights upward. In between each tracer, I knew, were at least four more unseen bullets. A commie

.51-caliber machine gun spat out slugs a half-inch in diameter and an inch long. They had incredible power and range when blasted out of a gun at better than 3,000 feet per second.

We were going to fly into *that*?

B-I-L-B-Y.

Blue raised the Cobra leader on VHF. "Apache Red, this is Blue." I couldn't help admiring the calm, firm tone of his voice. I wasn't sure I could even speak.

"Red, we're approaching now from about a mile out to your west."

"Roger Roger. I got you in sight, Blue."

"Red, we're going to do a fly-by to check out the situation."

"Stay to the north of us, Blue. Copy? That'll also put you north of our guys on the ground."

"Roger that, Red."

From the FM the LRRPs were screaming and sobbing. *"Hurry! Hurry! Goddamnit, hurry!"*

Our wing mate hovered at altitude, while we soared over low at full speed. Tracers were flying everywhere. I expected us to be riddled like a mallard on opening day of duck season.

I looked down through the tops of scattered big trees into a fairly open area, parklike with short grass, a few bushes, and a number of boulders scattered about. Little men in either black or greenish-brown garb, some wearing pith helmets, were darting and scurrying around all through the trees. They seemed heedless of the Cobras diving at them from the sky and peppering their ranks with rockets. Smoke swirled and eddied in the park.

Less than fifty yards down a slight incline from the enemy's leading soldiers, the LRRPs were making their stand behind a windfall of downed trees. We flew directly over them. Two GIs knelt behind the logs, returning fire uphill. The other three lay motionless on the ground in helter-skelter fashion, as though they had been dragged there on the run and dropped. They looked dead. One of the live grunts—I recognized Snider's face—stopped firing long enough to glance up as we buzzed over. There was a pleading, desperate expression on his face.

Charlie appeared bent on finishing off the other two GIs before we could get them out of there.

Shaky opened up with his M60, spraying the park with it, hammering hard. Frozen in my seat, I didn't glance back but it sounded like he was out on the skid. The noise impact of the gun was like someone rapidly slapping my ears with open palms. A mixture of odors assailed my nostrils—cordite, the bite of the acrid smoke from rocket explosions mixed with rich, pungent smells from the rain forest. Scents, sounds, and sights threatened to overwhelm my senses.

"Piss on you, motherfuckers!" Shaky screamed as he sprayed the park. "Piss on you! Piss on you!"

Blue's voice over the intercom jarred me back into my body. I felt like part of me had tried to escape it.

"There!" he said, trying to get my attention. *"There!"*

That shook me back into the game. I saw what he was pointing at. It was a small clearing about sixty feet to the rear of the LRRPs. I attempted to mentally record everything about it in the second or two it took to fly over before Blue pulled out in a fast, sweeping climb to the left. We dared not come back for a second look; the gooks would be ready for a repeat performance.

I estimated the opening in the trees to be about twice the length of a Huey one way and about one-and-a-half times its width the other. Some small stuff grew on it, saplings and grass, but I observed no major obstacles such as boulders or tree stumps.

Blue pulled up at altitude and asked through the intercom, "What do you think? Is it big enough for a PZ?" A pickup zone.

I shrugged. My voice sounded surprisingly calm. I couldn't believe I was saying it. "If you think we can do it, let's go for it. It's either that or nothing."

There wasn't another clearing of any size within five-hundred meters.

Beatty nodded. I saw him take a deep breath, as though girding himself for it, before he announced our decision over the air. He asked Farmer Farmer to stand by and hang loose, ready to make his own attempt in the event we failed. It occurred to me that if we crashed or got shot down going into the clearing, there wasn't enough room for another bird to try it. We would be marooned down there with the two surviving LRRPs. Charlie would surely get us all.

Cobra Red Leader was talking tactics. *"We're gonna run hot on enemy positions from east to west.... We're starting the run now.... We'll stay to the south side and try to give those guys some cover. Come in as soon as we get them pinned down...."*

"Affirmative, Red," Beatty responded. "We're going to make one sweeping left-hand turn and into the hole."

I wiped sweaty palms on my thighs and got on the controls with Blue, lightly. SOP required both pilots be on them when flying into a hot PZ or LZ, in case one of them took a hit.

I felt Blue bottom the collective. Over went the cyclic with the left pedal punched in. Around we came. We dropped out of the sky with dizzying speed and made one horrendously steep descent toward the clearing. No use providing the bad guys a floating target.

Confusion set in. Shaky's door gun crackled and pounded. "Piss on you! Piss on you!" It seemed everyone in the world, or at least in Asia, was yelling over the radios. Green tracks streaked all around us.

But then, suddenly, a fresh surge of adrenaline kicked in. Everything grew strangely quiet. I became detached from my surroundings. That was the only way to explain it. It was like I floated back out of the way and began observing the scene rather than participating in it. I glanced at my hands on the controls; they were no longer shaking. Above the ledge of the instrument panel, through the bright Plexiglas windshield, I saw the clearing telescoping toward us at a speed that should have been alarming but which at the moment seemed merely curious.

We decelerated at the last moment for landing, flaring with tail boom hanging low. Beatty pushed right pedal to swing the tail rotor away from the nearest trees. Then he squatted the machine. I spotted Shaky jump out and run around the left side of the bird with his M60. He fell to his knees at the edge of the jungle and rattled off a burst at targets unseen. Green tracers were bending and ricocheting everywhere.

I helped Blue quickly friction down the controls so the bird would sit by itself and continue to run at takeoff rpm. When we got ready to go, all we had to do was pull off friction, add more throttle, and we were out of there.

"I'm going in to get our guys," Blue called out, jumping to the ground with his M16. "You return their fire. Keep them pinned down."

Right. When I ripped off my helmet, the firefight sounded like my head was underneath a bucket with about a hundred kids pounding on it with steel bars. I snatched the grenade launcher from where it hung by its carrying strap over the back of my seat, grabbed a box of ammo, and dashed toward the nearest tree. Peeking around the trunk, I watched the two LRRPs making their desperate stand out in front of me and to my right. Blue was beating foot toward them, crouched over almost double as he ran.

Shaky shouted something. Then he darted back to the helicopter and tossed his machine gun inside before following the captain. I guess he thought he needed both hands free to drag the casualties. Two of the three guys on the ground lay dead still. The third writhed in agony. He looked to be crying out in pain and terror although I heard nothing he said because of the din of the firefight and the rush of blood in my ears.

Bad guys were jumping all around in the park, appearing and disappearing behind trees, bushes, and rocks. Muzzles flickered and smoked as the Vietnamese fought their way toward belly-to-belly contact in order to neutralize the air assault.

They were so near I smelled *nuc mam* on their breath. The sight of them stunned me. Somehow, I hadn't expected the enemy to be men like the rest of us. I expected phantoms or giants or *something* other than a bunch of little guys no bigger than me jumping all over the place like insane Jacks-in-boxes shooting at me.

One part of me saw it as so utterly unreal that it seemed surreal, while it encompassed such reality in another part of me that I heard the pounding of my own heart and blinked because the sun and the sky were so incredibly bright.

Blue and Shaky reached the deadfall. In all the excitement, Snider and the other grunt must not have heard the Huey's landing. They reacted by jumping to their feet and whirling around to confront a rear threat, almost getting shot themselves in the process. Blue yelled at them and I saw him pointing back at the helicopter.

By then I was busy myself. It was almost like I was on autopilot. I began peppering the enemy woods with exploding grenades, working without thinking, without feeling. I popped out grenades as fast as I could load the shotgunlike M79, squeeze the trigger, break it open, reload, and squeeze again. Mushroom clouds of smoke sprouted up everywhere with a popping like giant firecrackers as I attempted to lay down a flaming deadly wall of hot steel to cover our guys' escape.

The clatter of the responding AK-47s was deep-throated, more menacing-sounding than the tinny Mattie Mattell chatter of American M16s. Grunts said you never forgot the sound of a Kalishnikov rifle fired at you with purpose. Hell, I wouldn't forget the sound of an *air rifle* fired at me with purpose.

Captain Beatty grabbed a fallen trooper by his fighting harness. Shaky wrestled with the second body. Snider and the other LRRP latched on to the wounded man, dragging him out between them. He seemed to have gone mercifully unconscious. They kept firing back one-handed, John Wayne-ing it. Captain Blue and Shaky, stooping low, dragged their Sky Soldiers across the rough ground like sacks of heavy grain.

Eight or ten enemy soldiers, sensing their enemy's pending escape, charged flying through the forest, firing rapidly as they came. I blasted away in their direction with the chunker, sprigging their vicinity with mushrooms. An M79 when fired emitted only a mechanical *bloop!* easily drowned out by the din of battle. Apparently, not many of the bad guys even knew where I was. Although green tracers chewed viciously at the log barricade, only a few came my way.

I mushroomed hell out of the attackers. They had second thoughts about the charge and went to cover in the foliage.

We were giving a good accounting of ourselves in spite of our being outnumbered by at least ten to one.

Behind me I heard Blue shouting, "Get them in the ship! Get them in there!"

Like they needed encouragement. The bodies were torn and gray and bloody as they were hoisted into the cargo bay. Frantic grunts tumbled in on top of the corpses. Shaky went back to work with his M60. Blue was still yelling.

"Alexander! Come on! Let's move!"

I fired a last round, then tore for the chopper. I vaulted inside. Blue had everything unleashed. He pulled pitch and it was like he bodily lifted the Huey out of the clearing. As we soared out over the trees, dragging the skids through the tops of them, pissed-off enemy soldiers poured into the clearing behind, shouting furiously as they came. Lead and steel punched the air all around us.

Shaky hammered away with his machine gun. I leaned out the chopper's window and continued firing the chunker.

It was right out of *Terry and the Pirates*. The adrenaline rush was tremendous. I was scared, of course, scared shitless, but you didn't realize how scared you were until it was over. That was when your knees went wobbly, your hands trembled and you couldn't get your breath.

Blue was on the radio with Red Leader. "We're out! Everything left down there is prime target. Give the bastards hell!"

Cobras rolled and dived right over the top of us as we lifted out of the hole, unleashing all their awesome firepower now that no friendlies were left on the ground. Miniguns ripped like torn cloth, 3.5 rockets contrailed through the air. From toward Tay Ninh came more Cobras to weigh in on the fray and pulverize the earth, turn the entire area into a shredded cauldron of smoke and fire. I pitied the poor sonofabitching gooks. At the same time I hoped every one of them suffered the most excruciating of deaths.

28

I turned around once in the quiet and peace of altitude on the way back to Tay Ninh and looked into the cargo bay at the dead men. It was an image I would carry with me forever.

Shaky stood long-legged, leaning forward against his monkey line in the open door with his back to the carnage, as though distancing himself from it. Slipstream whistled past. Sergeant Snider sat cross-legged on the blood-smeared deck with the battered and bloodied head of his wounded teammate cradled in his lap. Blood oozed from a flesh wound in his upper arm. He stared wearily out the door past Shaky, his face flat and drawn and looking so old as to have gone beyond time. Like he too was attempting to separate himself from all that surrounded him.

The second live trooper appeared unscathed but exhausted. He lay belly down on the steel deck, too spent to move, his head turned toward the open door. He still clutched his M16 with one hand. It was difficult to tell him from the two dead guys who lay crumpled next to him like empty sacks of flesh, one almost on top of the other. They were all covered with blood. His free hand grasped the boot of one of the dead guys as though to prevent him from vibrating out. It was a tender and haunting gesture to see.

A thick puddle of blood seeped out of all that mangled humanity, pooled on the steel-riveted deck and quivered and throbbed from the vibration. I turned away quickly and concentrated on the green sweep of earth creeping past underneath and the wide stretch of sky above. I still smelled the rich, metallic odor of warm blood mixed with the acrid stench of cordite.

It was great to still be alive. That thought raced through my mind again and again. I felt bad about the dead guys, but wasn't it great that I was still alive? I felt vaguely guilty, but I couldn't help it. If somebody *had* to get it, wasn't it better that it was someone else rather than me? At least we got three of them out alive.

The odor of death stayed with me, cloying in my throat. Most people under normal circumstances failed to realize that blood had an odor. You didn't smell it when you cut yourself shaving. But when there was so much of it, pouring out all over everything, it had a primordial stink that seeped into your soul and memory banks and remained there forever.

It oozed into crevices and cracks in the helicopter. It took us weeks to get it all out. It dried and returned at unexpected times as a thin pink powder vibrating throughout the ship, triggering the sights and sounds and scents of that day. I had to glance back each time it happened to assure myself that the dead guys weren't still crumpled on the deck. It was like their ghosts stayed in the ship.

Blue still hadn't put on his helmet or fastened his seat belts, we had departed the PZ in such a hurry. Neither had I. He looked at me, his face pale and his wonderful mustache looking drooped. This guy had balls to drop a chopper in that hole.

"You got it?" It was a question.

He needed a break. I took a deep breath. Through the radios I heard the Snakes working out, mopping up what was left. *"Breaking right . . . breaking left . . . coming in hot . . ."*

"I got it," I said, and I flew it the rest of the way in.

LRRPs had had a bunch of wooden nickels made up somewhere which they gave to chopper crews that pulled them out of fires. They always made a big production of handing them out. It became a status thing among airmen to possess a pocketful of them. We may even have taken chances for wooden nickels that we would not have risked otherwise. It was sort of like what Napoleon said of ribbons: "If I had enough ribbon, I could conquer the world."

Blue, Shaky, and I were all recommended for medals. I eventually received my first Bronze Star with "V" for valor, but I placed a lot more value on the wooden nickel Sergeant Snider pressed into my palm after we reached Tay Ninh. There were tears in his eyes. The Bronze Star came from the impersonal bowels of the Department of Defense; that wooden nickel came from the heart.

Like Blue said at the O Club, "Hell, don't give me another goddamned medal. Give me a beer."

The action provided some nice stats for the brass. Twenty "confirmed kills" went up on the TOC's Vulture Board.

"How many did you kill with the blooper?" Sergeant Major Rogers asked me.

"How the hell should I know? I was too scared to notice. I was just shooting."

"Three," Blue said.

I looked at him. He shrugged.

"He killed three. That's confirmed."

"It is?" I said.

"What difference does it make?" Blue asked. "It doesn't mean anything. The brass add up all the numbers to claim we're winning the war."

The most amazing thing was that there was not a single bullet hole in our helicopter. Farmer Farmer and Miles landed directly behind us at Tay Ninh. Shaky was looking for bullet holes that might cause structural or mechanical damage while the dead and wounded were being loaded into a truck ambulance for transportation to the hospital and morgue. He stepped back in amazement.

The other pilots looked the ship over, even getting down on their knees and peering underneath. Blue and I checked it out.

"How in pea-picking hell did you manage that trick?" Farmer Farmer demanded. "From where we sat, it looked like you guys were flying into a spiderweb of green tracers. My Gawd!"

What could we say? That the gooks were bad shots?

29

Screening forces of the 1st Cavalry Division sometimes paid a high price in detecting and harassing large advancing enemy formations. One of the highest was paid by Company D, Second Battalion, 3d Brigade when, on the morning of December 3, 1968, the 116-man company airmobiled onto LZ Eleanor to operate against enemy supply lines.

The company met no initial resistance. The signal "LZ Green" was given, meaning a safe or secured LZ. Troops nonchalantly moved about in the waist-high grass on the two-hundred-yard-wide field. They were unaware that the LZ was ringed by more than four hundred NVA soldiers bunkered in the treeline with automatic weapons, heavy machine guns, mortars, and B-40 rockets.

On a given signal, the field was suddenly raked by a devastating barrage of bullets, mortar explosions, and rocket detonations. Dead and wounded cavalrymen dropped.

Rocket bursts ignited a raging grass fire. Troops frantically battled both the blazing grass and the ambushers while at the same time attempting to dig refuge in the parched soil. Many more were killed or wounded. Some of the wounded were burned alive. Their screams of agony and terror added to the hellish din.

Machine gun bullets riddled the first medevac helicopter to attempt a landing on the fire-swept field. The pilot, door gunner, and all the medics on board were shot. The copilot lifted the stricken helicopter from the LZ at once.

Immediate resupply and reinforcements were requested. Helicopters darted overhead as crews tossed out ammunition and other supplies. Many of the containers, dropped too high, landed beyond reach of the besieged defenders. A number of

GIs were killed or wounded while attempting to retrieve the precious cargo. Men crying for water and help lay sprawled in crumpled heaps all over the fire-blackened field. Three medics died attempting to aid the growing numbers of casualties.

After five hours of intense combat, only 36 of the original 116 cavalrymen were able to continue the fight. Field First Sergeant John Allison shouted for everyone to gather what ammunition and grenades he could and crawl to his position. The survivors formed a small perimeter and prepared for Custer's Last Stand.

They were saved only when slicks filled with airmobile calvary reinforcements began arriving and the North Vietnamese withdrew.

30

My war had started; I was now into it. It looked like Charlie was getting up for another offensive, pushing troops across the Cambodian border. We had heard the NVA had four divisions over there in sanctuary. We sent everything we had out there to look for them, to try to pin them down, harass, interdict, and kick shit out of them. So slow before, the war dramatically picked up and was becoming a confused and dangerous madhouse atmosphere.

Pilots scheduled to fly at dawn, hoping to catch Charlie with his morning ablutions down, were up and at 'em at Apache Sunrise. It was a rule that everybody, on-duty, off-duty, or standby, had to get up and get dressed, if only in shorts and T-shirts for the ongoing volleyball game. A Spec4 from ops came over to make sure we got out of bed. His duty was to shine his flashlight in our eyes until we opened them.

"Time to get up, Lieutenant."

"Did you wake up Captain Blue?"

"No, sir. He's off today. Schedule says you're flying with Mr. Farmer."

I turned on the light, swung my feet off the bunk onto the floor and hurried to dress to get in a cup of coffee before the briefing.

The S-3 came over and conducted briefings at the TOC either in the morning or the night before. Pilots scheduled to fly were informed of the night's activities. There had been some probing at FSB Phyllis, killing several soldiers; Blue Max flew all night, putting in air attacks. NVA dropped mortars on FSB Dot and probed the defenses with sappers; Miles as AC, aircraft commander, and Taylor would fly that area with Mosby from the White Platoon to see if they could find the tubes. A LRRP team made contact but broke off quickly without suffering casualties. Intelligence reported activity around the Dog's Head, but that was unconfirmed.

"Intelligence?" Mighty Morris scoffed. "Where do they get such shit? From Chinese fortune cookies?"

Two Pink Teams consisting of White Loaches and Red Cobras—white and red made pink; white, red, and blue made a Purple Team—were assigned to check out the area north of the Michelin plantation for signs of an NVA company reportedly passing through the area.

"Take down these grids," the S-3 said, "and steer clear of them. Artillery will be laying down fire throughout the day. Okay, here are the other missions. . . . Swede and Connolly in Snakes, Farmer and Alexander in lift, Gerard and Bird Dog in the Loach—you're a Purple Team. Here are your search coordinates. We understand there's heavy bicycle traffic in the area and a possible weapons stash. Go find it. . . ."

Before I came to Tay Ninh, the screening teams were all Pink. Whenever a Loach was shot down, which happened frequently, it took up to thirty minutes to get a lift out there to snatch them out. Accompanying Cobras sometimes expended all their ammunition trying to keep the bad guys back. I had heard stories of Cobras recovering Loach crews by landing, jettisoning ammunition out of the little compartments in the Snakes' bellies, and stuffing in airmen to lift them to safety. Somebody finally got smart and added Blue birds to the scouts and guns to make the team Purple. Fewer Loach crews were lost when a slick flew with the team ready to effect immediate deliverance.

"Activity is picking up," said the squadron CO, Major Calhoun. "Be careful out there—but the general wants a body count for the Vulture Board."

Everybody laughed. The body count was a joke. Most kills were estimates.

"Do you confirm five kills?" a pilot might ask a Blue ground platoon.

"Make that eight if you need the numbers," the grunt would respond. "I can see three dead rock apes."

"That's close enough. I'll confirm nine."

The scout pilot's mission hadn't changed much since the days when General Custer was looking for Crazy Horse and Sitting Bull. He could read a trail just as well as Kit Carson. He could tell if there had been use of a trail, when, how long ago, and by how many people, depending upon the condition of the ground and how close the trees allowed him to get to the trail—and all this while flying overhead. He was also looking for bunkers, rice and weapons caches, camps, and anything else that might provide information on the enemy, his movements, and his intentions.

The Loach, a "low bird," flew slow clockwise circles just above the treetops, while the "high birds"—the Cobra and the slick—circled in lazy counterclockwise circles at about 1,500 and 3,000 feet respectively. The scout relayed all information to the Cobra. The Cobra X-Ray, the gunner, recorded it and passed it on as a "spot intel" report.

"Apache Two-Four, there's been movement down here," Gerard radioed from the Loach.

"Watch your ass, George," Swede responded. *"Can you tell how long ago?"*

"It's recent. At least since the last rain."

Because the Loaches flew low and slow, they were sitting ducks for any dink hiding in a bush. They were particularly vulnerable to RPGs, rocket propelled grenades, the Russian equivalent of the bazooka. During "sniffer" missions I got a taste of what it was like being the low bird. Loach pilots had to have balls bigger than King Kong's.

A "sniffer" was a high-tech approach to scouting. Two hoses were corked into a Huey's drainage plugs and stretched back to a machine in the cargo bay operated by a couple of guys from special operations. Sensors were set to pick up odors from campfires and the ammonia in urine. We flew low above the jungle, skimming at dangerous treetop level over double and triple canopy while the machine sniffed. Another slick cruised at around 1,500 feet to guide the lower helicopter while a Cobra or two at our rear, also at treetop level, acted as guns. If we picked up anything, our job was to mark the target with smoke grenades and tracer bullets, then get the hell out of there. The Snakes followed the smoke grenades with miniguns and Willie Pete (white phosphorus) rockets.

A flight of slicks filled with Sky Troopers completed the arrangement. Their job was to land as near the action as possible, disgorge troops, and get a body count for Uncle Sam and the folks back home.

"We're getting close to them," the special ops guys would say over the intercom. "They're coming up. They should be coming up *now.*"

If you were the enemy down inside the forest, you couldn't tell by the sound of a low-flying helicopter where it was or which way it was heading. You never saw anything until it was directly overhead. The enemy always looked surprised. We came upon three VC, rifles slung over their shoulders, pedaling bicycles on a trail. The bicycles looked like they were loaded with a ton or two of rice, another ton of ammo, two mortars and a battle tank. I didn't see how these scrawny little guys could even pedal them. When they saw us, they dropped their wheels and ducked off the trail into the woods. Shaky popped a smoke grenade on them. Then he and O'Brien the door gunner, one on each side, got in a few licks for God and country with their M60s while I pulled pitch and climbed out of the way.

Snakes dived on the fleeing VC, chasing them like ducks after june bugs. They shredded and burned and tore hell out of the terrain. I almost felt sorry for the poor little bastards down there.

But who I *really* felt sorry for were the victims of Arc Light missions. During TOC briefings, we were provided the flight path info for attacking B-52 bombers and assigned safe zones.

The Guam-based B-52s flew so high you neither heard nor saw them. You didn't see the bombs falling either. The first and only sign you received was that awful Second Coming of awesome power. Air waves seemed to crack and shimmy from the force. The earth shuddered all the way to Saigon. I knew many guys on ships out in the South China Sea who swore the ocean even rippled from the concussions.

It was at dawn that I witnessed my first one. I thought the sun was either coming up brighter than ever before, that the horizon had suddenly erupted in flames, or that Jesus was coming back. Apparently my AC, Mighty Morris, also observing his first, felt the same way.

"Jesus God!" he murmured in awe.

Helicopters swarmed to the site as soon as the smoke and dust cleared in order to conduct a BDA, a bomb damage assessment. The jungle looked like a moonscape pocked with monstrous craters. A desertlike stretch of fresh dunes and holes and mangled vegetation was all that remained of a VC tunnel complex. I flew low over it, stunned, while Shaky leaned out the cargo door and counted isolated arms and a leg here and there or a face, all of which we reported and which was multiplied or divided by some factor at higher-higher to get a body count. I thought *nothing* could survive a pounding like that.

But survive the enemy did. Shaken and mud-caked and his ears undoubtedly ringing, he scurried out of the ground like rats in a city dump to open fire, still full of fight. I had to hand it to the little commie men. They were either brainwashed into becoming a bunch of fanatical nuts—or they possessed gonads down to about their ankles.

Door gunners worked out on them. Snakes followed. Then the little men packed what remained of their ditty bags, shook off the dust, hauled ass to Cambodia and returned the next night to dig more tunnels.

You bombed them, rocketed them, shot them with everything short of a nuclear device, and they just kept coming back. I figured there must be about sixty billion of them hiding underneath each and every one of the sixty billion trees in Cambodia.

"Nuke 'em little cotton-picking cocksuckers till they glow in the dark," Farmer Farmer suggested, "then use 'em for night targets."

We were never going to run out of targets. Our jobs, it seemed, would never become obsolete. As of June 1968, the Vietnam War became the longest war ever fought by the United States. Hell, I knew guys who had been over here since about 1959 and were making a career of the war.

During one incredible night and day I logged fifteen hours in the cockpit in support of an operation. It began with flare duty. Flying at night with a low cloud ceiling and without being able to clearly see the horizon was a terrifying experience. We had these big parachute flares that the crew chief kicked out over an FSB in order to light up the attack area where NVA were probing. Your night vision was shot once the first flare popped. The mission after that became damned near suicidal.

Elongated shadows shifted and streamed before your eyes in a greenish, liquid world as the flares floated toward earth under their parachutes. The entire experience became a fantasy from the bowels of hell. Everything turned black and scary when the last flare sputtered out. It made me want to pray. Maybe I did.

After a couple of hours' sleep, I was up again at Apache Sunrise and leapfrogging troops all over the AO, looking for the enemy. Grunts all helmeted and flak-jacketed and grim-faced piled into the cargo bay with their weapons. Three grunts would squeeze in on the canvas bench across the back of the cargo deck, three more onto the deck in front of them, while the remaining two filled up the two pockets. It was a load. Overloaded helicopters unable to hover could still fly if they made running takeoffs. Up on the collective and twist the throttle for maximum rpm. You had to keep it out of the red line, though, because otherwise you lost the tail rotor effect and the helicopter spun in the opposite direction. Up and out across the highway leading to Tay Ninh the city and over the river into Charlie country. We were mostly flying the newer, more powerful H-model Hueys; the old C and D models would never have made it.

Three or four Hueys loaded with troops echeloned off each other, each slightly behind, above and to the left of the one ahead. Snakes flew escort. Formation flying was tense. We flew so close you heard the buzzing of the tail rotor of the aircraft ahead. I lined up a point on my nose with the skid of the bird ahead. The two points moved slowly relative to each other as we surged through the air. We climbed at about ninety knots out past the Black Virgin, which in fact was no virgin. She was a whore raped so many times her entire womb was full of VC just waiting for the right time to spew forth like little demons from hell.

Apache Three-Four and Three-Six flew ahead of me, Apache Three-Five behind. I accelerated gently to maintain my position, overdid it, and backed off. Yo-yoing. The entire cavalcade began to bank in a turn toward me. I had to decelerate quickly to keep away, then accelerate to get back into position. Sort of like cracking the whip.

"Closer," urged Captain Blue, ever the patient instructor as I worked toward becoming an AC myself.

"Closer?"

It looked like our rotors were overlapped already. I turned and looked out at Farmer Farmer and Miles in Three-Five off my left rear, guiding on me. Farmer waved.

Getting into LZs and out again in formation proved scary at first, especially when each LZ or PZ might be hot and had the potential of turning into an active volcano. Too steep an approach could stack up the birds and cause problems in setting down. An approach too shallow left you hanging out like a skeet target. Disguised voices over the radio expressed their displeasure with mistakes by calling the lead bird several forms of asshole.

There were basically two ways to get into an LZ. A tight, fast, spiraling descent, or a long, fast, low approach. Sometimes we popped into two or three LZs to confuse the enemy about which one actually received troops. Air assault, even on a cold LZ, was exhilarating when everything worked right. Low-level flying was the exciting part.

You only flew low when there were trees or riverbeds or other cover, never over open rice paddies or fields. The flight would drop down on a long approach to the LZ, the whole gaggle really moving from speed gained in the dive, flashing along above the jungle canopy at more than one hundred knots an hour. Burning coal, hauling ass.

My heart pounded in cadence with the muffled *wop! wop! wop!* of the main rotor. Blood rushing in my ears drowned out the roar and vibrations. All three radios chattering at the same time created further confusion.

Going in at speed, busting out over the clearing, quickly decelerating for the landing. Back on the cycle and reduce collective to flare. Trying to see over the nose to get a glimpse of the LZ while Cobras dived and hammered in, prepping the surrounding treeline. All birds coming in and squatting simultaneously to reduce time on the ground and exposure to hostile fire. Both pilots in a ship with their hands on the controls in case one of them took a hit.

Grunts jumped out each door and bounded away toward the edge of the clearing. We waited ten seconds, then took off together, watching for the lead bird's tail to move. Lifting when he did, staying tight so as not to straggle and delay the others.

We were in and out like that all day. Out with a load of troops, fly back in to Tay Ninh, jump out and take a piss during refueling, then either back out with more troops or pick up soldiers out there and drop them somewhere else. Other than that, I had no idea what the operation was nor what its strategy was. Snuffy was seldom provided a look at the Big Picture.

"Fuck this. *Fuck this!*" Mighty Morris exclaimed, beat from too many hours in the cockpit. "I ain't taking it no more. I'm tired of all this chickenshit. I quit!"

But of course he couldn't quit. None of us could. He was up again at Apache Sunrise. We all were.

31

Squatty Body, which was what the other pilots dubbed me, somehow lacked the devil-may-care, yellow scarf—wearing élan associated with a flying cavalryman. I suppose it was better than being called *Shorty* or *Half Pint,* but none of this nomenclature befitted a pilot who would soon take Captain Blue's place as platoon leader when he DEROS'd back to the States.

"Why do you think the army sent us a lieutenant instead of another warrant officer?" Captain Beatty asked rhetorically when the question of his replacement came up. "Squatty Body's mustache is looking pretty good. Don't you think it looks *commanding*?"

Everyone guffawed. A man got no respect in this outfit.

"Looks a little *short* to me," Farmer Farmer ventured, launching another round of short jokes.

"My legs reach from my ass to the ground like everybody else's."

"Yeah, but our asses don't drag over bumps."

Because I was sent here to take Blue's place when he rotated didn't mean I automatically received the command. Probably I would, barring some fuckup. Everybody continued to look for a suitable sobriquet for the pending platoon leader. The question of what I would be called began resolving itself on the volleyball court. During one session of the ongoing game, Captain Brillo Pad, the tall, skinny S-3 with the kinky hair, spiked the ball flush into my face at the net.

"Why didn't you jump up and block it?" Gerard scolded.

"He *did* jump up," Brillo Pad chortled. "The problem is, he's a mini-man."

A few nights later, the scramble horn bleated us out of our bunks. A single long blast. A U.S. rifle squad out on patrol was about to be overrun. Although I wasn't yet an AC, I still took left seat and the controls whenever I was on the board with

Farmer. The Farmer was as clumsy in a helicopter as he was on the ground. Lloyd's of London would never have insured him even if he were riding a bicycle.

Shaky was crew chief; O'Brien was the gunner. It was a clear, starlit night with no moon. Three lifts took to the sky along with a pair of Snakes flown by Swede in one and Whoppa in the other. "Whoppa" had something to do with the Snake driver's genitals and a certain large hamburger from back home.

As we approached the scene, we learned that the rifle squad had fought its way in retrograde, which meant it hauled ass, to the edge of a clearing large enough for a PZ. There was a pretty good fight going on down there now as the GIs dug in to hold the clearing. It was their only chance of getting out. Grenade and rocket detonations flashed open the darkness. Erupting muzzles created a white, blinking rhythm. Red and green tracers crisscrossed in a crazy, confusing, and beautiful pattern. From the air, it resembled a silent light-and-shadow show with none of the sound and fury experienced by the grunts in the middle of it.

My ass was vacuum-cleaning, threatening to suck the seat up into my rectum, which at the moment had located itself near my esophagus. Anyone who claimed he could look down through the dark at that shit shimmering like a red and green animated spiderweb, knowing he was going to fly into it like a moth, and not be scared spitless was either a goddamned idiot or a liar.

I banked my ship off to the southeast to stay out of the sights of possible antiaircraft guns. Farmer and I were the first ship in the air on scramble; that made us head honcho on going in. I designated how we snatched up the grunts. I tagged myself Chalk One, the first ship on the ground, with Miles and Mighty Morris Chalk Two behind me. Two birds should be sufficient for ten grunts in the squad. Taylor and Mississippi would stand by at altitude in case one of us went down.

"Shoot a flare to give us your exact location," I radioed the embattled squad leader.

Those guys were in a hurry to get out. Almost instantly a flare streaked out of the treeline on the northeast edge of the clearing.

Swede asked if the situation was such that his Snakes could lay down cover-and-suppress fire.

The grunt leader was almost screaming. *"Negative, Red. Negative! The little yellow motherfuckers are all around us!"*

As always during action, all three radio frequencies were going bugfuck.

"I'm going down and coming in," I announced, then switched to FM to talk to the grunts. "Blue Four-Two? We have two birds coming down. Be ready to pile on. These elevators are going to be in a hurry."

"Three-Seven, you ain't nearly in the hurry we're in."

I swung wide to the northeast, Miles and Mighty Morris hot on my tail boom, then sank down to just above the black roll of the earth and poured on the coal. Swede popped down behind us and followed in from about a mile behind.

"Three-Seven, let me know the minute you get them aboard," he radioed, *"and I'll drop some shit in Charlie's face."*

"Roger that, Swede."

Trying to keep my voice calm and casual. Blue would probably be listening at the TOC. I hoped I didn't sound like a schoolboy about to undergo puberty.

We were really hauling ass, and low. The world went by in a black blur.

"Yee-ha!" O'Brien cheered through the intercom.

Crazy bastard.

"Yee-ha!" I echoed.

"We're all fucking bat-loco insane," Farmer Farmer decided.

You had to be insane to do this for a living. We shot out over the clearing and I pulled up cyclic. I had already picked out my landmark—a particularly large tree nearby from which the flare had originated. I came in hot and flared as near the tree as I dared. Streaks of green pierced the blackness all around. Shaky and O'Brien held their fire since we didn't know exactly where the good guys were.

Miles in Three-Four skidded in right behind me. Bullets were punching into his bird.

Hardly had we touched down than the squad appeared and tumbled aboard the two choppers. Door gunners opened up when everyone was aboard, pumping streams of red back at the flickering muzzle flashes in the woods. There was the smell of gunpowder, the sounds of grunts yelling, guns crackling, radios jabbering. In a helicopter on a hot LZ was a terrifying place to be.

I took off immediately through the live green web of rifle fire, soaring out shallow at first to reach max transitional lift, then pulling up hard on the collective. Enemy soldiers erupted onto the clearing, chasing after the helicopter, firing as they came. Shadows flitted and weapons sparked and flashed. Some nut was running underneath my chopper as I took off, firing directly up at it. I braced myself for the impact of his slugs. Tracers zipped past the cockpit.

While all this was going on, Swede's Wisconsin-accented voice rang through my helmet receiver: "Mini-Man, *lift your tail!*"

I automatically jerked more collective and almost ripped off the stick. I nearly split the needles and spun off my rotor cap as the Huey lifted straight up in a dizzying climb. At the same moment, Swede's Cobra streaked directly underneath as he planted rockets in the space I was vacating. They exploded among the hostiles with white flashes so brilliant the air itself seemed to catch fire, momentarily blinding me. The concussion shook the UH-1, rattling it to its bones, but at the same time nudging it higher into the sky and out of the enemy's reach. Unable to see, I held on and kept climbing until my vision returned.

"*Well done,* Mini-Man," Swede radioed.

The name stuck. No more *Squatty Body*. I adopted as my radio call sign *Apache Mini-Man*. Along with the name began a growing myth that *Mini-Man* flew charmed, that bullets couldn't touch any ship in which I flew. Miles and Mighty Morris had five bullet holes in Three-Four. Luckily, none had struck anyone or anything vital, although Miles claimed to have a bruise on his ass where a slug thumped the armor underneath his seat. In contrast, there wasn't a single dent in my Three-Seven. The guy running underneath shooting up at my belly must have emptied an entire clip, and missed every shot.

It became a bit embarrassing as word spread that *Mini-Man* flew charmed and that you were safe if you reached my bird. LRRPs stumbling into deep kimchi got on the radio and started yelping for help.

"We're in heavy shit! Get us out of here! Send us Mini-Man!*"*

I collected so many wooden nickels I had to keep them in my locker. Guys made a point of coming out to the flight line after every mission to check for themselves. It got to where the tower recognized my voice and the sight of the white visor cover with which I accessorized my OD helmet.

"How are you today, Mini-Man?*"* Tower would ask. *"Any bullet holes?"*

One of the crew chiefs was an excellent artist. On the back of my helmet he painted a sawed-off cartoon character wearing spit-shined paratrooper boots, a flight helmet, goggles, and a scarf like Snoopy wore chasing the Red Baron. Above it was the notation *Apache* while below appeared the other half of my call sign, *Mini-Man*.

Mini-Man, the smallest chopper pilot in the U.S. Army, now flew the unfriendly skies of Vietnam.

32

Endless hours of patrolling. Back and forth across the AO snooping and pooping, interdicting the enemy by day or night and poking at him to keep him from organizing to attack Saigon. It was believed that if Saigon fell, so fell the country. Events all seemed to run together after a while. Scramble alarm shrilling in the middle of the night. Apache Sunrise. Downed pilots. Trapped pilots. LRRPs under fire. In and out of LZs and PZs so hot the Devil brought ice water. A Blue Max gunship went down and both pilots were killed. Headhunters came in after missions and walked around their ships counting bullet holes.

"How about Three-Seven?" they asked each other. "Any bullet holes in *Mini-Man*?"

Like a wiseass, I made a big show of *not* checking for bullet holes. As though I knew there wouldn't be any, so why check. I took pride in being the little guy with a big set of balls. War was a game whose few and rudimentary rules I quickly mastered.

"Ol' Crazy Horse thought the spirits would protect him from General Custer's bullets," Mighty Morris mused. "*Mini-Man*, you ain't into the spirits, are you?"

"Crazy Horse finally got shot," Farmer Farmer pointed out.

"Spirits or not," Miles said with the old Headhunter spirit, "if *we* had been with General Custer's cavalry at the Little Big Horn, that river would still be known for nothing except trout."

"Don't get cocky," Captain Blue warned me. "There's only one way to keep bullets away—and that's a one-way airplane ticket home."

Which was where Captain Beatty would be heading shortly, leaving the platoon in my command. Thinking about taking over made me nervous. I had never commanded men before. Was I capable?

By the end of April I was an aircraft commander. Another three months or less and I would be an aircraft commander *and* platoon leader for the Blue lifts. Captain Beatty informally donated to me his lanky Texas crew chief. Shaky knew his stuff, and he knew helicopters. I was most grateful. So was Shaky. He and I began flying most missions together, I in the cockpit's left seat, he in the cargo bay with his machine gun and, on the ground, making sure my ship was always ready for takeoff.

"We've had six or eight downed helicopters and thirty or forty pilots, crew, or grunts killed in the AO in the last few months," Shaky philosophized through his south Texas drawl, "but we haven't had to patch a single bullet hole in any chopper you've flown, sir. Some guys can't even fly to Vung Tau for beer resupply without getting shot."

Whenever I thought deeply about it, which I tried not to do often for fear of changing my luck, I supposed I might have developed a different outlook on the war had I come over in artillery or infantry where I was actually down in there with the dinks and snakes. The war was different for each of us according to individual perspective.

Warplane crews in the fast movers and bombers took off from Da Nang or Ton Son Nhut or even Guam. They zipped in, dumped some bombs or rockets, then returned to base without experiencing the aftermath of their business. BDAs informed them they had destroyed so many enemy bunkers or inflicted damage on an NVA mortar platoon. They never saw the blood and smelled the guts and shit.

Although helicopter pilots were somewhat insulated from the full effects of the ground war, we were nonetheless much closer to the action than other aircraft jocks. We identified more with enlisted men and with grunts than we did with staff officers at MACV or other pilots. They were *them,* higher-higher, the brass, REMFs. We were *us,* the snuffies. Helicopters existed in that transition area between boonirats in the jungle and the rest of the war, fully a part of neither.

The helicopter made the war slightly more antiseptic for chopper jocks and crew. We had our moments of adrenaline and terror, of course, but they seldom lasted long. It was in and out, one round at a time. It was a lot of shooting and stuff, close enough to see and smell the corpses and blood and shit and snot and tears, but then we hauled ass and seldom had to experience the full aftermath. We could go back to the O Club for a cold beer and listen to Mighty Morris sing.

It was a crazy way to make a living. We all said so. Each of us had his own method of dealing with it. As I became a dues-paying member of the Headhunters' fraternity of fighting brothers, I found myself in a peculiar sort of way beginning to enjoy the job. From my first elaborate attempts at avoiding Vietnam, I now went the other way and embraced the war with a forced nonchalance and a certain pride in being good at my job as well as an object of some admiration.

Sometimes I wondered what happened to that other little guy I had been before I morphed into *Mini-Man,* hero of the oppressed and champion of truth, justice, and the American Way. How different a war it might indeed have been had my inbound flight not been diverted and I ended up with my original orders at Vung Tau flying generals and T-bones and playing the angles. Or, even more different, had I come over in artillery and ended up in the jungle as an FO.

Rather than writing letters home, I called Sandy regularly over a radio-telephone line through Japan. You could do that if you were stationed at a larger post. In one of my rare letters to her, however, I tried to explain things.

"I've changed since I've been in Vietnam," I wrote. "For the better, I think. Flying seems to be the thing I'm most suited for, that I was born to do. I feel like I'm doing an important job here. That's it's important to me, to you, to our children, and to our country. I really believe defeating communism will help keep the United States free, if the politicians and lawyers don't take away freedom first. I have to do everything I can to do my part. . . ."

33

The aim of the NVA "mini-Tet" offensive that began on February 23, 1969, was to overrun Saigon. The 1st and 7th NVA Divisions worked their way into the region north of the Michelin rubber plantation while the 5th VC Division moved into the Angel's Wing west of the capital. The 9th VC massed in southeastern War Zone D. Firefights and rocket and mortar barrages erupted over a wide front.

Cavalry operating out of FSB Grant near the Michelin plantation bottled up the 1st NVA Division by repeatedly interdicting the enemy's lines of communications. The NVA determined to clear the area for an unimpeded approach to Saigon. On the night of March 8, intense rocket and mortar barrages destroyed the headquarters of Second Battalion, 12th Cav at Grant, killing the battalion commander. Enemy troops stormed the FSB shortly after midnight.

Quad .50-caliber machine guns sliced through the human waves of charging NVA soldiers. Bee Hive rounds cut swaths through enemy ranks. Desperate artillerymen stuffed 175mm howitzers with powder charges, lowered the guns to troop level, and blasted flaming powder into the attackers' faces. The charge pellets were each about the size of a man's thumb. They came burning out of the muzzles at some hellacious rate of speed and penetrated into the guts and bodies of the enemy. Screams of pain and terror filled the night.

Concentrated defensive fires and air strikes smashed the attack a mere two hours after it began.

Three nights later, in the predawn hours of March 11, two NVA battalions again tried to overrun FSB Grant. They were driven back. Cavalry helicopters from the 1/9 at Tay Ninh pursued the remnants for the rest of the week.

The successful defense of Grant ensured that the cavalry would continue screening operations in War Zone C, III Corps, as it harassed, interdicted, and kept off-balance enemy elements attempting to push south and east toward Saigon.

34

If we were all a little crazy, the most insane of all were the pilots and crews who flew Loaches, the Hughes 500 OH6A LOHs. These guys were a strange bunch of ducks, a dangerous breed of loners who stayed off to themselves even when they were drinking at the club. They lost so many friends shot down that they simply stopped making friends. They had the option of transferring out of scouts once they accumulated five hundred hours of flight time or got shot down five times, whichever came first.

I often flew the Blue lift for Purple Teams, making large circles as the high-high bird, above the Snake below me and the Loach below him flying at treetop level. The low bird often acted as bait to draw fire in order to give the shark-jawed Cobra a workout. They were surprisingly hard to hit from the trees, but they got shot at so much that the gooks had to get lucky once in a while. If it was an RPG rocket, there was often nothing left but shards of metal and shreds of torn flesh. Hardly enough to even bury. *Sorry about that. This hand and this piece of scalp is your son. What's left of him. Bury him in good faith.*

Loaches flew with a three-man crew and all four doors removed. The "torque," or door gunner, sat directly behind the pilot, which enabled him to see whatever the pilot saw and to fire his M60 machine gun out either side. The observer, armed with an M16 rifle in one hand and a red smoke grenade in the other, sat in the left front seat. If a low bird took fire, all the observer had to do was drop smoke to mark the enemy's position. He already had the pin on the grenade pulled.

The Loach could sting when it had to. In addition to the machine gun and M16, the occupants were armed with frag and Willie Pete grenades and an entire box of M60 ammunition. Radio traffic between the low bird and the high bird Cobra, whose X-Ray pilot took down "spot" report information, continued at a running pace while the Loach sniffed around for enemy signs.

"Apache Red, looks like there's been recent movement down here. I'm going to let on down for a better look."

"Apache One-Three, keep an eye off to your left there."

"I'm watching it, Red. You help me with it. . . . Been some heavy traffic down here. Bicycles and troops. I'd say within the last day or so. . . ."

"You want me to pass it on to TOC?"

"You might tell TOC we have some Indians down here some-where. . . ."

"You want me to recon by fire, One-Three?"

"Might as well. Let me pull out of here. . . ."

You could always tell when the low bird took fire, even before he came up screaming on the radio and dropped smoke. Sometimes you saw muzzle flashes, particularly if it was heavy fire. But what was really telltale was the way the Loach's tail flickered up like he had been goosed when the pilot shoved in throttle and pulled pitch to get the hell out of there. If he were hit bad, say the loss of oil pressure or pedal control, he faced the prospect of either going down where he was, in which case Charlie was waiting to shoot him up, or he could attempt to nurse his crippled bird to the nearest clearing where the lift could get in to snatch the crew to safety.

Mosby took fire one afternoon. His gunner was hit in the arm. AK fire knocked out his hydraulics. The tiny helicopter wobbled and hawed across the air just above the trees as Mosby fought to keep it in the air. Swede in the Cobra dived with his minigun chewing forest. That left it to me to direct Mosby.

"One-Six, you read?"

"Affirmative, Mini-Man," Mosby said, his voice thin and strident. *"We got a man hurt. I don't know if I can keep us in the air."*

No time to waste with small talk. At Mosby's low altitude, all he could see were the tops of trees.

"Turn left right now," I barked. "Okay, okay, you got it. Just keep going straight ahead. You'll drop over a clearing in about five hundred meters. Set it down as soon as you can, but leave room for me to come in behind you. Got it?"

"If I can keep us up, Mini-Man . . ."

The Loach wobbled all over the air, engine sputtering out a thin mist that trailed behind, spreading out.

"You got two hundred meters to go, One-Six. Keep going. Be ready. I'm coming down behind you. . . ."

I dropped altitude. Shaky was on his M60, clapping my ears with its sound. The Loach broke out over the clearing choked with elephant grass. He did a good job bringing down his dying little ship. He dropped into the grass and the grass stopped him almost immediately. The Loach remained upright.

By the time I squatted behind it, the Loach's blades had stopped spinning. Mosby and his observer were helping the wounded gunner get out of the damaged chopper. Blood was spattered all over the interior. They grabbed their weapons and ran toward my Huey, looking back over their shoulders. Like someone was firing at them. Of course, I heard nothing. I saw no tracers. The crew tumbled into the cargo bay and Shaky signaled, *"Go! Go!"*

I pulled out so abruptly that Taylor, my copilot, called out, "5,800 rpm," which meant I was on the verge of losing tail rotor effect by exceeding maximum rpm. We were about to crash and burn. I tipped the nose to level out our rpm, but I kept going. Bad guys were all around us. My rotor blades tore into the tops of the trees as the Huey came out of the clearing. We sounded like a big weed eater.

Then we were into open sky. I glanced back into the bay. The wounded guy was sitting up holding his arm, which meant it was probably only a flesh wound. Shaky stood out on the skid, leaning against his monkey line and looking back and down. Mosby grinned and gave me thumbs up. He was lucky to get out of that one, and so grateful he bought me beers all night.

Ryberg a few days later wasn't so lucky. He was flying a

Purple Team low bird with Sergeant Brown as observer and Spec4 Norman as torque. They were looking around the Michelin plantation. NVA had attacked FSB Grant a month earlier. Two divisions of North Vietnamese were supposed to still be in the area working their way toward Saigon. The low bird reported cart and bicycle tracks leading in the direction of a nearby village that Blue infantry had searched a number of times already without finding anything. The tracks were deep. Something heavy had been hauled.

"I'm gonna follow them," Ryberg called to his high bird, piloted by Captain Jamison and his X-Ray Lieutenant Bleeker.

The Loach shuttled along above the trail sniffing like a coonhound on a track. Bleeker from above and the lift ship even higher suddenly saw red smoke go off. The Loach's tail lifted, but that was all. A ball of flame engulfed the little helicopter. It had been hit by an RPG. Pieces of it along with mangled bodies were blasted all over the surrounding real estate. The main cockpit plummeted in a smoking ball into a cloud of broken branches, leaves, dust and smoke.

"This is Two-Five, this is Two-Five!" Ryberg screamed to TOC. "Oh, my God! Our low bird has been shot down. Scramble the Blues . . . !"

Flickers of winking lights erupted from the dark underbrush at the edges of the trail. Ryberg uttered his last transmission to his X-Ray: *"Get on the minigun, Paul. Work over those assholes in the treeline when I come down . . ."*

The Snake rolled in hot, taking fire. Something happened. Something freakish. The Cobra lost its main rotor blade in the dive. The blade spun loose somehow. It hacked through the chopper between the pilot and his X-Ray. Bleeker, strapped above the red-and-white shark's jaws, tumbled out of the sky until he collided with the jungle. Ryberg rode the rest of the chopper straight down.

The 1/9 lost five brave men that day in the span of a few seconds. I scrambled to insert Blues and help recover the remains. The O Club was a silent place that night, with little

Author at the controls of his Huey Helicopter
(PHOTO: AUTHOR)

Author shortly after arriving in Vietnam
(PHOTO: AUTHOR)

Author, shortly after becoming platoon leader,
displays his "Cav mustache" (PHOTO: AUTHOR)

Author's Bird following a night VC mortar attack.
(PHOTO: AUTHOR)

Commendation awards. *Mini-Man* is the shortest man in the front rank facing to the right. (PHOTO: AUTHOR)

A partial view of Tay Ninh base camp, showing chopper pilot headquarters (PHOTO: AUTHOR)

Nui Ba Den, the Black Virgin Mountain, the most prominent feature in the area of operations (PHOTO: AUTHOR)

Viet Cong prisoner (sandbag over head) being transported to base camp (PHOTO: AUTHOR)

UH-1 Huey "slick"
(PHOTO: U.S. ARMY)

Trooper being inserted onto an LZ
(PHOTO: U.S. ARMY)

UH-1 door gunner provides covering fire for a squad of troopers under fire on the ground. (PHOTO: U.S. ARMY)

A "Red" hunter killer team, consisting of a "White" observation helicopter (center) and two "Red" Cobra gunships (PHOTO: U.S. ARMY)

Pathfinder guides in a flight of 1st Air Cav choppers.
(PHOTO: U.S. ARMY)

Skytroopers prepare to offload a Huey "slick."
(PHOTO: ARMY NEWS FEATURES)

talking and even less laughter. Even the mongooses, Sam and Pepe, seemed to be affected by the atmosphere. They curled up in a box in the corner and slept instead of begging for goodies.

H&I started soon after nightfall. Reverberations from the big guns shook dust from the rocket-box walls of the club. Flares lit up the sky and flickered morose shadows through the building's window screens. I kept thinking about what Captain Nice said at Fort Wolters when the two Iranian students creamed in and killed themselves.

"Get used to it," he advised.

Get used to it. I seldom drank much, but all of us drank more than normal. Mighty Morris broke out his guitar after a few drinks. His voice sounded thin and sad. There was none of his sarcastic takeoff tonight on popular songs. He sang "Red River Valley" straight. I got up from the table and walked to the screen and watched flares brightening the sky and winced at the lightning flashes of the big guns. In spite of the thunder of artillery outside, the club inside seemed as hushed and expectant as a funeral parlor.

> *"From this valley they say you are leaving;*
> *I shall miss your bright eyes and sweet smile...."*

35

One afternoon Loach pilot George Gerard was burning coal flying across a rice paddy. It was near the end of his mission, he was low on fuel, nothing much had happened, and he was heading back to Tay Ninh and a cold brew. Loaches generally stayed over trees so as not to expose themselves to open areas. It had been an uneventful afternoon, however, and George and his crew were in a hurry.

"*Taking fire! Taking fire!*" he suddenly shouted over the radio. "*My blades are coming off! I'm going in ... going in ... !*"

Taking fire or *taking hits* meant rounds were actually impacting. *Receiving fire* meant you only saw muzzle flashes and smoke.

The Loach went in hard, bellying into rice paddy water and mud. George and his two-man crew were banged up, bruised and shaken, but nothing serious. Lifts snatched them out of the rice paddy. A Huey airlifted the crashed Loach out of the mud and deposited it at Tay Ninh, where the maintenance officer looked it over.

"My engine quit suddenly," George explained. "I was taking fire when my engine quit."

"There are no bullet holes. You weren't shot down. You ran out of fuel."

"No. We were taking fire."

George's crew backed him up. Pilot error like running out of gas, while excusable with a hot date, got you grounded over here and slapped with a statement of charges. George would be paying for that helicopter for the next one hundred years. The AMOC, which was what we called the maintenance officer because he had completed the Aviation Maintenance Officer Course, asked me to sling-load the Loach underneath my Huey and take it to Cu Chi. Cu Chi was the site of the highest station of maintenance in Vietnam, a depot outfit that could determine the cause of engine failure. By now, we all suspected the Loach quit because of fuel starvation. George was sweating it out.

I burned up all the excuses I could think of not to do it, but was finally forced into submission. It was tricky enough slinging a load underneath a Huey, much less a broken chopper that would not streamline because the tail boom had been knocked off in the crash. Maintenance wired the tail boom back on.

"Now it'll streamline," the AMOC, Captain Stiner, assured me, satisfied.

I smoked a cigarette and looked it over, skeptical and more than a little uneasy. George came out and stood next to me, clearly worried, as a crew rigged lines to his broken bird.

"Hey, what else am I gonna do?" I asked in exasperation, throwing up my hands. I felt like I was about to deliver a fellow sky jock to the guillotine.

George shrugged. "Nothing you can do, *Mini-Man*." He turned and walked off slowly.

I ground out my cigarette butt underneath the sole of my boot and climbed into the Huey cockpit with Mighty Morris riding the second seat. I hovered the UH-1 above the smaller wreckage of the Loach. I felt the lines tug, then slowly lifted the bird off the ramp.

"So far, so good," Mighty Morris cheered.

"We ain't there yet."

I took off to the east, cleared base, and turned north between the outer wire perimeter and the river while I clawed for altitude. I wanted a couple of thousand feet of air between me and the ground before I cruised out over Indian country toward Cu Chi.

First, the Loach's wired-on tail boom came loose and fell off. Astonished, Mighty Morris and I watched it whistling down through space until it struck earth in an explosion of dust. Morris looked at me and shrugged.

"I don't guess we needed that," he said.

We needed it a lot more than we thought. Its loss altered the entire aerodynamic equation of our odd airborne configuration. Without its tail boom, the remaining bubble of the Loach started to gently swing back and forth underneath us. By the time we were at 1,200 feet, it was oscillating back and forth like a wrecking ball. It took control. I felt like I was in a rowboat hooked to a whale. It was jerking the Huey from one side of the sky to the other.

When I looked out my side window and saw the wreckage pendulum up to almost eye level, yanking the Huey toward it, I knew something had to be done quickly. I radioed TOC. I must have sounded desperate.

"This thing is not going," I complained. "It's dangerous."

"You're the aircraft commander," came the welcome response. *"If it's too dangerous, cut it loose."*

That was good enough for me. I needed no further encouragement. We were out over the cleared fields of fire surrounding the post. I hit the release button and dropped the Loach. A fall of 1,200 feet flattened it like a steel roadkill.

I thought George was going to kiss me. He was all grins. He bought beers for me all evening, and for the rest of the time we were there together. Nothing could convince him I hadn't destroyed the evidence on purpose. After a while I stopped trying and just enjoyed it. It was a lot cheaper on him buying beers for me than it would have been paying for the Loach.

36

Apache Troop and all its facilities were located near the more narrow tip of the air base's north end. The only things standing between Charlie and us, our barracks and mess hall and oil drum crappers, were a pair of 175mm cannon, two eight-inch guns, some 40mm antiaircraft pom-pom guns, a forty-foot-thick tangle of concertina wire laced with Claymores, trip flares and tin cans, and a width of about two hundred yards of cleared fields of fire. With all that, it wouldn't seem to matter that Headhunter pilots slept almost next to the perimeter's green line; it would appear that we were fairly secure. After all, it would have taken a White Sox prospect to hurl a satchel charge into the camp; it would require a *bunch* of the little mother-fuckers to overrun us. Still, I remembered Minh the sapper at An Khe, who sneaked up crawling through the wire without anyone seeing him until he tossed a satchel full of potential death into the midst of us wide-eyed FNGs.

All that artillery on base firing H&I almost every night should have been reassuring. Instead, sometimes, you got to hate it. It was tough trying to sleep with your bunk doing a Fred Astaire or Gene Kelly across the floor. If you turned on your bunk light and tried to read, air vibrations seemed to jar the words on the page into a scrambling mass of tiny cock-roaches. I stuffed cotton or plugs into my ears and lay on my bunk in the dark behind the mosquito netting and watched the artillery flicker in the dark all around, like heat lightning pre-ceding a storm.

So what if the poor grunts *out there* were sleeping in the rain, eating cold, greasy Cs mixed with rainwater and were scared to death because the only thing between *them* and Char-lie were their M16 rifles. You had to fight your own war. You couldn't fight everybody else's. Everything was relative.

"Psssst! *Mini-Man,* you awake?"

"Yeah, Farmer."

"Wanna make a run to the O Club to wet our whistles?"

"I'd rather make a run to Tulsa. But, yeah, let's go. They're gonna keep this shit up anyhow until Apache Sunrise."

Headhunters didn't have to settle for bleacher seats whenever there was stuff going on outside the wire. We had box seats, reserved, on the fifty-yard line. If there was a *really big shoo*, as Ed Sullivan put it, with guest performances by Spooky or Puff the Magic Dragon, we took our beers out on the chopper line and stood on top of the berms to smoke and joke and grab ass and cheer at appropriate times. The show was better than the Aurora Borealis, the Northern Lights, more spectacular than Fourth of July over the Potomac. Spooky and Puff were either AC-130 or AC-47 airplanes heavily armed with 20mm Vulcans, 7.62 miniguns, .50-cal machine guns, and even 105mm howitzers. Streams of red fire, like laser beams in the night, connected the battle planes in the air to the poor bastards down on the ground getting hosed. We made comments and jokes about the dinks getting fried and turned into crispy critters.

"Smell it! Just smell it!" Miles challenged. "There ain't no smell like the sweet scent of well-done gook."

"There *ain't*?" Mighty Morris countered. "What's the matter with you, Miles? You stupid? Ain't you never smelled pussy before?"

"I ain't never smelled it well-done."

"I know for a fact you've smelled it ripe, which is worse than well-done. I saw that cunt you were with in Tay Ninh. I smelled *her* as soon as I hit city limits."

"You smelled your own mustache, Morris."

Tay Ninh the base and the 1/9 Cavalry were *the* major obstacles preventing the enemy from marching on Saigon. In spite of the guns and wire and Claymores, Spooky and Puff and foot patrols and air strikes, in spite of it all, nothing kept Charlie from at least *trying* us, if for no other reason than to prove he was out there watching and waiting.

It ruined your whole night when Charlie decided to flex his muscles and awakened you with mortar shells going *Crump! Crump! Crump!* up and down the base. I envied the guy in his private bunker at the volleyball court who could just turn over and go back to sleep. I shot straight up in bed. Mighty Morris was already halfway to the door, carrying his guitar, while I was still fighting to extricate myself from the mosquito net.

"Better get your charmed mini-ass to the bunkers, Alexander!" he shouted as the screen door slammed behind him.

Pilots and crew in various stages of undress raced for the big culvert pipes buried in their berms of earth and sandbags. We scrambled into the open ends like mice seeking the nearest hole after being dusted out of an old mattress. An explosion thumped behind me, close, showering me with rock and gravel and dirt. I scrabbled into the pipe on hands and bare knees and didn't stop scrabbling until I reached as near the center of the pipe as I could.

About a dozen half-naked GIs were already inside. Mess cooks, clerks, pilots, crews . . . You couldn't stand up in the pipe, it was too low. Even for me. I flopped over onto my butt, drew my bare knees up to my chin, wrapped my arms around my shanks and tried to make the smallest target possible. Being small had certain advantages.

The *crumpling* continued at spaced intervals outside. Explosions flickered in the open ends of the pipe. The enemy seldom had enough spare shells to really carpet a target.

Cowering in the pipe reminded me of hiding from a tornado in a storm cellar in Oklahoma and Texas. It carried with it that same sense of waiting and expectation; of anxiousness that, while you might be all right in the cellar, what was the funnel doing to your home and to your neighbors and their homes?

Sergeant Major Rogers was one of the last men to seek cover. It was dark in the pipe, but I recognized his voice and his hulking Neanderthal silhouette framed against the flickering open end of the shelter. His breathing was raspy, excited.

"We got gooks in the wire!" he announced.

Oh, shit! Talk about elevating the pucker factor. I eyed the open end of the pipe, half expecting to see some vicious little bitty guy about my size pop up and yell *Banzai!* or whatever the hell it was the Vietnamese used for a war cry. I unexpectedly understood how it felt to be trapped in the *Titanic* when it went down.

"Anybody got a weapon?" a shrill voice demanded.

No one did. We were clerks and jerks and cooks and flyers. I thought about the M79 blooper behind the seat in my chopper. If I made a run for it, we could at least put up *some* fight. It was better than cowering in here waiting for a slant-eye to toss a bag full of Boom! in on top of us.

"Don't you think we ought to find weapons and put up a defense?" I asked of no one in particular.

Two things dissuaded me from leaving the pipe on that errand. First, a nearby explosion; Charlie would be trying for the helicopters, his primary target. Second, Sergeant Major Rogers had got his wind back.

He growled, "I said gooks were *in* the wire, not *through* the wire. Our grunts know what to do. Let them handle their job. The best thing we can do to help is just stay out of their way."

Bursts of small arms fire erupted out there somewhere on the line. If I sometimes felt vulnerable and exposed in the air, it was nothing like the feeling of helplessness I now experienced. I was so damned glad I gave up artillery for aviation.

Someone murmured a chant in the darkness: *"Oh, shit! Oh, shit! Oh, shit!"*

My sentiments exactly.

Any attack on a major installation automatically summoned the Air Force. All hell broke loose as fast movers screamed in overhead and dumped their bombs. Everything was going at once. The 175s were pounding. The forty mike-mike pompoms had two speeds, a slow speed and a slower speed: *K-thunk!* . . . *K-thunk!* . . . *K-thunk!* . . . C-130s overhead kicked out huge parachute flares that lit up the entire world like miniature greenish suns. Cobras took to the air with their 3.5 rockets armed. Because of the accuracy of their weapons, they could get in close and dirty on the enemy and prevent his closing with us.

Where do you want these rockets?

Five feet in front of us. Can you see where I'm pointing? That's where I want 'em.

We huddled together in the darkness of the culvert pipe, listening. I didn't realize Captain Beatty was inside until he flicked on his flashlight. He calmly groomed his magnificent mustache with one hand; he must have been sleeping and mussed it. Then he opened a newspaper on his knees and began reading by the light beam held in his free hand. Everyone stared at him.

"It says in the newspaper," he began reflectively, "and I quote, 'The Woodstock generation is staging an antiwar moratorium in Washington.' It says here the war is 'corrupt, immoral, and feeds the American arms industry.'"

"Well, fuck 'em and the black horse they rode in on," Farmer Farmer snorted. "Their asses ain't out here getting shot at. As far as this ol' southern boy is concerned, I'd just as soon waste an antiwar hippie as shoot a gook or eat turnip greens."

That produced a titter of laughter. Tension immediately dissolved. A big discussion soon started in which almost everyone sided against the draft-dodging protesters and politicians who refused to let GIs win the war. Everyone had his own opinion on what should be done with the dope-smoking hippies, starting with castration. I worked my way down to Blue.

"Can I look at the Sports section?" I asked.

He grinned at me.

The probe on the wire lasted only a short time. Soon, a stillness descended upon the base like the aftermath of a storm. We ventured cautiously out of the pipe. A single parachute flare remained stuck in the sky, blocking out the stars with its bright light. We began checking for damage, looking a little stunned as people do who have survived a storm.

"Lieutenant Alexander?" someone said.

"Yeah?"

"They blew all the windows out of your Huey."

From the looks of the flight line, it appeared mortars had walked down one side of the line and up the other. Three out of our eight slicks were damaged, one of which looked totaled beyond salvage. It would have to be cannibalized for parts. A Loach was also destroyed and three Cobras busted up. Maintenance had to start work immediately if the Headhunters were going to stay in business.

My chopper was out of commission temporarily. Shrapnel ate holes in its one side while the concussion of an exploding round shattered the Plexiglas windshield. Shaky came and stood beside me.

"It's all right, sir," he commiserated. "It don't count if it gets shot when you're not in it. *Mini-Man* is still charmed."

37

Enemy mortar damage grounded half of Apache Troop's Hueys and Cobras and one of its Loaches. The AMOC, Captain Stiner, and his maintenance section worked twenty-four hours straight to get us back in the air. It led to Captain Stiner's receiving the only Distinguished Service Cross I ever knew to be awarded for noncombat action.

Other than being a maintenance officer, Captain Stiner was also a certified test pilot. He sometimes went out to fly X-Ray in Snakes when he got bored with being stuck in the repair shed. He decided to test one of the repaired Cobras by taking it up and flying around the pattern.

He got it up with no trouble and was scooting along the downwind leg of the long airstrip when suddenly his tail rotor came off in-flight. It whizzed past him in the air like a Frisbee.

Losing a helicopter's tail rotor was something like dropping a wing on a standard airplane. It virtually assured you of a crash. Instead of panicking, however, Captain Stiner put all his experience to work. He used throttle, cyclic, and collective in combination to overcome the loss of countertorque and balance normally provided by the tail rotor. He actually *landed* the Cobra in the cleared field of fire about one hundred yards from the base without additional damage to either the aircraft or himself. I heard it was the first time such a feat had ever been accomplished.

Captain Stiner stood by the helicopter nonchalantly munching on a candy bar when a truck came out to pull the Cobra back to the maintenance shed. That guy had cool. I wished I had cool like that.

38

Apache Troop infantry from Tay Ninh put a big dent in the enemy's transportation system when GIs blew up a bicycle factory containing seventy-five bicycles. The number of nearby bunkers indicated a regimental-sized base camp had also been established there.

The Blues encountered withering fire from an NVA platoon as they withdrew after blowing up the factory. They scattered the enemy by employing their machine guns in a crossfire, only to be attacked by a second enemy platoon near their extraction PZ. Artillery and air strikes broke up this attack. Huey slicks snatched the Blues out of the jungle and returned them to Tay Ninh.

That night, B-52s from Guam made final work of the Communist positions with an Arc Light mission. It cracked and blazed on the horizon like a severe electrical storm while troops at Tay Ninh watched in awe.

39

Mighty Morris ragged Farmer Farmer about having fallen off his Alabama turnip wagon too many times. It wasn't that Warrant Officer Farmer suffered from spatial or perspective problems; he was merely clumsy. During the continuing volleyball game, he spiked the ball against the net and back into his own face. The scramble alarm sounded and he jumped up, made a break for the door, and crashed into the door frame. I wondered how he survived flight school. If he had had Captain Nice, he surely wouldn't have made it.

The fact was that at times he was absolutely brilliant at the controls of a helicopter. He did things with a chopper that machines weren't supposed to do. But then he suddenly had an attention span lapse and did something stupid. You never knew which of the two Farmer Farmers you were flying with. I kept a wary eye on him whenever we flew together. He was okay at safe altitudes, but I contrived to take the sticks myself whenever we dropped down on the contours to snoop and poop, sneak and peek.

Shaky was as jittery about him as I was. He took me aside when Farmer volunteered to fly right seat with us on a sniffer mission. He looked worried.

"Sir, you ain't letting Mr. Farmer fly down low, are you?"

"Don't worry," I reassured him. "I don't feel *that* charmed."

Every pilot enjoyed flying low level, skimming the air on that cushion right above the treetops. There was a "dead man's zone" that covered the area between about 100 feet above the ground up to 1,000-foot altitude. Above 1,000 feet, you were out of effective reach of most ground fire. Below 100 feet, the bad guys couldn't see you until you flew directly overhead. Strange in that the *lower* you were or the *higher* you were, the *safer* you were.

"I feel as sharp as a hen's tooth today," Farmer Farmer affirmed in his slow southern vernacular.

"*I'll* fly," I said quickly.

Shaky let out a breath of relief. The sniffer team was already aboard with its bloodhound machine. Farmer, Shaky, and I climbed into our places. I took off and flew out toward the Saigon Corridor where George Gerard flying his Loach had located a VC bicycle factory a few weeks before. There had been a big firefight followed by an Arc Light B-52 attack that left a huge scorched gash across the jungle.

If there were hills, you tried to stay close to them for protection when you flew low. Since there were no hills in our AO except the Black Virgin, I grazed just above triple canopy jungle. Shaky braced himself spread-legged in the door with his umbilical monkey line secured and his M60 ready to rock 'n' roll.

"Okay, I got a scent," one of the sniffer guys said through the intercom.

"Did you read that, Shaky?" I asked.

"I'm ready for 'em, *Mini-Man*."

"We should be coming up on them," Sniffer said, getting excited.

Occasionally I glimpsed sections of a pathway down through the tree canopy. Hunting men was exciting. Anyone who claimed differently was not being honest.

Shaky spotted movement the same instant I did. Some guy hauling ass on a motorbike. I paced the guy, peering down through my chin bubble and watching him flicker in and out of view. Shaky got a clear sight picture and opened up with his M60. Leaves and limbs exploded as the machine gun fire cut into the foliage.

"He's down!" Shaky exclaimed.

I didn't see him go down, but I didn't see him riding anymore either.

"Down for good?" I asked.

"He's *down*. Sir, come back around. There! Do you see him?"

Although we were generally credited with several kills a day when our boonirats were in contact with the enemy, I knew for a fact that the Vulture Board received many kills that were only estimates. There was no doubt about this guy, though. He was dead, ripped all apart and lying in a thick pool of his own blood mixed with spilled gasoline from the bullet-riddled motorbike.

"Do we count that as a confirmed, sir?" Shaky asked.

"His hide is on the Vulture board," Farmer declared.

I lifted the chopper away. One dead enemy was a good day's work. You lost interest after that. We were all ready to declare victory and go home. The sniffers wanted to continue work on the way back, make a token effort anyhow. I stayed low and headed over the green sweep of jungle toward Nui Ba Den rising like a giant tit to our left front.

"I got it?" Farmer Farmer asked.

I looked at him. I saw a brace of Cobras from out his window working out on something a mile or so away. Rockets shot from their stubby wings like slivers of fire. "Okay," I said, relinquishing the controls. "You got it. Ease off to the south away from them Cobras, will you? It's not our fight."

He continued flying a few feet above the top of the jungle for the benefit of the sniffers. I relaxed, hands folded in my lap, and watched the forest slide rapidly past below us. An unbroken carpet of the deepest green, almost iridescent under the tropical sun. I expected nothing between here and Tay Ninh. I realized I was hungry.

"Hunting gooks all day makes me famished," Mighty Morris once put it. "And when I'm famished, nothing satisfies my appetite like a big bowl of hog entrails and beef tripe from an army dining facility."

I glanced ahead and saw a dead treetop sticking up above the green. It was a gray and twisted snag about five hundred meters ahead. We were heading directly for it at about eighty knots an hour. I didn't think anything about it. I figured Farmer would pop the collective and hop over it the way we always did.

The next time I glanced up, the snag loomed about 100 meters directly ahead. Farmer was looking squarely at it. He seemed relaxed and aware. Although I was sure he knew what he was doing, I still felt the muscles in my legs tense.

I watched mesmerized as we approached.

I started to cry out at the last moment. *"Farmer—!"*

Too late. That hillbilly didn't hop and pop at all. We busted right through the dead treetop in an explosion of gray wood. The chin bubble at my feet splintered with a crack like a rifle. The chopper shuttered dangerously to one side, dumping the two sniffer guys on top of each other and throwing Shaky lunging against his monkey line. It was the only thing that saved him from sailing out the door.

"Taking fire?" Shaky yelled through the intercom, surprised.

"Taking a tree!" I corrected, fuming with astonishment and indignation.

Farmer *had* to have seen the damn tree. His visor concealed his face, but his body language betrayed him. He was as astonished as the rest of us. I waited until he got the Huey straightened out again before I reclaimed the controls. I quickly checked the instrument panel to make sure no red lights were on.

"Did you see the tree?" I asked once I had myself under control along with the helicopter.

He allowed he had.

"Why did you hit it then?"

"I don't rightly know."

That was the only explanation he ever gave. I reported the incident to Captain Blue. Blue talked to him and let it go. No real harm done. He was just careless. Besides, we were always short on pilots.

I ordered him, not the crew chief, to replace the chin bubble. I figured his putting in 180 screws that held the Plexiglas in place might give him time to contemplate his error. He looked puzzled and a little dumbfounded.

"I oughta have you put a piece of the Plexiglas in your navel so you can see when you got your head stuck up your ass," I scolded.

"It was an idiot thing to do," he admitted.

I agreed with him.

40

Occasionally, as a change of pace, I flew X-Ray in the Cobra with Swede. Unlike the UH-1, which was a utility helicopter designed to carry payloads, the AH-1 Cobra was the first helicopter designed from the skids up as a rotorcraft gunship. A Cobra traveled almost twice as fast as a Huey. It was slim, only thirty-six inches wide, and as agile as a dragonfly over a pond. The crew of two sat in tandem. The aircraft commander flew from the rear cockpit, which was elevated above the front pilot in order that the AC could get a good all-around view over the head of the X-Ray.

"Let's go hunting," Swede might say when I had some down time.

Out we went into the AO, flying the VC and NVA infiltration trails. The X-Cache Route, Jolly Trail, Saigon Corridor . . . Hunting for troops, bunkers, rice hooches, "mules" on bicycles loaded down with RPGs, carts full of rice or medical supplies . . . Anything that moved. Although we had to abide by the rules of engagement which said you pinpointed your precise target and didn't go around shooting up hooches at random, hunting was almost always good in War Zone C.

As X-Ray, I sat way out over the shark's jaw with clear cockpit all around and a wonderful view. The X-Ray read the map, recorded intel from the low bird if we were operating as a Pink or Purple Team, kept an eye peeled for movement, and stayed prepared to employ the bird's formidable weapons. In addition to 3.5 rockets bristling on its stubby wings, the Cobra was mounted with a 40mm automatic grenade launcher and a 7.62 Gatling-style minigun mounted on a turret underneath the shark's nose.

The firepower it carried was awesome. There was a sighting mark on the windscreen which you lined up with the target. You rotated the guns up or down and sideways. The 40mm blooper fired forty rounds a minute, laying down a solid chunking row of explosions like a mini–Arc Light. The minigun fired so rapidly, six thousand rounds a minute in a solid wall of steel, that tracers blurred into a single red stream as from a fire hose.

"See him! There!" Swede exclaimed through the intercom. "He's running for the woods. I'm going in hot!"

He tilted the aircraft into a dizzying dive and swooped down like a hawk chasing a field mouse. The prey had abandoned his bike and *di-di'd* into a copse of bamboo and palm. He disappeared into it. I opened up with the minigun. You could chew a patch of jungle into sticks and kindling in ten seconds. Not always did you know whether or not you hit your target as he ducked and dodged through the trees, but if the poor sonofabitch survived you could bet your ass he was one scared and impressed gook.

Swede was loudly lip-playing the *William Tell Overture,* the Lone Ranger's theme song, as we chased the poor Vietnamese. He pulled out of the dive.

"If he lived through that," Swede said with his accent and a chuckle, "he'll be trying to *chieu hoi* tomorrow."

I wasn't the only pilot who liked to fly the Cobra; it was the latest thing on the market at the time. Less than two years before, our gunships had been converted Hueys. Bronco pilots who flew FAC—Forward Air Control—for jet fighters landed at Tay Ninh every once in a while and wanted to go Cobra flying. They reciprocated and took us up in their Broncos.

A Bronco was a tandem-seated turbo prop that resembled the P-38 fighter-trainer used by the air force. It flew at a speed somewhere between two hundred and three hundred mph. FACs derived a big thrill in taking up chopper pilots and subjecting them to G-forces until they passed out. Gs were something new to most helicopter jocks.

I hopped a ride with one of the FACs. He was grinning as we buckled up and took off. He tried everything. Loops, dives, steep climbs . . . I hung in there with him and chatted over the intercom. I was feeling pretty cocky, pretty *Mini-Man,* when he gave up.

"We'll take her on in," he said, lining up about five miles out for a straight-in approach.

He was really booking, screaming in. He did a couple of fast barrel rolls. Next thing I knew we were taxiing up to the hangar. He was grinning again when I came to, still a little queasy, and staggered away from the airplane.

"You keep that thing," I told him. "I'll stick to Hueys."

41

Nui Ba Den, the Black Virgin, rose out of the jungle, as Farmer Farmer put it, like a huge pimple on a pig's asshole. Beyond the mountain to the northeast hung a thick black column of smoke stretched between earth and sky, its silhouette etched dark and ominous against the blood red of the rising Vietnam sun. When I came out of the mess hall with Captain Blue and Farmer Farmer, Mighty Morris was standing on one of the berms which were supposed to protect our helicopters from mortar fire. He gazed reflectively at the rising smoke while he drank a cup of coffee and drew slowly on a cigarette. He looked at us, then looked back toward the smoke.

"What's with him?" Blue said.

I pointed at the smoke.

"Damn!" the captain said.

The three of us climbed the berm revetment and stood with Mighty Morris. He squatted on his haunches like a Vietnamese and silently smoked his cigarette. His short-cropped yellow hair and his handlebar cavalry mustache glowed almost like gold in the morning light.

"They attacked an FSB last night," Mighty Morris finally said.

"Looks like our poor ol' boys really caught some of the Devil," Farmer Farmer commented sympathetically.

"I was over at the TOC," Mighty Morris said. "They told me Sabre Troop has been flying GI body bags and WIAs into Phuoc Vinh since before first light."

I put a match to three cigarettes and gave one each to Blue and Farmer and kept the last for myself.

"Who was it that got hit?" I asked.

Mighty Morris stood up and stretched. "That must be the Eighth Cav over that way, isn't it?"

"Looks about right," Blue said. "Poor bastards."

We all smoked and watched the smoke. Farmer said, "We've got the North Vietnamese outnumbered and outpowered. Wouldn't you think these ol' boys would finally see where the corn grows and yell uncle?"

"They're never going to quit," Captain Beatty said. "They've been fighting in this part of the world since Genghis Khan. I've run into Vietnamese who fought the Japanese in 1944 and the French at Dien Bien Phu in '54. Now they're fighting us. Some of them will probably live to fight our grandchildren."

"Not mine," Mighty Morris said. "I'm sending them to Canada."

We stood on the berm as the sun burned off the fog on the river that we saw glinting through the forest, talking of the war, smoking cigarettes, drinking coffee and watching the black smoke lift straight up from the FSB, then curl at the top from a slight breeze aloft. FSBs and LZs with romantic names like Grant and Jamie and Phyllis and Carolyn were attacked and fought savage battles—and those of us not involved stood and watched the smoke. For you personally, the war was only that part of it that you saw immediately around you.

We were like cops working our own precinct. We had more than enough to keep us busy. We fought our own skirmishes out there in our own AO and seldom knew what was happening in neighboring AOs, much less how the war in general was going. Seldom did anyone talk about winning anymore. The war had gone on far too long for that. In the same way that cops never won their war on crime, we didn't expect to win ours. It would just keep going on, day after day, month after month into the foreseeable future.

Occasionally, one or two or three of us vanished from the ranks and showed up no more at volleyball or at the O Club. Like when the Loach exploded and the Cobra lost its rotor blades and cut the bird in half. Five guys gone all at once. Mighty Morris sang songs for them. Then they were just gone and we tried not to think about them anymore. Dwelling on your losses turned you morbid and made you start considering your own mortality. That was something you never wanted to consider in a war zone.

Seeing only what was around you, not knowing what was going on in the rest of the war or in the rest of the world, was a bit tough on morale. We saw smoke rising after a battle, but we only heard rumors about how it went. Like, thirteen grunts died in a firefight near Cu Chi, a helicopter went down and all eight aboard were killed, a pilot was lost and captured by the VC, who tortured him, cut off his genitals and left him strung heels up in a tree... We had TV in the O Club, but programming came through the Armed Forces Network and was sanitized for our viewing so as not to affect morale. Care packages from home included newspapers with headlines about war protesters, draft dodgers, and dope-smoking campus hippies. How much of it was true and how much exaggeration, we had no way of knowing.

"Doesn't it frost your balls," Miles once complained, "that while we're over here getting killed, one of these dope-smoking scumbags is dodging the draft and will grow up to be president of the United States or something?"

Thought of it frosted *my* balls.

Mighty Morris glanced at the column of smoke a last time, stamped out his cigarette, then climbed down from the berm and kept his back to the smoke as he strode away.

"I'm getting to be a short-timer," Captain Blue said, sounding weary and relieved at the same time. "I'll be out of here in less than six weeks."

The war would never end. Only our tours of duty ended. One year in-country and then we left. Others took our places and the war continued. Forever and ever, amen.

Captain Beatty looked at me. "The platoon will soon be yours, *Mini-Man*. At least it'll be yours until it's your turn to go." He shook his head and sighed. "Ain't this a hell of a way to run a war?"

42

The day after Major General Elvy Benton Roberts took command of the 1st Cavalry Division on May 5, 1969, the North Vietnamese decided to annihilate LZ Carolyn, which stood on a site near the abandoned Prek Klok Special Forces camp. NVA began the assault in the early morning darkness with rocket and mortar barrages, followed an hour later by a pincer ground assault against two sides of the base. Enemy soldiers broke through the wire and stormed onto the LZ, overrunning six perimeter bunkers and capturing a medium howitzer. They threatened to cut the camp in half.

American defenses were reduced to only two companies since several other companies of the occupying Second Battalion, 8th Cav, were out on patrol when the attack began. Artillerymen, supply and signal personnel, engineers and clerks all took up arms in a counterattack to hurl back enemy penetrations and save the camp. The most violent fighting raged on the northern side of the base. A 155mm howitzer position exchanged hands three times in fierce hand-to-hand fighting with rifles, pistols, knives, and entrenching tools.

Air support that included Cobras, fighters, AC-47 "Spooky" and AC-119 "Shadow" gunships rolled in against enemy anti-aircraft weapons ringing the perimeter. American defenders shot holes in fuel drums at the aviation gas dump and ignited fuel to form flaming barriers. A howitzer gun pit received three direct hits from rockets, touching off a fire in its powder bunker. Two 105mm artillery ammunition points exploded around 3:30 A.M. Cook-off of the ammunition in the resulting fires sprayed the LZ continuously for the next four hours. Grass and forest fires raged everywhere. Flames licking high into the night air created a sky glow visible from as far away as Tay Ninh and Phuoc Vinh.

Desperate 155mm gun sections lowered their cannon, packed them with Bee Hive rounds or powder charges and blasted the attackers at point-blank range. Blazing pellets discharged in solid walls of flame pierced skin and flesh and continued to burn inside body cavities. Screams of terror and pain added to the hellish din of battle on the LZ.

Cut off by loss of communications, small pockets of Americans fought on in isolated desperation. The mortar platoon's four tubes fired 1,500 rounds of illumination during the night. Everywhere there were shortages of ammunition. Volunteers dashed through fire-swept open areas to look for more rounds in storage bunkers. Cannoneers redistributed ammo by crawling from gun section to gun section under a hail of enemy fire and exploding shrapnel.

Gradually, as dawn approached, cavalry counterattackers reestablished Carolyn's perimeter. Air assets continued to pound enemy reserves and antiaircraft and mortar positions. By 6:00 A.M., the NVA force was retreating, leaving blood trails for Cav helicopters to follow. Columns of black smoke bellowed into the dawn from shattered LZ Carolyn, but the base had held against considerable odds.

During a period of twenty-four days following the attack on Carolyn, Cav forces used helicopters, Blue infantry, and two batteries of artillery to force sixty-two separate contacts with NVA/VC units and put pressure on the X-Cache Trail and its route to Saigon.

43

The LZs the LRRPs selected for their insertions were never very big. They looked for the smallest, least-conspicuous clearings they could find on the assumption that since Charlie hadn't enough people to spike welcoming parties on every prospective LZ, he would probably stick to the larger ones. Common pilot reaction to the LRRP choices went something like, "You want *me* to put this machine *where*?"

Add to the small size of the LZs the fact that most insertions were conducted just before dark when vision was poorest and you had a formula for complicating everybody's life. You needed all the lift you could get to put the team in. These guys carried with them everything except the oil can crappers. Many times, for these reasons, we split the team members between two lift ships. Two or three in one slick, the remaining two or three in the other, with a pair of Snakes flying shotgun.

TOC scheduled me for an LRRP insertion at 1800 hours flying with a new kid, a warrant named Stockton. Stockton replaced a short-timer called Cowboy whom we had seen off at the last hail-and-farewell at Phuoc Vinh. Because of our staggered one-year tours, guys were always coming and going. You never had a chance to get to know some of them very well.

Stockton looked about nineteen, although he claimed to be twenty-two. He hadn't shaved *that* many times. He surveyed my cavalry mustache with envy. His, so far and perhaps forever, was a mere shading of the upper lip. He was still the FNG with his hands digging in his pockets and his eyes curious and amazed and nervous.

"You're the old-timer I wanted to fly with," he allowed deferentially.

I started to laugh but held it back to a grin. Imagine. I hadn't been in-country much more than five months myself and yet, considering the speed with which guys rotated in and out of Vietnam, I was already the "old-timer." *Don't you see the irony of it?* I wanted to ask him, wiseassed as always. But I didn't. I remembered the awe with which I regarded Captain Beatty when I first reported here as the FNG. Now it was my turn to break in the incoming cherries; I would soon be their commander. The thought was still a little disconcerting.

"Everybody says *Mini-Man* never gets hit," Stockton asserted, as though hoping it were true.

"Everybody says that, huh?"

"That's what they say. They say you haven't been hit even once. They say *Mini-Man* could fly straight into Hanoi and come out with nothing more than a good scare."

"Maybe that's what we ought to do then."

He looked at me sharply to see if I were serious. I smiled to show him I wasn't stupid.

"They say you're *charmed*."

"I prefer *charming*." I twisted the ends of my mustache.

It was hard for an FNG to see humor in things at first, he was so intense and scared.

"I expected you to be a lot taller," Stockton said.

I looked at him. It wasn't at attempt at humor; he was serious.

"Yeah. Well, we all can't be six feet tall."

"I didn't mean anything by it, sir. Did you know Alan Ladd is shorter than you are?"

"Let's just drop it, Stockton."

"Yes, sir."

Farmer Farmer and Miles would fly the second lift ship. At sunset, the LRRPs waddled out with all their gear taped to prevent rattling and their faces blackened with cammie. They clambered aboard the two choppers, three guys in mine, three in Farmer's. The patrol leader held up a wooden nickel.

"You coming back in to get us tomorrow night and pick up this, *Mini-Man*?" he asked.

"You betchum, Red Ryder."

They all laughed. Stockton looked at them like they were crazy. How could they laugh when they were going *out there*?

It was supposed to be a routine mission, if anything could be routine in Vietnam. All we had to do was take these guys out there, drop them off and come back home. Like a bus driver. It was a nice evening for it too. Vietnam was such pretty country that I often thought I would like to come back some day after the war was over. If the war was ever over.

The sun hung red and low in the west. It reflected ruby-red from scattered sheets of water in rice paddies over by Nui Ba Den. It was already getting dark down there. I used a high overhead approach to the LZ, starting my spiral from about 1,500 feet and screwing us in tight and dizzying. My skids hadn't even touched earth, with the grass whipping below and the forest black and overwhelming around us, than Shaky chirped through the intercom, "They're gone!"

I pulled pitch to get out of there. The longer you stayed on the ground, the greater chance you had of being compromised. I did a cyclic climb by coming out over the treetops to pick up lift speed, then pulled back and popped up. You gained 1,000 feet real quick and were out of small arms range almost in a single breath.

As soon as I jumped out of the tiny clearing, Farmer plunged toward it. One bird leaving the nest, a second taking its place.

Suddenly, Farmer's distinctive drawl crashed through the air waves: *"Taking fire! Taking fire down here!"*

Instead of pulling out of his approach as he should have, he continued on in. His three grunts bailed out automatically and beat it toward the trees. Apparently they didn't realize the LZ was hot until their taxi was already back in the air. Farmer came out of the nest through another hail of small arms fire.

Radios started going bugfuck. Everybody tried to talk at once. Our two Snakes circled overhead, chattering to each other as they attempted to determine the source of the fire. The grunts on the ground were screaming and swearing. Miles was shouting at me that they had taken some hits. I calmed him down and asked if he had any red lights on his instruments. He didn't.

This entire situation now stunk. The LRRPs were compromised. We couldn't leave them down there. We had to go back in and get them. It would take both helicopters. I was afraid that a single chopper wouldn't have enough lift in a vertical hover to pull all six men out of that small clearing.

I explained all this to Farmer and Miles as I circled the LZ. Charlie had stopped firing, not wanting to unnecessarily give away his position. Farmer quickly regained his composure.

"Them cotton pickers," he said in his strongest epithet. *"Okay, Mini-Man, we're with you. I think them little dudes was shooting at us from the southwest."*

An anxious plea came from the ground. "Mini-Man, *we need out of here pronto."*

"Are you in contact?" I asked him.

"That's a negative at this point. We heard the firing from about two hundred meters to our southwest."

At least the LRRPs weren't at risk of being overrun within the next few minutes. The real danger right now lay to the choppers, not the grunts. Charlie knew what we had done; he knew also we wouldn't leave our guys. He was down there right now getting set up and ready for when we returned for the extraction. Apparently, wherever he was, he had an open view of helicopters approaching and departing the clearing.

"I think I might have a location," Red Leader reported. *"Ready, Mad Dog?"* he asked his wing mate.

"I can almost smell the little motherfuckers."

"We'll cover you, Mini-Man," Red Leader promised.

I swung west to where the sun had already gone down to leave the sky bruised with color and the earth below purple with darkness. I dropped down low above the forest and poured on the coal; Farmer and Miles were about a mile behind me. I rode so close to the treetops that they chattered in the slipstream of our passing. A few taller branches slapped our belly. Stockton scrunched down as though trying to hide inside his seat armor. I knew how he felt. There were times when I felt like melting into my helmet. This was one of them. I would rather have taken a beating than go back, but someone had to do it.

Dumbass Farmer. Why the hell did that Alabama hick let his guys off when he knew he was taking fire?

The Snakes were rolling in hot, delivering ordnance off the southwest edge of the clearing, ahead of us and to our right. Rocket explosions flared bright. I ignored them, concentrating on my job and the clearing rapidly approaching.

"Get on the controls with me," I instructed Stockton. "Just in case . . ."

"Yes, sir."

I wondered, wryly, if he thought *Mini-Man* was so charmed now.

"We're receiving fire from the right!" Shaky called out.

Such was my concentration that I was only peripherally aware of scattered tracers zippering the purpling air.

"Gunner, have you got a target?" I asked. "Have you got a target?"

Shaky's M60 opened up, slapping against my ears.

Stockton was praying. This was his first action. He appeared frozen. *"Oh, God! Oh, God! Oh, God!"*

As always when adrenaline started pumping, I experienced that sudden calmness as though I were a mere spectator instead of a participant. I brought the slick in, decelerated at the last moment and squatted it down into the clearing. I had already advised the LRRPs of their loading arrangement. They were ready. I didn't even see them bound out of the jungle, but all of a sudden Shaky gave that exclamation I was relieved to hear: "They're on!"

It was in and out. As I pulled up and out in a cyclic climb, accompanied by tracers streaking past, Farmer slid in underneath me. Unfortunately, this was not one of those evenings when he was absolutely brilliant at the controls. It was like he was driving the turnip wagon instead of falling off it.

"We're hit!" he screeched over the radio. *"Going down!"*

44

From later piecing together the action, it was clear that Farmer, flying right seat instead of the customary left, saw rifle flashes winking at him from his side of the helicopter and tracers coming like bright jet-propelled basketballs. Instinctively, without realizing it, he pushed his bird over to the left away from the fire as he landed. The clearing wasn't big enough for evasive maneuvers.

Scrubby trees surrounded the opening. In the dark, the tip of his blade whacked one of the trees, knocking about eight inches off the rotor's tip. There was a sudden blade stall that vibrated the aircraft so violently that it shook loose rivets and rattled teeth. The engine quit momentarily, dropping the Huey about ten feet to the ground. Farmer and Miles both thought they were in for good. Farmer was already on the radio yelling, *"Mayday! Mayday!"*

He couldn't stay out of the trees. They were like a magnet to him.

The engine caught again immediately; the loss of part of the rotor blade made it run as rough as an old Alabama Ford truck chugging along with only six of its eight cylinders firing. Not realizing what had happened, the three remaining LRRPs piled aboard while Farmer's gunner hammered at the treeline with his machine gun.

By all rights, the aircraft should never have flown out of the clearing. But such was the flow of adrenaline in all the excitement that Farmer Farmer experienced one of his moments of brilliance, or perhaps desperation, and pulled pitch. Slowly, nursing the wounded bird, he lifted it off the ground. Miles later remarked how calm the Farmer was, like he was sitting in his rocking chair on his front porch, in spite of the radio's going ape shit, his machine guns pounding, tracers streaking past or *tick!*ing as they pierced the bird's skin, and Cobras race-tracking off his flank shooting their rockets and miniguns. Fortunately for Farmer, perhaps, he didn't have to think; all he had to do was fall back on training and instinct.

From aloft, I watched him bring the Huey up wobbling like a duck with a wounded wing. He had his red-and-green running lights on to let the Cobras know where he was. They also illuminated him for the enemy. I expected him to go down in a ball of flames at any instant. Stockton still sat frozen in his seat, staring in horror.

By some extreme stretching of luck and fate, the slick limped away through all that ordnance out to get it. Unable to climb, it flopped slowly along at treetop level until it cleared the kill zone. Farmer's voice over the radio was strained and thin but also controlled. I asked him if he wanted to set down somewhere. I had already notified TOC of the situation and more slicks and Cobras were being scrambled. Farmer informed me they were going to try to ride the crippled bird back to Tay Ninh.

"It's awful dark down there, Mini-Man," he said. *"I'm afraid of boogers."*

His thinking was that if he stayed low and they had to go into the trees, they had a chance of surviving the crash. I couldn't understand how the chopper stayed aloft. It wobbled, pitched, and jerked as though on the strings of a mad and drunken puppeteer. It was a tribute to Farmer's often-undemonstrated skills that he kept it limping forward. I was amazed.

"Mini-Man, *are you still up there?"* he kept asking.

"Don't worry, Farm Boy. I got you covered."

I followed him in case he went down, hovering overhead at about one thousand feet altitude. It was a long flight. A long, long flight filled with tension, uncertainty, and the expectation that the bird had to crash at any moment. I could imagine the anxiety inside Farmer's aircraft.

Full darkness came quickly as it did in the tropics. The lights of Tay Ninh sparkled on the horizon. Taylor and Mississippi joined the cavalcade, along with Swede in his Cobra. Two

Snakes from Blue Max kept going to join the action at the rejected LZ.

"We're going to make it, Mini-Man!"

Watching him continue to flounder his way home was a little grisly. Like watching a dog injured on the expressway dragging his hindquarters while attempting to avoid onrushing eighteen-wheelers. The question was not whether the dog got hit, but *when.*

He made it across the river, then above the outer perimeter wire. Tower cleared the runway for his emergency landing. Farmer plopped down his chopper with its final gasp. Grateful LRRPs forced wooden nickels into everybody's hands. Stockton got out, a little unsteady on his feet, and looked for bullet holes. He found none. He stood looking at me.

AMOC's inspection of Farmer's helicopter revealed a warped frame, while centrifugal force had twisted what remained of the blades.

"That helicopter *couldn't* fly," Captain Stiner said.

But it did.

45

They tried to kill us, we tried to kill them. That was the name of the game over here, and I learned the rules well. I had certainly changed from my first days in Vietnam. I was losing some of my initial gung-ho, having second thoughts about the job. I accepted the war now instead of embracing it. I would do my job, of course. It was an insane job and we were all crazy in doing it, but I would do it. I was no hero, though. Another term for the CMH—Congressional Medal of Honor—was Casket with Metal Handles. There were times when I sat on my bunk and seriously considered my own mortality. I was afraid that one day the law of averages was going to catch up with me. I had a premonition that I was going to die a fiery death in the debris of my own chopper—or that a mortar round would land in bed with me. I cast an eye toward the private bunker at the volleyball court and even considered building one of my own.

Everyone wanted to fly with me. I seemed to fly unscathed into and out of all the garbage in the world while other guys were bullet magnets. I wished like hell this whole "charmed" thing had never got started. It felt like a curse now because I knew, I *knew,* it couldn't last forever. One of these days, one of these fucking days, "charmed" was going to get its ass shot off.

"You live a charmed life," the other pilots said. "There's no way you can do this shit without getting at least one bullet and not live charmed."

Whatever it was, luck or charm, I hoped it saw me through the rest of my war and back to Sandy and the girls. There were so damned many ways to get killed here. It happened every day. This one guy came running down a hill to a helicopter waiting to pick up his squad. Because of the angle of the hill and the way the chopper was sitting, the blade was rotating about head high. The guy ran right into the blade. It chopped off his head.

The enemy had a real incentive to bring us out of the sky. Charlie out there with a gun was given a month's pay, a new bicycle, and a thirty-day R&R leave whenever he succeeded in shooting down a helicopter. That was why he shot at us so much.

Captain Blue was leaving a big pair of boots for me to fill as platoon leader. I recalled his composure under fire, his attention to detail and correct procedure when it came to flying. You might possess all the luck in the world, the Archangel Gabriel might even ride on your shoulder, you might even be "charmed," but it certainly hurt nothing to give luck a hand every chance you got. Blue had drilled that into me.

Out of a feeling of obligation and pending leadership, I volunteered myself for many of the tough missions. As a commander, you never asked anyone under you to do something you wouldn't or couldn't do yourself. It was my sacred duty, I felt, to learn everything I could so that when I took over the Blue Lift Platoon I could carry out its mission and lose as few men and machines as possible.

Because of the total concentration required to fly helicopters in combat, pilots were restricted to four hours of actual flight time a day, 120 hours a month. That didn't mean if you started flying at 0600 you automatically quit at 1000 even if there was a big ops going on. You had to bend the rules to fit the situation. There were many times when I flew all night looking for enemy mortar tubes, conducting flare missions, or lifting troops in and out. I staggered out of the cockpit. The flight surgeon grounded you for three days once you exceeded 120 hours within a thirty-day period; it was a good way to get some rest.

Fatigue was setting in. I was getting homesick. I was never much of a letter writer. I sent Sandy a postcard now and then—*Love you, miss you, doing fine, be home soon*—and I sent her a real letter and a dozen roses when the dog got sick. What happened was she mailed me an audiotape of her and the girls talking. Sandy said that Pooh had gotten sick with pneumonia. "Pooh" didn't come out clearly. I thought one of the girls had pneumonia. Sandy thought I was exceptionally thoughtful and sympathetic over her pooch's illness.

I didn't find out my mistake until the next time I patched in a call to her on the radio-telephone link.

"How's my daughter? Over."

You had to say "Over" in order to let the operator know to switch back the conversation to go the other way. It was a bit disconcerting for someone not in the military.

"Our daughters are doing fine. Ronnie, I want you to know ..." And she was rattling on. Sandy was a talker.

"You have to say 'Over' when you're through," I reminded her.

"Over."

"Which one had pneumonia? Over."

"Neither one. Over."

"But you said ... ? Over"

"It was Pooh ... Over."

"Who? Over."

"Pooh. Pooh had pneumonia. Over."

"Who? Pooh? Over."

"Yes. Pooh. The dog. Over."

Such conversations were entirely unsatisfactory. I wanted to *see* Sandy. Touch her. Hold her. In-country soldiers were granted two R&R leaves during a tour of duty. I was almost halfway through my tour. I requested R&R to meet Sandy in Hawaii. When I returned in two weeks, Captain Beatty would ship out stateside, leaving me to take his place as platoon leader. I thought I needed some downtime to chill out and work off a little of Vietnam before I came back to the war to assume the additional responsibilities and duties.

46

The airlines had gone on strike. Sandy sat at the Los Angeles airport for six hours on standby trying to get a flight out to meet me in Honolulu. Tired and cross, she began mumbling and grumbling about being a combat vet's wife and here she was stuck in California and it wasn't fair because her husband had to go back to Vietnam afterward and . . . Other than being small and blond and cute, Sandy was also persistent to the point of being annoying when she didn't get her way. Especially when it was something important like meeting me after I had been gone so long. It was virtually the first time we were separated since I met her at Butch's funeral nearly three years ago.

She finally got a seat to Honolulu, in first class, sitting next to a pretty Hawaiian girl. They got to talking. When the stewardess came by with the drink cart, Sandy politely declined. She had no tolerance for alcohol. Her mother said the smell of a wet bar rag was enough to knock her knee-wobbling drunk.

The Hawaiian girl smiled. "You must have a Hawaiian drink on your way to Hawaii," she said.

"I don't drink."

"You'll like a mai tai. We'll have one together. It's like drinking punch."

Sure enough, it was like drinking punch. Sandy didn't decline the next time the drink cart came by, nor the next. When the plane landed in Honolulu late that afternoon, she was knee-wobbling drunk, just like her mother said, and jabbering away about not receiving a welcoming lei like she had seen everyone getting in the movies. Flight stewardesses, laughing, helped her down the ramp, scrounged up a lei for her and put her in a taxi to take her to our hotel.

The hotel was a big resort overlooking the beach. Still jabbering and giggling, Sandy checked in. She tipped the bellboy after he set down her bag and then looked around the room.

It was a small suite with the living room and bedroom combined, a kitchenette and a bathroom. It contained a sofa, a table and chairs, a lamp stand, a cook stove and refrigerator. Panicked, Sandy snatched up the phone.

"Where's the bed? I can't find the bed! My husband is coming in from Vietnam at five tomorrow morning and I can't find the bed! Why don't I have a bed?"

"Ma'am, if you'll just calm down, we'll send somebody up."

An employee folded out a large double bed from the sofa and left. Sandy collapsed on it. She simply could not hold her liquor. It was now six P.M. She had to be at the R&R Center at five A.M. to meet me. There was no alarm clock in the room. She was afraid that, having drunk so much, she wouldn't wake up on time. It never occurred to her to phone downstairs and post a wake-up call. She was, after all, a small-town girl out in the big world all on her own.

The cook stove was equipped with a timer. Aha! An hour was its maximum setting. She got up every hour all night long to reset it every time it went off. But she made it to the R&R Center in time.

I was just coming down the ramp from the Center, in khakis with my bag on my shoulder, when she got out of the taxi in a miniskirt and came running and screaming and sobbing to throw herself into my arms. What *America* meant to me, what the war and everything else was reduced to at that moment, was the girl in my arms and the two little girls at home in Tulsa.

That evening when everybody on the R&R plane met on the beach for a drink, one of the women commented, "Let's have a mai tai. I understand they're great."

Sandy looked aghast. "Never again will I drink another mai tai."

47

There seemed to be no end in sight for America's longest war. It was rapidly losing credibility as a cause. Disillusionment was setting in. President Nixon decided that the war could not be won by force alone and called for "Vietnamization." He warned that it might take "days and even years of patient and prolonged diplomacy" to end it. Diplomats argued over the size and shape of the negotiating table and who sat where.

In response to "Vietnamization," American troop withdrawals began in June 1969, albeit slowly. It signaled to GIs in Vietnam that the goal of winning was over. Although the war would go on, wasting lives and time, it became clear that its outcome would not be settled in the jungles and air of Vietnam but instead in the corridors of power elsewhere. Soldier morale plummeted. TV no longer reported victories to disenchanted viewers back home; it showed only endless footage of bloody and stubborn fighting. A new motto cropped up throughout Vietnam. It was scrawled on helmets, on hooch walls, stuck to bulletin boards and scribbled inside helicopters.

Don't be the last GI to die in Nam.

In July, wherever TV satellite relay was available in base camps, pilots, crews, and grunts of the 1st Air Cavalry watched astronauts landing on the surface of the moon. Neil Armstrong took his first step and uttered the quote that became famous: "That's one small step for a man, one giant leap for mankind." Angry grunts openly scoffed. "Let that motherfucker come here and take a step with me."

"Search and destroy" tactics gave way to the endless jungle patrols and ambushes of guerrilla warfare. Routines of fighting and killing, fear, boredom, body bags, weariness, and disillusionment produced reluctant warriors whose primary thoughts were of survival. Get through one desperate year's tour of duty and go home. More and more men simply refused to fight. Open rebellion was threatened in some units. Even the elite 1st Air Cav chalked up thirty-five combat refusals over a twelve-month period. One thought was everywhere.

Don't be the last GI to die in Nam.

48

It was tough returning to Vietnam after two weeks lying on the beach during the day and lying in bed with Sandy at night. It was almost like heaven in Hawaii. No H&I every evening or the *Crump! Crump!* impacting of VC mortar rounds. Sandy dropped a pot in the kitchenette one evening while I was sleeping and I scared her half to death by springing out of bed and making a rush for the door and the culvert bunkers.

"I'll be seeing you soon, kid," I said to her in a light tone as I caught the big bird back to the war.

I stood for a long time at the R&R Center before leaving, simply looking at her lovely, tear-stained face. I might never see her again, might never bounce my daughters on my knees. The second time going back, after you knew what it was like and the possibilities that existed for your personal disaster, was much harder than the first time, when you didn't know what to expect. This "charmed" stuff and the curse I now considered as part of it was beginning to affect my entire attitude. I thought fate might be playing some kind of cruel joke, letting me think I was skating through while waiting until the last minute to slam the lid on me. It might have been better were I getting regular bullet holes like all the other guys.

I grinned at Sandy to hide what I was really thinking, to keep her from seeing my own tears and fears. Lieutenants in the By-God U.S, Army 1st Cavalry Division never cried. I watched her from the airliner's porthole until the plane taxied away and I couldn't see her any longer.

Change of command for a platoon leader wasn't much of a ceremony. The platoon fell in for formation and Major Calhoun came out and announced that Lieutenant *Mini-Man* Alexander was now assuming Captain William Cody Beatty's position. I was the new "Blue." Captain Beatty had already been "hail'd and farewell'd." He left Tay Ninh that very day for Ton Son

Nhut to catch the Freedom Bird back to "The World." Major Calhoun wouldn't be far behind.

Mighty Morris slapped me on the back. "You owe us all a round tonight at the O Club," he said, and that was all there was to it.

With command came an increased feeling of responsibility. I felt it heavy on my shoulders, along with a certain aloneness. It wasn't, I realized, only because of my promotion and being set apart from the rest of the guys as their leader; it was also because I was fast becoming among the last of the flyers of the first batch that were here when I arrived in February. Mississippi and Taylor were both leaving the same month. Miles was about to be transferred stateside to instruct new helicopter pilots. Mighty Morris's DEROS came up before Christmas. Only Farmer Farmer was thinking about extending his tour of duty past my own departure. He would be the last of the "old guys."

Yet, while I dreaded the rotation of the "old guys," another part of me was relieved whenever they made it out in one piece. If I had to make life-and-death decisions affecting my men, it was easier on me that they all be FNGs like Stockton and Rouse and the others with whom the platoon was gradually filling up. You didn't get buddy-buddy with the FNGs. You felt the responsibility for them but not the personal attachments. You knew what could happen to them *out there* and you didn't want to be emotionally connected when and if it did happen.

"That's Nui Ba Den, the Black Virgin Mountain," I narrated to Rouse as I conducted his platoon leader's orientation flight out over the AO. "It's a landmark you can see from about anywhere in War Zone C. You're not lost as long as you can see it...."

"Where you from, sir?" Rouse asked through the intercom.

"Maryland and Oklahoma."

"I'm from New Mexico. I got a wife and a kid..."

And off he went attempting to establish a personal link between us. I remembered having attempted the same thing with Captain Blue Beatty. And I remembered Captain Blue having interrupted me, as I now interrupted Rouse. Stick to business. Don't let it become personal. What if he went down out there in a month or so? B-I-L-B-Y.

"I expect you to memorize every fuse box in the aircraft," I said, cutting him off. "Sooner or later, something will happen— a malfunction, a bullet through the electrical system or the hydraulics—and there won't be time to get your head out of your ass."

Responsibility for these guys was enough. They didn't have to like me, and I didn't have to like them. I watched the same kind of transaction occurring between my crew chief Shaky and the enlisted FNGs who sometimes flew their breaking-in period with him and me. Shaky was not only the best crew chief in the platoon and in Apache Troop but also the best hand with an M60 machine gun. I liked him to show our enlisted cherries the ropes. The better they were, the better the entire platoon and the better prepared we all were to survive.

There were a number of abandoned hooches north of the Michelin plantation that Shaky used as target practice for FNGs whenever we were in the area. I flew over them at about three hundred feet. I heard Shaky's Texas drawl over the intercom explaining to a new crew chief/gunner, a Cuban from Miami named Autberto Palma, how things worked.

"When you're shooting into the hooches," he said, "you want to keep the little fuckers in there. Every fifth round you fire is a tracer incendiary round. So you get a rhythm going and keep the little fuckers in their hooches, set the hooches afire with the tracers, and make crispy critters of them. Like this . . ."

The gun began clapping as Shaky chanted. "One in the door, two in the window, three in the roof . . . One in the door, two in the window, three in the roof . . ."

"Jesús, mi madre y—"

Shaky locked a belt of nothing but tracers into the M60 and began firing to make his point that the rounds were going where he said they were going. He poured a broken stream of red into the hooch. "One in the door, two in the window, three in the roof . . ."

"That is incredible, Sergeant Shaky. How did you learn to do this? You will teach me and we will be friends and—"

Shaky blocked him. "The last friend I had was shot out of his helicopter. Don't make friends, Palma. It ain't a smart thing to do while you're over here."

Friendly, yes. Friendship, no. After I became platoon leader, I found myself increasingly taking many of the most hazardous missions myself. It wasn't out of friendships or because I figured I was *charmed* and had the best chance of getting back. It was because I felt *responsible* for the lives of my men. I understood now why Captain Beatty personally flew and led so many missions.

"A leader cannot lead from the back of the pack," he always said.

49

One of the FNGs was a West Point grad, a ring knocker captain named Williams who was in Vietnam to get his combat ticket punched for swift advancement to general. He was an arrogant asshole who went to headquarters platoon as Apache Troop's executive officer under Major Calhoun. Rumor said, and it was always passed along with a groan, that Captain Williams was up for promotion and would replace Major Calhoun as Troop commander.

All officers and warrants in the Headhunters were also aviators. After only two weeks in-country, Captain Williams already felt bullish and ready to take over the herd. He liked to go out with the lift ships. I suspected it was because he thought a few air medals would look good in his personnel file. Although it was a rule that nobody, regardless of rank, was AC before he had three months' combat experience, the good captain had the attitude that *Hey, I'm a West Point grad, by God. I'm a captain, and therefore I'm an AC.*

Mosby and one of my new warrants named Meeker were shot down near the Cambodian border. Because of so much activity in that corner of the AO, we scrambled two Cobras and four of my lifts carrying a platoon of infantry split among us. Captain Williams took one of the ships with Farmer Farmer. Palma the Cuban flew with them as crew chief/gunner. When we lifted infantry, we didn't always carry a second crew member because of load restrictions.

Rouse flew right seat with me. Shaky, of course, was my crew.

The AO, indeed all of Vietnam, was divided into sectors and quadrants. All a pilot in trouble had to do was radio in his sector number and everybody knew where to start looking. Rouse broke a map out of his SOI saddle bags and found the sector and grid coordinates. We didn't know at the time if the bird went down in the middle of an enemy nest or what. Tower on the UHF hook advised the 2/20th Infantry to stand by, we might need additional support.

The airmada swarmed off the base and over the river like mosquitoes. From high in the air when we arrived above the site, the crashed Huey resembled a child's toy cast aside after a play session. It sat skid-crunched into an opening not much larger than its fuselage, blade wrapped into the branches of a small tree. It had probably been downed by a .51-caliber radar-controlled machine gun; the round had blown a large hole through the belly of the aircraft before knocking out the hydraulics system.

The clearing was too small for a rescue out of it. The four-man crew was okay, on the radio, out of the ship and hiding nearby. They appeared next to the crippled bird and waved frantically when they heard us. We circled above them like a flock of vultures.

"There's a clearing about two hundred meters to your front," I radioed Mosby on the ground. "Maybe we can put down there. Are you receiving fire, Three-Four?"

"Negative, Mini-Man, *but stay away from the north. There's a fifty-one pit somewhere around."*

"Stand by, Three-Four."

I dropped down to contours and flew over the larger clearing so fast it was a blur. It looked acceptable. I advised Mosby that all four lifts were landing in the clearing to disgorge troops and secure the area. I would be Chalk One, first ship in, followed by Captain Williams and Farmer in Chalk Two, then the other two birds. We formed up and came in low and fast. I floated over a felled tree and rotor-whipped elephant grass into a frenzy. I hovered to the edge of the field and sat down while the other three ships assembled on the grass behind me.

Troops scrambled out of Huey bellies and hurried to form a security perimeter. I didn't like the idea of sitting there waiting, like ducks on a pond, but we had little choice. At any rate, it didn't take Mosby and his unfortunate crew more than a few minutes to cover the two hundred meters from their crash to us. They burst out of the woodline and tumbled into the nearest Huey, which happened to be Chalk Two piloted by Williams and Farmer.

Everything still seemed quiet—for about five more seconds. All of a sudden, I heard a distinct *Pop!* It sounded like a pressure stall, except it couldn't be. My skids were still on the ground.

"He's hit!" Shaky yelled through the intercom.

"Who's hit?" I yelled back.

"One of the grunts—he's hit!"

I was starting to make the ship light for takeoff. I glanced back into the cargo bay. One of the boonirats who had come back to the helicopter for something had taken a round. The impact knocked him completely out of the chopper.

"Throw him back on!" I shouted.

Shaky and another grunt tossed him inside. He was squirming and sobbing from pain and fear. I pulled collective and pushed in cyclic, lifting and shooting the Huey forward, gaining momentum and transitional lift. I expected airframe Plexiglas to start smashing and instrument panels to erupt in sparks and smoke. Instead, there was only the single sniper's shot.

I soared out above the treeline, leading the Hueys to altitude and out of the danger zone. I radioed Captain Williams to take the flight to nearby FSB Barber, drop off Mosby's bunch, and wait there for me. We had to retrieve the infantry platoon once maintenance came out with a Chinook to recover the wreckage. I would deliver the wounded trooper to the hospital at Tay Ninh and return.

Halfway back to post, Shaky chuckled through the intercom.

"Sir, you ain't gonna believe this."

"What's wrong?"

"This guy ain't hurt bad. All he's got is a bruised ass. One of his ammo pouches stopped the round."

Rouse looked at me with something like awe. "Everybody's right," he said. "Even when *Mini-Man* takes a hit, nobody gets hurt."

I concentrated on flying. How much longer could my luck possibly hold out?

50

A twin-rotored Chinook flew out from Phuoc Vinh, hooked sling lines to the disabled chopper and pulled it out for repairs and salvage. By that time, I had dropped the bruised soldier off for first aid, refueled, and met Captain Ring Knocker and the others at LZ Barber. We returned to pick up the security platoon at the clearing, where we found soldiers relaxing, smoking and joking in the trees around the PZ. The sniper had apparently *di-di'd* after firing his one shot.

Again, I went in as Chalk One with Williams and Farmer as Chalk Two. It was a routine extraction until we lifted off with the troops. I had noticed while on the ground that Captain Williams was flying the helicopter from the right seat. Nothing wrong with that. It was just that most guys preferred the left because of the better view down through the chin bubble. In flight school, IPs always flew left while students took the right. Williams obviously felt more comfortable in the student position.

I elevatored out of the PZ and was well on my way to altitude when Williams behind me broke to the right, which was a natural thing to do for a pilot flying from that side of the ship. Instead of gathering steam and altitude immediately, popping out of there, he mushed along at an altitude of about a thousand feet at a slow sixty knots. Slow and low, a matter of inexperience. A .51-caliber antiaircraft gun had an effective range of well over a thousand meters. Williams at three hundred meters high was dead in the center of a kill zone.

He passed directly over a .51 pit. Something was going on down there, a small base camp maybe, or a platoon patrol. Blue infantry hadn't located it while securing the crash site and the PZ.

The first round smashed through Williams's left chin bubble. Startled, Williams immediately pulled to the left, which turned him directly into the antiaircraft fire instead of away from it. Shaky happened to be looking back from the bay door of my lead ship when what looked like a solid stream of green tethered the second Huey to the ground. Tracers smoked and chewed at the chopper, batting it about in the sky. It shuddered and began rolling to the left and right while its nose pitched up and down. It seemed to be disintegrating before Shaky's eyes. It took thirty-six hits in less than three seconds.

"We're hit! We're hit real bad!" Williams yelled into his mike, a statement immediately followed by a horrific scream of agony.

Armor-piercing rounds nearly ate off the nose of the wounded helicopter. One struck Williams's right leg. It splintered the bone from shin to above the knee and made hamburger of his leg. The point of the round stuck out through the skin of his right thigh, having been prevented from going all the way through by his seat armor. Blood exploded inside the cockpit.

Worse yet, Williams's leg and foot got wedged in the pedals, making them inoperable. The aircraft went crazy all over the sky, like a balloon spurting out air. Farmer Farmer fought with the controls. He completely freaked out. He was screaming his head off.

"We're taking hits! I can't control it! We're going down ... down! ..."

Fortunately, his crew chief, Palma, trained by Shaky, was fast becoming one of the best and coolest crewmen in the platoon. He kept his head. Each pilot's seat had two little red handles with safety wires, one on each side. The handles released the seat and let the back fold down. Palma lunged over the top of the panicked troops in the bay, jerked the red handles and dragged Williams howling with pain into the back. That freed the pedals, allowing Farmer to regain control of the bird before it blasted into the jungle.

Miraculously, the Huey remained airworthy.

"Farmer, are you okay?" I shouted at him through the radio. Once out of the kill zone, Farmer's composure returned. *"I'm okay. Just scared. Oh, God. I really think I got the calf scours and messed my pants."*

In the meantime, the third ship in line took eighteen hits but continued to fly. Mighty Morris at tail end instantly jiggered to the left and poured on the coal, escaping without damage. Snakes rolled in hot on the .51s while my forlorn little squadron limped back to base. Two of my ships were shot all to hell, having accumulated fifty-four bullet holes between them. It was unbelievable that they could still fly. Even more unbelievable, considering that both birds were stuffed with crew and troops, the only man wounded was Captain Williams. Which proved that helicopters were harder to bring down than some people supposed and that guys were pretty hard to kill, all in all.

My helicopter hadn't been fired upon.

None of us ever saw Captain Ring Knocker again after that. His replacement, a captain named Powdrill, was a muscular young redheaded guy who arrived with enough good common sense to realize he didn't know it all. He soon replaced Major Calhoun as Troop commander and became a good leader.

51

Lieutenant Dave Stegall was flying his Loach as part of a Pink Team sneaking and peeking on enemy activity about ten miles north of Tay Ninh. Spec4 Larry Kempers was crew chief and observer, Sergeant John Binegar was torque with the machine gun. They were skimming the treetops and peering down into the jungle when they encountered automatic weapons fire. Plexiglas shattered. Bullets *ticked!* through metal. Muzzles flickered and smoked from the trees. All three men suffered wounds, none of which were life threatening, all of which were scary nonetheless because of the blood spattering each other and the interior of the little whirlybird.

"Taking fire! Taking fire!" Stegall screamed at his high bird.

Kempers dropped red smoke; he had the canister in his hand, ring already pulled. Binegar, nursing an arm wound, opened fire with his M60, the muzzle stuck out the open door, shooting at the enemy in the trees directly below.

Bullets thudding into the tiny scout chopper severed the helicopter's push-pull levers fore and aft. The bird lurched in and out of the treeline as Stegall fought to keep it in the air. They were dead men if they went down here into the guns of their ambushers.

Stegall increased lateral thrust to overcome the ague that threatened to shake the bird right out of the sky. This caused the Loach to fly sideways. It skipped awkwardly above the trees, swooping and falling and rising and sputtering, but managing to flee from its attackers.

"I don't know how long I can keep it in the air!" Stegall cried over the radio.

He ordered Kempers and Binegar to get rid of weight. Lighten the bird in order to gain lift. They started tossing equipment out the door—a case of smoke grenades, a fire extinguisher, chicken plate, their lunches . . . They jettisoned everything loose inside the aircraft except their weapons. Those they were going to need *when* they went down. That they *were* going to crash was a foregone conclusion. Stegall strove to get as far away from the ambush site as he could before they went in.

He gained a hundred feet of altitude, then lost most of it. The ship shook so hard he could hardly hold on to the controls. It was like it was a dog and they were fleas it was trying to get rid of. Behind, the high bird Snake rolled in hot over the red smoke, making the enemy pay for his little indiscretion of opening fire on a helicopter. It afforded little consolation to the wounded men inside the even more seriously wounded Loach fluttering painfully through the air. They were not going to make it back. Not in this ship.

"Tighten your belts," Stegall warned his crew. "I'm going to take her down. We're going to hit hard."

His alarm went into the air: *"Mayday! Mayday!"* And at Tay Ninh, the scramble horn sounded three blasts.

He desperately searched for an opening in the thick forest cover. Ahead and to the right he spotted a break in the treeline and headed for it. He came upon a small clearing clotted with six-foot-tall elephant grass, bamboo, and dead tree stumps spiked around like gray tombstones. He would never have selected it for a landing under any other circumstances, but he had little choice now.

"Going in!" he exclaimed. *"We're going down!"*

He crash-landed the Loach in grass and brackish underlying water. After the initial impact, it listed to one side against a stump but remained on its skids. The crew, shaken but without additional injuries, bailed out and huddled in the trees at the edge of the clearing.

It became now a matter of which side reached them first.

"You can't imagine how happy we were to see crossed sabers and Headhunters," Lieutenant Stegall roared in the O Club after his wounds were patched up. "It was certainly a better sight than seeing sandals and black pajamas."

He jumped onto a chair with both boots and hoisted his beer. "A toast!" he cheered.

Pilots crowded around, laughing and grabassing. "Hear! Hear! A toast!"

"A toast to the best and bravest bunch of guys in Vietnam. Who put their own asses on the line to snatch Larry, John, and me right out from under ol' Charlie's nose. Down the hatch, guys."

Kempers and Binegar over at their NCO Club were undoubtedly undergoing a similar "debriefing." They would be dropping by later to collect their free beers. Loach flyers normally stuck to themselves, but an experience like this constituted a special occasion.

When we lost somebody *out there,* when we brought back full body bags, the O Club that night was a little quieter than normal and Mighty Morris strummed his guitar and sang "Red River Valley." But when we had a downed bird and got the crew out and back safely, the O Club was full of drinking down and away the bad that could have happened.

Laugh, laugh, laugh. Rough banter. Machoing away fear and anxiety. Everyone getting a little loud and a little wild in affirmation of still being alive. A celebration of survival. Whooping it up tonight because tomorrow we would all be back *out there.* And for whom did the TOC alarm toll? It tolled for thee.

"Hey, Dave. Did you ruin a pair of skivvies? Anything brown floating around inside the cockpit?"

"Hey, Dave. Did your life flash before your eyes?"

What everybody really wanted to know was, *Tell us about it, Dave. What was it like to get shot and go down? Tell us about it so we'll know when it happens to us. Tell us, but don't get too heavy. Keep it light and joke and bullshit about it. Let us all whistle through the graveyard, because that way it ain't nearly so scary.*

He told his story and things grew quieter and more serious. Silence crept in like fog through cracks to dampen spirits. The bullshitting and grabassing ceased. I leaned against the rocket crate bar with Farmer Farmer, who had almost gone down twice, and sipped my beer and listened. Each of us nursed his own fears and apprehensions as he fought back unspoken nightmares which threatened the possibility that tomorrow it could be *me* out there.

We listened and we felt the worms crawling in our guts. Afterward, it was again laugh, laugh, laugh. Getting rid of all that awful silence. Mighty Morris took up his guitar and started to sing. It was one of those macabre songs with an unlimited number of verses that continued to accumulate night after night.

> *"Eighteen kids in a free-fire zone,*
> *Books in hand going home;*
> *Last in line goes home alone.*
> *Napalm sticks to kids.*

> *"Vietcong woman on the run,*
> *Struck by napalm from the sun.*
> *When they're pregnant, you get two for one.*
> *Napalm sticks to kids.*

> *"Charlie in his boat sitting in the stern.*
> *Thinks his goddamned boat won't burn.*
> *Those fucking gooks will never learn.*
> *Napalm sticks to kids."*

Whoops and laughter of encouragement once again filled the club. Beer cans sailed around like mortar rounds. I finished my beer, slapped Stegall on the shoulder and walked outside into the Vietnam night. The 175s were also silent, for a change, no H&I tonight. Dark cloud banks formed on the horizon. I smelled rain and I smelled pollution from the river. I smelled fish and human shit and kerosene smoke from Tay Ninh the city five miles away.

I wondered if Charlie kept a Vulture Board like we did on which to record his kills.

52

Although the "Nixon Doctrine" proclaimed on Guam on July 25, 1969, emphasized "Vietnamization" and the incremental withdrawal of U.S. troops, President Nixon refused to commit to total disengagement. To do so at this stage would have amounted to defeat for both America and the South Vietnamese. He was determined by the use of air power to keep up the pressure on Hanoi for a cease-fire and for stabilization.

General Creighton Abrams oversaw America's withdrawal from the war. He drew up a "glide path" of fourteen stages for the return of troops to the United States, beginning July 1 and ending at a projected date in November 1972 when America would be extricated from the Vietnam quagmire.

The first phase ended on August 31, 1969, when the first promised increment of 25,000 men, primarily from the 9th Infantry Division, was withdrawn. Between September 18 and December 15, 1969, another 40,500 men from the 82d Airborne and the U.S. Marines were pulled out. By the end of 1969, nearly 52,000 soldiers would have left Vietnam.

For those left behind, however, the war continued as before—with the exception that they now realized they were on hold, fighting a war in which America had lost interest.

53

You had to be a little crazy in order to avoid going a lot insane. Everybody said it, and everybody laughed about it. Of course, we were all young—a year ago some of the gunners and crew chiefs were still in high school; Shaky was barely nineteen—and when you were young you did foolish and dangerous things. The Headhunters as a college jock fraternity could have been pulling panty raids. Instead, we pulled air raids. Instead of water balloons, we had rockets and machine guns. Dangerous frat brothers, we were, whose sense of perspective became a bit warped from the war, whose humor turned to the dark side.

Tales of particularly funny and curious events spiced evenings at the O Club as guys spun their favorite "no shit, there I was" stories. At least they were funny to us "old-timers." The FNGs looked at us a little strangely, but it wouldn't be long before they came around.

Swede recalled dropping fleschettes on a VC bunker complex. Fleschettes were like razor-sharp horseshoe nails, thousands of which burst from a single explosion. Blue infantry later found a dead NVA left behind in one of the bunkers. A burst directly outside the bunker propelled fleschettes through a gun slit and through tiny cracks to pin the VC to the opposite wall inside. Stuck there on the wall like an animal's hide, his feet off the floor and his arms tacked spread away from his sides. His pith helmet had been nailed to his head. It must have been a damn funny sight, Swede allowed, seeing that gook up on the wall like that.

There were always the flyers who pushed the envelope. Like the ones who got caught in flight school and kicked out for buzzing farmers' cows or flying underneath bridges. These same daredevils who didn't get caught got bored in Vietnam when nobody shot at them and therefore they couldn't have any fun shooting back. Lacking human targets, they expended ammo shooting at elephants or buffalo. They got right down on the deck and tested their skills by trying to place rockets directly up the beasts' assholes.

Bird Dog in the White Platoon spotted a gook running across a rice paddy. He brought his Loach right down above the field and flew alongside the panicked VC, pinging at him out the window with his pistol until he knocked him down. He and his torque had made a bet that Bird Dog couldn't add to the Vulture Board using nothing but his pistol. It was a confirmed kill.

Pilots on river patrol looking for VC sampans smuggling weapons and supplies liked to buzz women and girls bathing in the river to see them run away naked. One afternoon when it was raining and the enemy foolishly thought choppers wouldn't be flying, a Purple Team caught three sampans in a little flotilla heading south. It was always difficult to tell bad guys from good guys or neutral guys. Everybody wore black pajamas.

However, it was unusual enough to see three boats together that it looked suspicious. The Loach of the team flew over to check them out. First time he buzzed over, the boatmen held. The second time he came around, they apparently thought their cover had been blown and they were made. They opened fire on the low bird with automatic weapons and RPGs. All three boats were full of munitions and rode heavy in the water.

The high bird immediately radioed for backup. Cobras scrambled from Tay Ninh base camp less than two miles away. It was a turkey shoot there on the river. Everybody wanted to get in his licks. Pilots were whooping and shouting over the air. One loudly sang "These Boots Are Made for Walking" as he made his weapon runs. It was great sport for everyone, a major overkill that turned the boats into kindling, sank the munitions and left a wide pool of blood and gore drifting south with the current. Everybody returned to base laughing and joking and still on a high.

No pilot adhered strictly to the rules of engagement, which stated we had to precisely pinpoint an enemy firing at us before we could shoot back. It became a joke between Shaky and me.

"Receiving fire! Receiving fire!" Shaky would shout over the intercom.

"Can you see where it's coming from?"

"Roger that." It was always, "Roger that."

"Then *fire!*"

One night when we were returning to base from a flare mission, flying above a section of Tay Ninh the city that happened to lie within the base's traffic pattern, we received fire from the suburbs. O'Brien was flying gunner in one door of the ship, Shaky in the other.

"Receiving fire!" Shaky notified.

I gave him the routine. "Can you see where it's coming from?"

"Damn right I can. It's coming from the city."

I laughed. Close enough. "Then return fire."

No chopper received further fire from the city for the rest of the time I was there.

We told our "no shit" stories in the O Club, embellished them a bit, laughed over them, and sipped suds. When we got tired of watching old reruns of *I Love Lucy* and *Art Linkletter*, we took beers out to the mongoose compound. The Blues were always bringing in a snake of some sort. Whenever it was a big cobra, a boisterous crowd of drinking pilots and crew gathered to wager on exactly how long it took Pepe or Yosemite Sam to dispatch the serpent. Whoppa the morose Cobra pilot always bet on the snake. Some day, he said, it was going to win.

"You can't keep doing it," he said, "without the reptile getting you sooner or later."

54

A battalion of NVA and VC main force struck FSB Candy north of Nui Ba Den for three or four nights in a row. It was nip and tuck, come and go. Some of us at Tay Ninh hung around the TOC listening to the fight on the radio at night instead of drinking beer at the O Club or watching Pepe and Sam fight snakes. Holding on to the FSB soon proved untenable. Chinooks rushed in during the day while the enemy was pulled back in the jungle resting for another bout that night and jerked the GI company out, abandoning the support base.

LRRPs were to go in after dark and booby-trap everything with C-4 plastic explosives. They figured Charlie wouldn't come back that night since he knew everybody was gone. When he ventured in to scavenge at first light, the base would be all fixed up for him— Surprise! Surprise!—and the LRRPs would have been extracted.

Rouse and I volunteered to insert the five-man team with Shaky flying crew chief/gunner. Farmer Farmer and Stockton the baby face supported me at wing in a backup slick while a Cobra from Blue Max flew shotgun. The LRRPs must have had a ton of plastic distributed among them in their rucks. They grunted like beasts of burden when they climbed into my helicopter shortly after nightfall. Night always came quickly in the tropics. One moment there was a glorious sunset, the next purple darkness fell like a curtain.

A misty overcast hung over the jungle, penetrated by a quarter-moon. Gerard had flown his Loach over the FSB several times in the late afternoon after it was abandoned and had seen no activity among the bunkers and hooches. The perimeter wire hadn't yet been cut. The FSB remained a dark flatland when I arrived with my load of LRRPs, seemingly undisturbed from when the GIs pulled out.

It was supposed to be a quick in and out. Drop off the troops, then come back for them before first light after their job was done.

The FSB was about two hundred feet across with the helipad on the east side next to the defensive berms. I blinked my landing lights on and off quickly as I flared to make sure nothing was sticking up. I touched down.

"They're gone!" Shaky said.

I hadn't much more than hit collective and rose out over the wire and the forest than the entire treeline began that white blinking silent rhythm of erupting muzzles. Green tracer tracks lit up the darkness. Their intensity as they flashed past the helicopter windshield was almost blinding.

"Receiving fire!" Shaky exclaimed, and right away he was hammering with his M60, pouring a stream of red tracers back at the forest.

I throttled out of range and circled the FSB at a distance. By this time, tracer tracks had lowered and were darting in a psychedelic rage across the flats of the FSB. I had no choice but to go back for the team. Our guys were going to get the shit kicked out of them.

The LRRP leader came up on the radio. "Mini-Man, *come right back to the same place. We'll meet you there.*"

Normally when the adrenaline began surging, I went into my calm spectator mode. It was different this time. I was so scared I almost went into convulsions. I nearly stopped breathing from the tightening band around my chest. I had to go back into that madhouse of steel and fire—and all I could think of was that, sooner or later, like Whoppa said, the reptile was going to get me. Charmed or not, it just couldn't last.

The panic attack went away almost as soon as it occurred. However, I couldn't help feeling, later, that this was only the beginning. The pressure was starting to build. It was like I was standing at one end of a field while somebody at the other end was shooting at me with a machine gun. The bullets ate their way closer and closer and there was nothing I could do to get out of the way.

"Mini-Man, *did you read?*" the LRRP leader cried, sounding urgent.

I shook myself out of it. Rouse looked at me. "Roger that," I said.

Blue Max Cobra radioed that he would roll on the west side of the FSB, from which the enemy fire originated, in order to take some heat off me when I made my second run. I had to keep my red-and-green position lights on to let Blue Max know where I was. I felt like a lighted target as I swung the Huey wide and poured on the coal on approach.

The Cobra rolled hot. I became peripherally aware of his rocket explosions and red laser-like minigun streams to my left flank. Shaky hammered away from his door. We scooted at maximum speed dangerously low to the ground toward Candy. Blue Max's run suppressed little of the enemy fire. *"My God!"* Rouse shouted, and we flew directly into the light show of streaking tracers.

The weight of the chopper hadn't even settled on the skids before Shaky yelled, "They're on!"

I pulled collective and shoved cyclic hard forward, putting so much stress on the engine and blades that the hands on the rpm gauge shot momentarily into the red *Never Exceed*. Rouse, whose duty as copilot was to help watch the gauges as well as to be ready to take over in case I bought the farm, exhaled sharply through the intercom as though to shout a warning, but then he shut up and held on. I popped the Huey up and out in a cyclic climb through the pulsating rhythm of the tracers probing to knock us out of the air.

"Color us *gone*!" Shaky cheered—and we were gone.

Back at base camp, Rouse climbed out of his seat like an old rickety man. The LRRPs pressed wooden nickels on us and Rouse walked twice around the helicopter, shaking his head in disbelief.

"There must have been eight thousand rounds coming at us," he said.

Shaky grinned. "Bullets can't touch *Mini-Man*," he said. "Not our little bitty lieutenant with the big set of balls."

I looked at my hands. They were trembling.

55

We had live entertainment form time to time for the sake of the troops' morale. Nothing like Bob Hope or the big USO shows. Those were confined to Saigon or Vung Tau or the larger posts where security could be provided. This wasn't World War II where battle lines were drawn and everybody knew where they were. There were no battle lines here. Your own hooch maid could be the enemy. What we had instead were Korean rock 'n' rollers who sang with funny, outrageous loss of their *Ls*—*love* became *ruv*—and go-go dancers. Mighty Morris complained that the Korean dancers had mosquito bites for tits. Nonetheless, there was always lots of jeering and encouragement for the girls to "take it all off."

A couple of times *Playboy* Playmates came out to hand out pictures, sign autographs, and then get the hell out of there and away from all those drooling horny GIs before it got dark again.

Red Cross blood donor days were events as well attended as the Playmate visits. Guys were always hungry to see round female eyes. Besides, the Red Cross Dollies, surely selected as much for their looks as for their abilities, gave you orange juice and donuts and actually held your hand, even while sticking a needle into your arm to draw blood.

RHIP—rank has its privilege. As platoon leader, I flew the Dollies to the top of Black Virgin Mountain to draw blood from the radio relay detachment. Miles quipped that he bet there *still* weren't any virgins on the mountain. Landing on top of the mountain was a trick. The helipad was about the size of a basketball court, with just enough room to one side for the relay station. The mountain dropped off precipitously from there on all sides.

When I took off again, I eased off the mountain in a hover and then let the bottom fall out as on a roller coaster, showing off and giving the girls a thrill ride. They screamed with excitement.

"One of them wore a short dress," Shaky exclaimed, "and I almost saw her *panties*."

"Know what I'd do if I were an ugly girl?" baby-faced Stockton asked rhetorically. "I'd go to war and hang around army posts. You'd get your ass screwed off every night, no matter how ugly you were. GIs ain't particular."

Any event gave cause for much excitement and preparation, a welcome respite from routine. Sometimes we had to make a trip into Tay Ninh the city for supplies that could only be purchased there. The club refrigerators never made enough ice for an occasion when everybody showed up to hoot and holler at the girls.

Farmer Farmer, Mighty Morris, Shaky, and I piled into Sergeant Major Rogers's quarter-ton jeep one morning for an ice run. All such visits had to be made in the daytime. Standing orders. No GIs were allowed in town after nightfall when the VC started venturing out.

Shaky drove. Mighty Morris only half-jokingly said he had rather stay on base if the Farmer took the wheel, considering the way he flew helicopters. I took the front passenger's seat and let my boot hang outside the Jeep.

"You're not going to leave your foot out like that, are you, sir?" Morris asked.

"Why not?"

"I've heard stories about kraits attacking jeeps and trying to bite through the tires. Imagine what a really big snake could do to a boot."

"Bullshit," I scoffed, but I retracted my foot.

The base camp's main gate opened onto a long track that led through the wire to the highway to Tay Ninh. The highway was a fairly decent road of patched tarmac lined with palms and rice paddies and hooches. Even from five miles away, when the wind was right and sometimes when it wasn't, you picked up the stench of the brown river and the city on the other side of the river. The odor was a peculiar mixture of stagnant water, cook fires, water buffalo dung, human shit, garbage, and air pollution.

Open souvenir stands outside the wire on the road clustered in ambush of emerging GIs. Coke stands and cribs for the "Three P" girls. Ragged kids, whores, and crones with red betel nut juice staining deeply the crevices in their chins. They waited like crows around a roadkill to mob every vehicle that left base camp. Butchered English raised a cacophony of crow sounds.

"Coke-Cola, GI?"

"You souvenir me, GI?"

"Want have good time, GI? Me good time girl. Me do all you like, GI. Chop-chop, doggie . . ."

I had heard stories about how VC deliberately infected whores with an incurable strain of black syphilis or about how VC whores concealed razor blades in their twats. I never knew if the stories were true or not; they were enough to deter me even if I had been so inclined to experiment. Everybody teased Shaky about his testing to find out. As far as we knew, he still had his dick.

"It was my Texas duty," Shaky drawled good-naturedly. "I couldn't let the poor troops loose on these girls without making sure they were all right. Strictly altruistic, you understand? Nothing is too good for the troops—and nothing is generally what they get."

Farmer Farmer took out a handful of C-rat chocolates and tossed them into the ditch gutter. When the kids and whores scrambled for the candy, Shaky goosed the jeep and squealed out onto the tarmac toward town.

Nearer the city, shops appeared vending everything from tire tread Ho Chi Minh sandals and patched bicycle tires to fish head sauce, rice, Cokes, and souvenirs. Old men wearing black pajama bottoms squatted alongside the highway, looking as wizened and wise as temple monkeys. Women tended cook fires. Whores looking young and pathetically brazen in mini-skirts and bright makeup waved and wriggled their butts. Ragged kids ran everywhere, shouting and playing. Women washing clothes lined the river while their children swam. Some guy might be taking a leak in the stream while a few yards downriver a woman filled her clay jar with drinking and cooking water.

Unlike the ground-pounding grunts who spent a lot of time among the Vietnamese and developed a near-contempt and disgust for their way of life, we pilots associated with the natives sparingly. We therefore regarded them with curiosity, interest, and, of course, suspicion.

It was common knowledge that VC and VC sympathizers infected most towns and cities in Vietnam. VC were everywhere, but you could seldom tell them from anyone else. It wasn't like they wore uniforms or signs on their backs. Only Americans did that.

Surprisingly enough, however, we encountered very little trouble in Tay Ninh. Charlie liked to come to town as much as we did to have a few cool ones and chase pussy. Neither side wanted to upset the status quo. Both sides appreciated the benefit of a neutral ground.

Shaky slowed to thirty-five mph as we approached the river, traveling between the hooches alongside the road. You wouldn't want to hit one of the kids and cause a big incident. Ahead of us, a group of four or five urchins, the oldest of which appeared to be about twelve, was playing the Vietnamese equivalent of stickball in the road. The kids parted to let us through.

As the jeep eased past, I suddenly heard the distinctive *Spang!* of a grenade handle being released. I was an old 82d Airborne trooper and I *knew* what a grenade sounded like when you pulled the pin. I caught my breath sharply.

Mesmerized, I watched a grenade sail out of the huddle of kids. It arced high into the air, twisting slowly in the sunlight, seemingly in slow motion, and dropped toward the open jeep. The kids broke running for the nearest hooch.

The grenade bounced off the jeep's hood and landed inside on the floorboard between my feet.

"Oh, shit!"

A frag grenade has a fuse of about five seconds. I knew beyond all hope that I was a goner, charmed or not. The charm had all run out.

No one ever knew how he would react when staring at his own death. I simply acted instinctively out of self-survival. There was no time to think about it.

Shaky's first impulse was the same as mine—to either get rid of the grenade or get away from it. Irrationally, he goosed gas to the jeep and it lurched forward. At the same moment, I scraped the little bomb off the floorboard and flung it out as hard as I could. I didn't care where it landed; I only wanted to get rid of it before it detonated.

The kids who threw it ducked through the open door of a hut next to the road. By some freak coincidence, the grenade went in right behind them, as if it was a yo-yo attached to a string.

It exploded immediately with an ear-cracking *Crump!* We ducked as debris and shrapnel whistled past the jeep.

Shaky kept going, speeding until he reached the bridge. None of us looked back. We bounced over the bridge and got lost in the city among all the other jeeps and GIs. Shaky pulled to the side of the street. His hands shook on the wheel. Mighty Morris emitted a quivering sigh. I was still stunned.

"I'll be a corn-shucking redneck hillbilly!" Farmer Farmer declared finally. "Did you see *that*? It blew *them* up."

They all stared at me. "You meant to do that?" Mighty Morris accused, looking amazed.

"I didn't. I swear. It just happened."

"Goddamn!" Shaky said. *"That* was poetic justice."

We got our ice and went back to base, not even looking at the destroyed hooch as we drove back by. People were all around and there were some white mice—Vietnamese policemen—investigating. They waved as though to stop us, but we kept going. A GI couldn't win in a deal like this. We dared not report what happened. It meant a long, involved investigation by CID resulting in the town likely being placed off-limits to all GIs. That would make us exceedingly popular.

We felt like criminals on the lam for a few days, expecting to be apprehended. But none of us said anything about it to anyone outside our group and that was the last we heard about it. I don't know if the kids were killed or not. Probably they were. The stats never went up on our Vulture Board.

"You saved our butts," Shaky said. "I'm a short-timer. I'm gonna stick to you like glue, sir, until I get my Texas ass out of this goofy shitpot country."

56

The dinks brought into the AO these radar-controlled .51-caliber antiaircraft machine guns and scattered them around at random in attempts to pick off helicopters and hamper our screening ops. They were terrifying. They had such range that you weren't safe from them even at three thousand feet.

For some reason, our FM radios picked up the .51's particular radar signature when it tried to home in on us. You had about five seconds to take evasive action from when you heard the first *beep!* By the time you heard the third *beep!* it was already too late. You didn't encounter the .51s often, but when you did your blood formed instant ice crystals.

Werner, one of my new warrants—it seemed almost everyone was an FNG—and I were working a Purple Team up north. We heard over radio traffic that a second team farther south had encountered a .51. A grunt on the ground broadcast a warning over the radio. *"Huey bound for the south toward FSB Phyllis, be warned. You are under fire from a fifty-one-cal to your north."*

You rarely heard gunfire inside helicopters.

A few minutes later I heard the *beep!* I almost slung Shaky and O'Brien out of the helicopter. I slammed the cyclic forward and dropped the collective, putting the chopper into a nose dive to both gain speed and lose altitude. You had two chances for survival; hesitating got you shot out of the sky. First, you wanted to move faster than the .51 could track you. Second, you dropped low to get out of his line of fire.

If a 7.62mm tracer looked like a flaming basketball coming at you, the .51 cal was a burning trash can. A silent stream of green trash cans lazily sailed above and in front of us as I maintained the dive. I pulled up short above the treetops and shagged out of range before I returned to altitude.

We had the ability to call for air strikes when the target

appeared hardened and beyond the capabilities of our Snakes. Often, .51 antiaircraft guns protected important food and arms bunkers or tunnel complexes that could withstand anything short of an Arc Light or a few loads of fast-mover napalm. I located the target. I talked it over with Connolly and Mad Dog in the Red Bird. They agreed with me that we should summon fast movers to obliterate an area next to an abandoned rice paddy.

Requests for air generally took about a half-hour of relaying it up through echelons. I remained over station, circling, while my Loach and Cobra swept on to the west as a Pink Team. The FAC always arrived ahead of the jet fighters to pinpoint and mark the target for them.

We made lazy chandelles in the air, bullshitting over the intercom and listening to a rock 'n' roll AEFES radio station out of Saigon. Some DJ REMF-type who opened his program with a rousing *Good morning, Vietnam!* All of a sudden, Shaky blurted out, *"Son of a bitch!"*

I did a double take. Right outside my window, flying next to us, was a Bronco. It was so close it looked like Shaky could have stepped out the Huey's door onto its wing. I knew how fast those things could fly, having been rendered unconscious by excessive Gs during my own experience flying in one. Stall speed must have been next to nothing since this one had slowed enough to fly formation on me.

"Hello there!" the FAC pilot said cheerfully, grinning from his cockpit and waving at us. *"I hear you got some excitement for me. What are you shooting at and where is it?"*

When I found my voice again, I identified the target and showed him where it was. He in turn chatted with the fast movers.

"F-4s from Vung Tau will be here in about five mikes," he relayed. *"They're gonna make their runs from east to west, so you need to move to the north. You can come in later for a BDA and see if we killed anything. Okay, I'm going in. Let me know if this is the right place . . ."*

He tilted his opposite wing and plunged away into a screaming dive. He really burned along next to the ground. Willie Pete smoked up next to the field and the Bronco seemed to shoot straight up away from it. WP—white phosphorus—was heavy, easy to see from the air and remained in a cloud for a long time.

"Is that the place?" FAC asked.

"Close," I responded. "Maybe thirty, forty meters to the south."

He chuckled. *"I got it spotted then."*

It was absolutely spectacular. I felt like cheering for our side. Two F-4 Phantoms streaking through the sky like bullets dived from out of the invisible distance, flattened out and dumped their loads in and around the WP smoke. A fiery bright cauldron of flames blossomed in the forest next to the rice paddy as the jets rocketed out of sight.

The Phantoms made one more screaming pass, adding to flames erupting within an area roughly two hundred meters wide by a klick long. *Boom! Boom!* Like that, it was over and the fighter jets were gone back to wherever they came from.

"Okay, Mini-Man," the FAC chirped. *"We enjoyed it. Call us again if you need us."*

My God, we had that kind of power and yet these little bastards fought on! Didn't they know they were licked?

57

A single blast on the TOC alarm—troops in contact—was one thing, and you hustled. But *three* blasts . . . Bird down. That could be *you* out there. I beat feet for the TOC every time it sounded if I wasn't already in the air or scrambling as part of the duty ready force. Now that I was platoon leader, those crazy, magnificent bastards out there were *my* guys. I stayed next to the radios until aircrews were rescued or bodies recovered. The waiting was an unnerving experience.

When White Platoon leader Captain Cotner went down on the edge of the Michelin plantation, we knew he was a goner. The rubber farm always teemed with enemy because of the overhead cover against air surveillance. I would have been out there with the Blues looking for him except the flight surgeon had red-lined me for three days for excessive flight hours. Instead, all I could do was listen to the radios as the drama played itself out.

Cotner and his two-man crew, Gonzalez and Washington, were low-sniffing for bad guys around the edges of the plantation when enemy machine gun fire riddled the Loach with bullets. Their high bird Cobra rolled in hot on the machine gun while the Loach attempted to limp away. It was so badly damaged, however, that it didn't get far before it crashed into the rubber trees. Their spreading branches helped cushion the impact. It dropped on through to the ground below.

Soon after the TOC alarm wailed at Tay Ninh, Cotner came up on the air to give his grid location. He reported that all three members of the flight crew were alive but that he heard enemy closing in on them. The problem now lay in finding the downed bird beneath the thick rubber tree foliage before the Vietnamese discovered it.

Although shaken and stunned, the three airmen quickly recovered from the crash as dust and leaves settled. None had been wounded in the fusillade of fire that brought down their Loach. At first, there was only the sudden silence following the pandemonium and adrenaline rush of the smashup. Then they heard the Cobra buzzing past looking for them. At the same moment, they detected Vietnamese voices coming their way.

They found themselves in one hell of a predicament. It was going to be tough for rescuers to see them in the trees; Cotner dared not drop smoke to mark their location because of the proximity of the enemy. There were also no clearings suitable for a PZ anywhere in the vicinity.

Before abandoning the crash site, Cotner grabbed all the Willie Pete grenades he could carry. He didn't have time to destroy the radios and other gear as SOP required. He sent the torque and observer ahead while he waited in the surrounding trees for the approaching Vietnamese soldiers.

Minutes later, Charlie appeared in a cautious six-man NVA squad. Caution, however, quickly turned to recklessness when the soldiers saw no one around the bird. They began crawling all over it, trying to rip out the radios and anything else they could turn to good use in their own cause. So absorbed were they in their tasks that no one observed Cotner sneaking up on them.

When he was within range, he pulled the pin on a white phosphorus grenade and hurled it at the wreckage. One guy glanced up in time to see it hurtling through the air. He screamed a warning, but it was too late. The Willie Pete exploded with a horrifying flash of smoke and flame hot enough to instantly melt magnesium.

Cotner immediately tossed two more grenades into the blazing conflagration. Flames consumed the Loach, six NVA soldiers, and the surrounding rubber trees. All would soon be reduced to smoldering ashes.

Fire and smoke marked the site for rescuers. An hour later, Farmer Farmer and Stockton snatched all three Whites out of the rubber trees. There was a great deal of celebrating at the

O Club and the NCO Club that night. Mighty Morris sang his songs and beer cans sailed through the air. I must have been growing a crop of melancholy. I kept thinking, *There's always tomorrow and another chance for these brave men to die.*

58

General Elvy Benton Roberts's 1st Air Cavalry Division retained the offensive throughout the summer as the monsoon season approached. Units of the 1/9 saw much of the action as they struck enemy troops, supply lines, and assembly areas throughout War Zone C. The 1st Squadron accounted for 25 percent of casualties inflicted upon the enemy during the month of September. The NVA lost 149 soldiers to the 1st Cav in a single week; the 1/9 accounted for 100 of these kills.

Air power pounded War Zone C. Fighter jets dropped tear gas to run the enemy out of his holes, then massed B-52 bombing runs smashed him with Arc Light attacks. Large amounts of chemical gas crystals fell from the air to contaminate enemy supplies and channel enemy movement. Helicopter gunships constantly harassed the enemy.

Air assaults, "bunker busting," and search-and-destroy missions continued as the 1st Cav stretched its screen entirely across northern III Corps, systematically whittling down the offensive momentum of the four NVA/VC divisions in the AO and rendering them incapable of inflicting damage on Saigon. This activity cost the lives of 567 cavalry troopers. Another 3,555 were wounded.

59

Mr. Miles left, DEROSing back to the United States. Mighty Morris counted down to within seventy days of rotating out. He posted his short-timer calendar above his bunk and marked off the day every morning at Apache Sunrise, announcing his remaining time in a loud voice. "Seventy-one days and a wake-up..."

"Seventy days and a wake-up..."

"Sixty-nine days and a wake-up..."

He started getting paranoid, a common malady for the short-timers. The dinks were going to get him before he went home. He made a bid on the private bunker by the volleyball court, whose current occupant was about to DEROS, but another short-timer Cobra jock from Blue Max bought it and moved in.

I was also about to lose my crew chief, Shaky. He was DEROSing stateside, then getting discharged from the army and moving back to Texas. I stood with Farmer Farmer on the flight line smoking a cigarette and watching his crew wash blood and sweep expended cartridge casings from the cargo bay of his helicopter. A hot landing killed one trooper and wounded another. The odor of blood was diluted now, the water used in the cleaning having turned from dark rose to pink. I listened to it riveting onto the tarmac.

"There wasn't a lot of blood," said O'Brien, who had flown with Farmer as door gunner. "I've seen the whole floor an inch thick with it."

Shaky came walking out to the flight line with his hay straw cowlick freshly barbered and his lanky form encased in newly pressed khakis. He had even shaved his mustache. His shoes were shined. I hardly recognized him out of his soiled flight suit, greasy combat boots and flight helmet. He leaned against the chopper.

"Cap'n," he greeted me, looking wistful. I had just received my promotion to captain.

"Shaky."

We watched water running out of the helicopter until it turned from pink to clear. Shaky stuck out his hand suddenly. I took it.

"Is it today so soon?" I asked.

"I feel guilty about leaving you, sir."

"Don't. You did your part. Now go home and forget it."

"We did some stuff, didn't we, Cap'n *Mini-Man?*"

"We did some stuff, Shaky."

Neither of us knew what else to say after that. We stood awkwardly looking at each other, smiling. Finally, he shook my hand again, looked emotional, then turned and strode away.

"Stay charmed, *Mini-Man,*" he said.

After a few minutes, I walked to the mess hall for a cup of coffee. With the passing of each day, especially after a day like this, I felt increasingly alone and isolated. I was only twenty-four, but for the first time I felt *old.*

60

The tapping of rain on the tin roof awoke me. It amused me that I had become so accustomed to nightly H&I that I slept right through the pounding of the big guns while the gentle sound of rain disturbed my sleep. I rolled my feet off the bunk, pushing the mosquito net aside, and shook myself out a cigarette. I lit it by cupping my hands around the lighter to keep the flash from awakening the other pilots.

The guns were silent. I heard Stockton and Conrad snore-dueling. The gentle rain fell harder, beginning to thunder against the roof. So this was how the monsoons began?

Mighty Morris jerked awake. "It's raining!" he exclaimed.

I chuckled. "What was your first clue, Dick Tracy?"

He yawned loudly. The stretched springs on his bunk protested as he turned over. "Won't be much flying tomorrow," he announced gratefully and went back to sleep.

Farmer Farmer farted loudly. "A kiss for you, Morris."

"Christ. Go outside to do that," Conrad scolded. "What were you, born in a barn?"

"As a matter of fact he was," Mosby said.

Then there was just the sound of the rain again and Stockton and Conrad snoring. I sat in the dark on the side of my bunk and listened to the rain and watched it crawling on the barracks screen where breezes had blown it underneath the awning. Drops oozed down the screen and they were like liquid golden marbles against the watery yellow glow of a light marking the mess hall. I liked the cool clean smell of the earth being washed.

It had rained one evening on my R&R in Hawaii with Sandy. I liked to remember those days because there were nights when I thought I might never see her again. We had lived an entire lifetime in those two weeks, tanning on the beaches, swimming, dancing in the evenings and then lying in bed afterward talking. She brought pictures of April and Angela.

They were growing so fast. Angela was six months old when I left for Vietnam. She wouldn't recognize her own father when I got back.

"You're not quite the smart-ass you used to be," Sandy observed.

"It'll all come back. I'm saving up wisecracks."

"You are going to be all right?" Wanting me to reassure her.

"Why shouldn't I be?"

Because it was a *war,* stupid. I didn't want to talk about it. What could I say that might change anything. There was no need to cause her worry. I let her think I spent most of my time safely hanging around base camp smoking and joking. After all, *Mini-Man* hadn't suffered a single hit.

She laughed with delight over my call sign and the cartoonish *Mini-Man* character I described as adorning the back of my flight helmet. She giggled and came up with call sign suggestions of her own.

"How about *Mighty Mite* or *Puny Buns? Pygmy Pilot?*"

"Smart-ass," I countered.

Truth be told, Sandy probably knew more about the war than I did. After all, she and the American public received the "Big Picture" via television every night as dinner fare in the United States. Right from the comfort of their own living rooms they watched silver caskets being unloaded from C-141 Starlifters, GIs patrolling and battling for their lives, Phantom jets and B-52 bombers striking the DMZ, helicopters *wop-wop-wop*ping across the Vietnam skyline.

They also saw a side of the war that we GIs knew little about until we returned home. It disturbed Sandy that antiwar activists and protesters were mobbing in the streets while her husband was fighting for them in Vietnam. The nation had filled with shrill, dope-smoking, love-beaded, unwashed, draft card–burning hippies. The world really had gone insane with Dr. Spock, Jane Fonda, the Black Panthers and SDS and riots in the cities and on college campuses.

Stunned veterans returning from the war were confronted

at airports with BABY KILLER signs and chants of *Ho-Ho-Ho! Ho Chi Minh is gonna win.* They got off the planes on stretchers or in wheelchairs with limbs missing and were spat on and called names. It was a different America from the one we left. Ashamed, some of them slunk off to airport latrines to change out of their uniforms as quickly as they could. They looked at the stumps where legs and arms had been traumatically amputated and wondered what it was all about.

Sandy saw the war from that broader angle, albeit second-hand via the electronic marvel of TV. I saw only my small part of it at Tay Ninh. Sandy filled me in on it all because she said she wanted me to be prepared when I came home. America was going to hell.

We refused to speak of what *could* happen and darken the time we had together. She held on to me hard when it was time for me to return to Vietnam. I knew she was as afraid as I that this might be our last good-bye. We were leaving so much of our lives unlived and so much unsaid between us. But still we didn't talk about it, and now there wasn't time left. Besides, if you talked about it, you might make it happen.

"Please stay *charmed,*" she pleaded through tears.

I forced a grin. "I thought charm was why you married me."

"No," she said, trying to lighten the moment. "It was your uniform and your money. But mostly it was because I could beat you at pool. Ronnie . . . Ronnie, please come back home."

Now I listened to the cleansing rain and smoked my cigarette in the dark, drawing the smoke in deep. I pitied the poor grunts out there in the jungle in the rain, crouching miserably underneath their ponchos while they tried to keep their cigarettes dry and lit. By comparison, we pilots had it dicked. For us it was hours and hours of utter boredom followed by raw terror. Then we went back to the O Club for a beer and slept in our dry, warm bunks.

The boonirats were almost always in combat, living with constant fear and dread right in Charlie's backyard. For them there were no beers and rarely a warm, dry place to sleep. A guy could eat himself alive with guilt if he dwelled on comparing who in this war had it dicked and who didn't.

"You couldn't *pay* me enough money in all the world to fly a Huey onto a hot LZ," proclaimed a LRRP sergeant after I snatched his team out of the jungle and away from trackers close on his trail. "I'll take the ground any day. You guys have to be crazy to do this."

I supposed it all depended upon your perspective.

From the relative security and comfort of Tay Ninh base camp, we heard of things going on out there among the ground troops that puzzled, shocked, and confused us. Stuff like dope smoking and officers being fragged, deliberately slain by their own men. Mutinies and disobedience of orders. Poor morale and passive or not-so-passive resistance to the war. There were also rumors of atrocities. Men cutting off ears or noses as war souvenirs. Torturing prisoners and gang-raping women. Few people realized how brutalizing war could be.

Not that the ground troops had a monopoly on decomposition. I had heard stories of similar atrocities in aviation. Of guys tossing captured NVA or VC up into the whirling rotor blades of choppers sitting on the ground; of "half a helicopter ride" interrogations in which a pair of prisoners were taken up in a helicopter and one guy thrown out to encourage the other to talk; of women and kids in VC villages being mowed down by machine gun fire. I had heard all this, and didn't know how much of it was true and how much exaggeration. Of course, we sometimes attacked villages with rockets and miniguns and I was certain women and kids were killed. In a war of attrition such as this, everybody got tossed into the meat grinder.

Casualties inflicted on the enemy from the air carried less impact than shooting them personally face to face. I thought of the kids who tossed the grenade into our jeep. I hadn't intended to kill them, but I probably had. I was glad I hadn't actually seen the corpses afterward. It might have troubled me more had I actually *known* the kids were dead.

One thing, though, it taught me to empathize with the

ground troops. Frustrated soldiers complained about how hard it was to find the enemy out there and how much harder it was to determine *who* he was. A six-year-old kid could blow you up with a grenade. A teenage whore set you up for ambush. *Everybody,* they said, was the enemy. Old people, women, kids. A favorite GI quote went *Kill 'em all, let God sort 'em out.*

I understood this better after my incident with the kids and the grenade. Not that I condoned it, not that any of us did. We *understood* it.

"It's easy enough for us and everybody else back in the States to judge him," Mighty Morris commented when news reached us in September about Lieutenant William Calley Jr. and the so-called My Lai Massacre. Calley had just been charged with war crimes. "None of us was out there with him."

The poor damned grunts.

Apparently a series of situations conspired to rob Calley's cursed platoon of the Americal Division of its humanity. It all began in February 1968 during the Tet offensive. The enemy was picking Calley's men off one by one. His RTO was shot, two of his men were killed by booby traps, three more hit by sniper fire. The company of which his platoon was an element stumbled into a minefield. Explosion after explosion decimated the company as men rushed to aid wounded buddies or make escape attempts. Severed limbs flew through the air. The terror lasted for almost two hours, leaving thirty-two men killed or wounded.

The company was then mortared, suffering even more casualties. Four soldiers were blown to pieces by a booby trap two days before My Lai. During a period of one month, the company whose field strength was approximately one hundred soldiers suffered forty-two casualties and had rarely even seen the enemy.

Then came My Lai. Lieutenant Calley led his platoon into My Lai full of rage and frustration—and vented it within the moral vacuum that was Vietnam. The operation spontaneously turned into a blood orgy as men went temporarily insane. There could be no other explanation.

The maddened platoon shot anyone who tried to escape, bayoneting others, gang-raping women, shooting pigs, ducks, and water buffalo and laying waste like Genghis Khan. Survivors were rounded up and herded into a ditch where GIs massacred them.

A two-year-old child crawled out of the carnage, crying. Calley kicked him back and shot him. A *mamasan* was so riddled with bullets that her bones exploded chip by chip. Another woman had her baby slashed open with bayonets while she watched. Then she was shot. A GI raped a young girl, then rammed the barrel of his M16 into her vagina and squeezed the trigger. An old man was flung into a dug well and tossed a grenade; it was his choice to either drown or blow himself up with the grenade.

When it was all over, somewhere between 170 and 350 people had been slaughtered, all of them unarmed old men, women, and children. The toll would have been higher had it not been for slick pilots who put an end to it. A pilot and a gunner received medals for a bizarre incident in which Americans rescued people from getting killed by other Americans.

The most amazing thing about it was that back in the States war protesters actually defended Calley, as though he were merely the fall guy for behavior both common and officially sanctioned in Vietnam. It was like we were *all* guilty if the truth be known. Even future president Jimmy Carter defended him.

I was as horrified by what happened at My Lai as anyone else—if, in fact, the details were as they were purported to be. We were all being branded in broad strokes as war criminals, dope smokers, mutineers . . . It simply wasn't true. I wanted to believe that in spite of the brutalizing effects of war most soldiers who fought it were honorable and decent.

I was sent here to do a job for which I was trained—fly helicopters in combat. I never received orders whose legality I would have questioned, was never ordered to kill babies or bomb innocent villagers. There was no dope smoking among flyers that I knew of. We were a team when we went *out there*. Our safe return depended upon all of us being alert and working together. Morale remained relatively high in the 1/9. Perhaps it was because we were unique and suffered fewer of the problems incurred by other units, particularly the infantry companies. Whatever, I was grateful for it.

All I wanted now that I had been sent to Vietnam was to do my war—then go home to Sandy and my daughters. Safely. With all my limbs and body parts intact.

A cool moist breeze blew through the barracks as I sat smoking on the side of my bunk. I snubbed out my cigarette in a 175mm shell casing that I used for a butt can. I lay back down and listened to the rain.

"Good night, Sandy," I murmured.

61

Rain fell for three days. Great billowing clouds rushed angrily in from the South China Sea and dark grayness covered the land. A violent two-hour torrential downpour, followed by an hour or so of sun and steam, then another two-hour downpour. It fell in driving sheets that pounded the jungles and rice fields until every stream, every canal, every river swelled and overflowed. Men and machines bogged down. The runways at Tay Ninh flash-flooded. Streams of water almost knee-deep gushed through the culvert pipes that were our bomb shelters and pooled in lakes underneath hooch barracks. Now I understood why everything was built on blocks above the ground.

Mighty Morris stood on the little overhanging porch of our hooch and gazed out toward the Black Virgin. The mountain was invisible in the overcast.

"You'd think weather like this would drive the dinks to their holes," he said. "It won't. The little fuckers'll take advantage of our being grounded to start moving shit forward out of Cambodia for another round of fighting."

It wasn't like monsoon season appeared suddenly one day and rained continuously for the next forty days and forty nights. It came incrementally in a series of weather fronts. In the beginning, there would be more sunny days, broken only by normal tropical showers, then monsoon ones in which the clouds opened. Later, however, as the season got into full swing, the rainy days would take over. That meant a lot of pilot downtime. Charlie brought out his canoelike sampans and went to work.

As soon as the weather broke, a patrol from FSB Jamie made contact with a large NVA force. The FSB sent out a reaction element on foot and requested help from Tay Ninh. Red Platoon dispatched Cobras while I loaded four of my slicks with our Blue infantry platoon.

By the time my airmada reached station, Swede and a couple of other Snakes were darting and diving at the enemy. The North Vietnamese were attempting to close "belly to belly" with our grunt patrol and wipe it out.

"Dalton Four-Six?" Swede's unmistakable accent came up on FM, talking to the patrol. *"I'm running hot. Danger close! Danger close! I'm gonna shoot over your heads!"*

Most of the time, gunships made their runs parallel to friendly lines and out front of them in order to reduce accidental "friendly fire" against our own guys. But because of the L-shaped defensive configuration of the GI defenders and the nearness of enemy soldiers, the Snakes were forced to dive in behind friendlies and shoot over their heads. Swede later described how he placed rockets ten meters in front of the battling grunts. Ten meters was about three steps.

The bursting radius of a 3.5 rocket was about twenty-five meters. However, because of momentum, the burst and shrapnel traveled forward and away from the defenders. It was dangerous business and called for precision, but it kept the NVA at bay.

My ships dumped Blue infantry into a clearing about three-hundred meters to the rear. I then led my helicopters to the FSB about three klicks away where we sat down on the road to wait to pick up our platoon after the firefight. Most of us broke out C-rats and heated them over pinches of C-4 explosives. C-4 burned with a hot blue flame and would not explode unless you added a concussion to the fire. That meant you didn't want to try to stomp out the flame. Every pilot carried a half-pound of plastics underneath his seat for fuel; we spent a lot of time like this parked and waiting to go somewhere else.

When the excitement ended a couple of hours later, we lit up the choppers to go back out to get our platoon. The four Hueys were not much more than off the ground than we were socked in by rain and fog. Weather often moved in quickly during the tropical monsoons, suddenly dropping down from high blowing clouds to make pea soup in the jungle. During times like that, there might not be a top for five thousand feet.

Scattered across our AO was the wreckage of thirty or forty downed birds, most of which had been picked out of the air by enemy fire. Some of them, however, were victims of weather. Pilots sometimes suffered vertigo, refused to believe their instruments and actually flew into the earth. Disorientation in weather or at night increased your pucker factor at least tenfold. While you grew accustomed to Charlie duck-shooting at you, if you could actually get used to something like that, vertigo struck by total surprise and left you dizzy, short of breath and with sweating palms. It was damned near as scary as getting shot at. You could almost be flying upside down and not realize it.

Wouldn't that be a hell of a note—*Mini-Man,* impervious to enemy fire, brought down by vertigo and his own stupidity?

I hated flying instruments. I better interpreted IFR, Instrument Flight Rules, as I Fly Roads. I hadn't done well under the hood during flight training. Half the time my body told me I was flying upside down while my instruments assured me I was straight and steady. I *knew* the instruments had to be lying.

But you had to go with them in this kind of weather—the turn-and-bank indicator, the artificial horizon, air speed indicator, altimeter, and compass. It was white knuckle flying at its finest. Conrad flew my second seat. He sat stiff and silent, his eyes glued to the instruments, hands gripping his thighs. *He* was white-knuckled. Flying in formation doubled or tripled the danger.

I tried to appear casual and unconcerned, like I did this all the time.

There was heavy rain inside the cloud cover. Rain didn't *fall;* it was just *there* swirling around inside the fog. I switched on my windshield wipers, for all the good that did, and kept trucking. It wasn't like you could pull over to the side of the road. The Farmer was my wingman. I radioed him to back off a little. I didn't trust him not to blunder into my blades and bring us both down.

"*If I back off too much,* Mini-Man," he responded, "*I'll be like a chicken with its head cut off. I won't be able to see you at all.*"

Mighty Morris flew wingman to Farmer Farmer while an FNG warrant from California named Hal Bijorian brought up Tailend Charlie. By twisting my head and looking back, I made out the ghostly form of Farmer's bird riding slightly higher and to my right. All I saw of Mighty Morris was the dim blinking of his red-and-green position lights. For all I knew of Bijorian, he was lost in the fog. I kept track of everyone over the radio.

"*See anything,* Mini-Man?" Bijorian asked.

"Fog," I said.

I almost whooped with relief when I broke out of the storm. Suddenly, the earth appeared wet and green below and stretched off toward the horizon and the sun shone through the recent rain like burnished copper. Rays of light stabbed translucent through the high clouds and gashed splashes of gold on the forest. I thought the world absolutely beautiful.

Mighty Morris, always the poet and itinerant minstrel, came up on the radio. "*And He saw what He had made and declared it good. . . .*"

"*Amen,*" said the new guy, Bijorian.

62

Vung Tau, where I would have spent my war in comfort and safety if Charlie hadn't mortared the runway at Bien Hoa the day I arrived in-country, was an R&R site and home of the main Post Exchange in Vietnam. Hotels lined the beach, next door to French restaurants and nightclubs. U.S. and ARVN generals relaxed and rubbed shoulders with NVA generals and Viet Cong cadre leaders on downtime. Everybody screwed the same goodtime girls, and, of course, the goodtime girls spied for everybody.

On a lazy day when not much was going on, Swede the Cobra jock, who wanted to get in a little stick time in the UH-1, and I made a beer run to Vung Tau for the O and NCO Clubs. Although we intended flying high and dry at above two thousand feet, O'Brien the gunner went with us. Our pockets were stuffed with military scrip to buy beer and sodas. We would return with the Huey packed full of cases.

It was a relaxing forty-five minute flight on a sunny day. Swede took the controls and landed at the big airfield on post. We bought cases of beverages at the PX. A forklift hauled them out to the chopper and stacked them aboard. There was barely enough room for O'Brien to belly in on top of the cargo.

"Are you sure this thing will fly a load like this?" he worried.

"If it'll hover, it'll fly," I cracked.

I might have been concerned if this were a UH-1C model instead of the UH-1H. When loaded down with either cargo as a slick or with gun pods, armament, and ammunition as a gunship, the 1C was so underpowered that pilots had to make a run with it, bouncing off the ground, in order to get it in the air. It was said that crew chiefs ran alongside the helicopter for a bounce or two to let it build up speed and lift before they jumped aboard.

The 1H had considerably more power, but I thought I heard

it groaning nonetheless as I hovered it out to the runway and received tower clearance for takeoff. I bounced it once to gain lift, then slowly throttled it out of Vung Tau with the blue sweep of the ocean and the jumble of the city behind us. We would burn off some weight on the way back through fuel consumption.

Swede took over after we were airborne. Less than a mile later, a caution light flickered on. Nothing caught your attention quite like a sudden red light on the panel. It was always an *Oh, shit!* moment. Swede stiffened.

"I've got it," I said.

"Or has it got us?" Swede retorted in his typical cavalier manner.

I went through the segment lights on the console, checking for specific problems. Some times the problem lay in the instruments, not in the machine. Standard emergency procedure called for recycling a switch in order to test it. The hydraulics light blinked twice, then went out. The Huey seemed to be flying okay. I shrugged.

"Bad switch," I said to Swede.

"Looks that way."

Thirty seconds later the hydraulics caution light came back on, glaring at us. It was for real. There was definitely trouble somewhere in the hydraulics system. The *Oh, shit!* moment turned to *Oh, God!* Flying a Huey without hydraulics was like attempting to drive an eighteen-wheeler at seventy mph without power steering. To do it, you had better have arms like a weight lifter and weigh ten pounds more than a new Buick— not be five-three and three-quarters and maybe 125 pounds wearing chicken plate and a *Mini-Man* helmet.

If this bird conked out on us, what with the weight we carried . . . Could anyone say anvil?

We were going to have to make an emergency landing. Hopefully, I could get us back to the airport. The runway was still within sight.

I pulled the circuit breaker to prevent hydraulics surges. You didn't want your "power steering" going in and out to cause you to alternately over-and under-compensate when you were trying to make an emergency landing. That was the fastest way for you to end up in the scrap heap. Well, maybe not the fastest. The fastest was getting shot with a Soviet-made RPG.

I fought the Huey into a 180-degree turn and headed back to Vung Tau. I raised Tower on UHF.

"Are you declaring an emergency, Mini-Man?"

"Roger that, Tower. I have hydraulics failure. Request permission to make a straight-in approach and a running landing?"

Since you couldn't hover without hydraulics, you had to make an approach like a regular airplane and slide in on your skids. You came in low and slow, holding only enough speed to maintain transitional lift, and greased the chopper in at about forty knots an hour. Because the controls were stiff, it took both pilots on the sticks to manhandle it to the runway and keep it going straight after touchdown so it didn't swerve, catch a skid and flip over.

"Make your one-eighty and come straight in, Mini-Man," Tower advised. *"We're waving off other traffic. Do you want Crash Rescue standing by?"*

"It might not hurt, Tower," I said.

It was just like in the movies. Ambulances and crash trucks raced out to the runway to wait for us. Lights flashed and blinked all over the airport. On his side of the cockpit, Swede gripped cyclic and collective and had both feet on the pedals. Together, straining with muscles in arms, legs and backs, we battled the Huey to line it up with the runway. I could never have done it alone. Sweat from tension and exertion poured from our faces. I felt like I was sitting in a sauna.

The procedure for landing either a hydraulics-stricken Huey or a Cobra was the same up until the skids touched the earth. Then the procedure changed. You attempted to keep a Huey going straight ahead on the runway; but because of the Cobra's high center of gravity and its tendency to roll, you took the controls with it whichever direction it went. You didn't fight it. If it veered to either the right or left, you not only let it go there, you helped it.

I didn't realize that while I was thinking Huey for the emergency landing, Swede was thinking Cobra.

For the type of landing we made, it was perfect. Directly in the center of the strip. Sparks crackled from the skids. Metal howled sliding against concrete.

The chopper drifted to the right. I compensated by pulling controls to the left to keep it moving straight on the runway. At the same time, Swede the Cobra jock pulled controls to the right.

Each of us fought the machine desperately, little realizing that we were also fighting each other as well as the helicopter. I thought the controls must have frozen up. The aircraft continued to skid to the right no matter how hard I struggled to rudder and cyclic it left. Swede was a big man with bull shoulders; he was simply stronger than I.

The Huey swerved off the strip and began clipping off the heads of running lights in the grass alongside. It finally came to a standstill. By some miracle it remained right side up. I killed the engine and systematically turned off all switches. Then I collapsed in my seat as the blades slowly ran down. Muscles quivered. I was too spent to move.

Swede looked equally drained. O'Brien held on to the top of the cargo like a cat on a screen door. He expelled breath in a great sigh of relief. No one said anything for a long moment. Ambulances and crash trucks rushed to surround us.

"Whew!" Swede exclaimed at last. "Damn! I thought the controls had completely frozen. I thought I was never going to get it to turn right like it wanted to."

I stared at him. "You mean you—?"

Then it struck him what we had done. "Jesus God, *Mini-Man*. It's a *Huey*. You were trying to bring it back left!"

The emergency crews at Vung Tau must have thought all

helicopter jocks were crazy. They bailed off their vehicles to find two flyers who had just escaped disaster still sitting belted in their seats while a third peered down from a pile of boxes. All three were laughing their fool asses off.

63

Not long after our crash landing at Vung Tau, I was flying X-Ray for the Swede on a river sweep for sampans south of Tay Ninh. I had accumulated about twenty hours total in a Snake, most of it in the nose as X-Ray, but some of it as AC when I occasionally volunteered to fly one to Cu Chi for higher-echelon maintenance. Swede and I had also gone out a few times to shoot up a "mule" or practice firing on a VC hooch with his miniguns, just for fun. You didn't get much opportunity in a Huey slick to personally get your licks in. Door gunners saw most of that action. Once or twice, I chunked grenades out the helicopter window with my M79 at smoke, flitting figures in the jungle, or a bunker, but that didn't really count as aerial combat.

It was a perfect day for flying after last night's rain. The world glistened. Swede and I chattered over the intercom and were having a pleasant time of it when an alarm went out over the emergency guard freq.

A truck convoy of the 82d Airborne Division, my old outfit, had driven into a major ambush on the highway between Cu Chi and Bien Hoa. The on-site commander was desperately requesting air support. Anything he could get, but it had to be fast. The convoy was stalled at a U in the road and under heavy enemy fire.

A call like that was akin to an "officer needs help" plea in a police precinct. Everybody within a certain radius scrambled to get there. Swede poured on the coal. We were twenty minutes away. We arrived along with about ten other Cobras and some lift and medevac ships from various other units. The scene from a distance looked like vultures circling in the air above a roadkill. I spotted the smoke from ten miles out.

A Blue Max Cobra on his way back from Cu Chi had taken charge in the air and was attempting to traffic-cop things into some kind of order. He got the gunships racetracked out to start making gun runs while the dustoffs and slicks floated high in orbit prepared to medevac wounded men or rescue downed aircrews.

About thirty or so deuce-and-a-half trucks were dispersed around a horseshoe bend in the road. Some were pulled off into ditches in a defensive posture while others had nosed into jungle cover. A number were abandoned on the road. Several appeared damaged. At least one suffered a direct hit from a mortar round. It looked crumpled like an empty tin can. Flames licking from its engine coughed oily black smoke high into the air.

The ambushers were concealed in forest in the center of the horseshoe in such a way that they could bring fire upon the entire convoy, from front to rear. Paratroops sprawled among the trucks anywhere they could find cover. Muzzles winked and flickered. Tongues and snippets of rifle fire licked back and forth. Green tracers webbing across the road drew red tracers in retaliation. There seemed to be a lot of shooting down there, judging from the thickness of dueling tracers. A haze of gunsmoke and black fuel smoke obscured the action.

Swede brought the Snake low and fast over the site, checking it out as we took our place in the racetrack with the other gunships. Flying front seat in a Cobra was like being inside a plastic bubble stuck out in the sky with a wide-open view of the entire world. The road passed below my feet. GIs glanced anxiously up at us. One grunt was dragging a wounded comrade across the road away from the horseshoe toward a ditch on the other side. A few green streaks traced across the sky in the midst of the massing helicopters. I heard nothing of the battle, of course, because of the vibrations and roar of our aircraft and the excited chatter of radios in our ears.

Blue Max was talking to the guys on the ground, asking them where the hottest fire was coming from.

"Where?" he asked. *"Where do you want us to shoot?"*

"Them, Blue Max!" the convoy commander snapped back. *"Shoot* them! *They're in the woods!"*

I was really pumped up for this. I had my legs stuck straight out and braced and my thumbs on the triggers. I controlled through a robotic arm–looking apparatus inside the cockpit both the 40mm automatic grenade launcher in the aircraft's nose and the 7.62 minigun below it on a turret that could be rotated up or down, right to left. The minigun looked like a Gatling gun from an old western movie. It had six spinning barrels and two electric motors to pull ammo into the gun. It fired six thousand rounds a minute, making a low wailing sound as it did. The pilot had sole control of the 3.5 rockets. When he fired a rocket, it overrode the other weapons systems.

Swede edged our Snake into the racetrack pattern with the others, all one behind the other at intervals. Like sharks closing in on a kill. The lead chopper dived and made its run with the long axis of the convoy to reduce the chance of erratic fire. It was fast and nimble, cutting through the air at around two hundred mph. Rockets emitting smoke contrails stabbed toward the trees with their tails blazing. Tracer tracks from the minigun resembled a red laser beam that arced delicately as it chewed through the treeline like a tornado, blasting timber and vegetation. Pure destruction gnawing pathways through the jungle.

When it came our turn, Swede poised the Cobra an instant at its highest apex of the racetrack, as though gathering himself for the attack. Then he dropped it out of the sky to build speed for sweeping past the enemy position.

"Hold on, *Mini-Man.*"

Earth rushed up at me with dizzying swiftness. I glimpsed a black-clad figure below darting, then disappearing. The rats were in there. I lay on the minigun trigger. A minigun for *Mini-Man.* I heard the low groan and purring sound of the Gatling-like barrels turning. That was the only sound of firing inside the cockpit.

I ate at the forest with my red laser beam. My God, that gun was awesome!

Swede released a brace of rockets. His interrupter switch cut off my guns when he fired to keep me from nailing our own rockets in the air. Rockets streaked in twin flames into the thick foliage. They exploded with white resounding puffs, silent to us, and brought down trees.

My gun cut back in, startling me. My thumb was still pressed on the button and both hands gripped the aiming and firing mechanism. I let off as the helicopter's nose began to rise.

"Say hello to Ho Chi Minh for me," Swede cracked as we sailed by, ascending out of the action on the other side and crossing above the road and the burning truck. Smoke left an oily film on the windshield.

"Ho Chi Minh is dead," I shouted back through the intercom.

"When did that happen?"

"A coupla months ago."

"Damn. I wanted to shoot him myself."

Adrenaline surged through my body. Aerial combat was a hell of a high. I was so excited I almost forgot to be scared for a change.

Swede brought the Snake back up onto the apex, all the birds flying around and around in a tilted elliptical circle, like a twisted merry-go-round. Smoking the dinks. I looked back and down in time to watch the next chopper in line make its run. Trees toppled and the forest filled with smoke, like a textile comb clotted with wool. A couple of green tracers searched for it, but didn't even come close. They sailed high into the sky until they burned out and vanished.

We made a second run. I chunked 40mm grenades in a mini-Arc Light. As we broke out on the other side, I glanced off to my left and spotted a strange Cobra racing to join the fun. It was painted flat black and bore no markings or numbers of any kind. It sailed across our bow so near the X-Ray gave me thumbs up. He and the pilot wore international orange flight suits in contrast to the dull green ones we wore.

"Rooster One," intoned the new arrival, coming up on the air to Blue Max with his call sign. *"You guys need some help?"*

"Rooster, *this is* Max. *Whatta ya got?"*

"I got pods full of eight-pounders with fleschettes."

"Fleschettes?" Max sounded cautious. *"We got friendlies near."*

"I see that, Max *We can put fleschettes into the eye of a needle."*

"If you can do it, welcome to the party, Rooster One."

The black Cobra swept down and screamed past the target lower than any of the other birds, releasing rockets. As each rocket detonated, it scattered smaller charges which themselves exploded to deliver about ten thousand razor nails into anything within its radius. Big pink clouds hovered in the aftermath.

"Max, *let me make three more quick passes,"* Rooster One requested.

He jumped rotation and made his runs. He climbed out of the fray after expending his munitions.

"See you later, Blue Max," he said. *"I hope we were some help."*

"Who *was* that masked man?" Swede quipped.

We had heard rumors of unmarked CIA Cobras running clandestine attack missions across the border into Cambodia. The only thing we could figure was that it had to be one of them. It was the only Cobra of its kind I ever saw in Vietnam.

What with a half-score of shark-grinning Snakes working out on enemy positions, the center of the horseshoe was reduced to smoldering wreckage within a few minutes. How could anyone live through a pounding like that?

> *"Them goddamn gooks will never learn . . .*
> *Napalm sticks to kids . . ."*

After exhausting a cool accumulative million dollars or so of ammunition, the original Cobras took off for home while other

Cobras took our place and continued thumping Charlie. Nui Ba Den loomed green-crusted on the horizon ahead of us. We navigated to the left of it. Swede gave an exaggerated sigh.

"Another day at the office, *Mini-Man,*" he said.

I sighed back. "Yeah. We could always be one of them poor bastards with a stuffy nine-to-five job. Ain't we lucky?"

64

In late 1969 and into the first months of 1970, as part of President Nixon's "Vietnamization" efforts, selected units of the 1st Air Cav mated up with ARVN airborne brigades to develop the South Vietnamese airborne division into an airmobile strike force. Pressure was placed on the Cambodian border in III Corps in an effort to neutralize the enemy and "level the playing field" for eventual ARVN takeover.

The 1/9 became especially busy with screening operations, traveling light and fast in the air and on the ground to interdict foot, bike, cart, and truck traffic on the interlocking maze of the "Ho Chi Minh Trail." Division patrols penetrated deep into uncharted territory to scout out the trails and bunker complexes and report on enemy movement.

Behind the air and foot patrols came airmobile companies and platoons of the division's brigades, many of which were integrated with ARVN paratroopers. They established temporary fire bases as launching points for deeper penetrations. Once ops were firmly established, the fire bases were closed and fresh ones opened in new territory. The goal was to run the NVA and VC completely out of III Corps, especially in the northwestern area and its corridors leading to Saigon. It was dangerous business, pushed forward beneath an umbrella of B-52 bombers, fighter bombers, aerial artillery, and helicopters.

65

It was the strangest damn thing, everybody said so. George Gerard in his Loach spotted them. He was sniffing around on top of triple canopy as low bird for a Purple Team that included Hal Bijorian and me in the lift and Mad Dog in the Cobra.

He suddenly interrupted a long exchange of mostly bull-shitting on the radios. We had been out an hour so far without seeing anything.

"Apache Red Two-Two?" he said to Mad Dog, his voice suddenly gone tense. *"There's something shiny down in the trees. We can't tell what it is, but it's big."*

"Want me to make a run on it, George?" Mad Dog asked.

"Nobody's shooting at me. It's just there. It's not moving."

The sighting warranted enough interest at TOC that our CO, Major Powdrill, decided to put the Blue Platoon on the ground to check it out. It was a three-bird insertion onto a clearing less than two hundred meters away. I took my Hueys to the nearest FSB to await developments.

The platoon worked its way to the location without encountering resistance. Soon, it came upon a Cobra that had crashed through the jungle canopy and come to rest inside the moist womb of the forest. Finding a crash site in III Corps wasn't that big a deal normally. There were dozens of helicopter wrecks scattered about. What made this one different was that it was not plotted on any of our charts. It was a bird from Bravo Troop that had been MIA, missing in action, for about a month, along with its pilot and X-Ray.

Jungle vines and lianas grew and crawled all over it. Another month and it would have been completely overgrown and probably never found. Other than the blade having been sheared off, the Cobra appeared virtually intact. There were no bullet holes in it. GIs climbed up on the stubby stabilizers and looked inside the cockpit. What they saw startled them.

A Cobra cockpit was air-conditioned and airtight. That seal had not been broken in the crash. Insects and animals had therefore not gotten to the corpses. They looked to be dried out by the heat and remarkably preserved, almost like mummies. They sat in their seats, still wearing helmets, hands on the controls and open eyes staring straight ahead. Some of the grunts said it was the eeriest thing they had ever beheld.

I carried out the body bags. They had no odor or anything. The mystery continued to grow and was a topic of conversation and speculation at the O Club for many weeks. Nobody could figure out how the jocks died or what caused the crash. The aircraft seemed to have simply mushed in. It was solid and not broken, not blown up or shot up or anything. At least one of the pilots should have survived; the impact didn't appear to have been that violent.

Swede speculated that they had made a gun run, failed to pull out in time and flew the Snake right into the jungle. But what killed the pilots? They weren't shot, cut, smashed, or broken.

"It was a heart attack," Whoppa guessed.

"Both of them at the same time?" Mosby countered.

"You explain it then."

Swede got up, went to the fridge and got himself another brew. He came back to the table and popped the top as he sat down.

"There's only one explanation," he said in his crisp accent. "It could happen to any of us. Whatever occurred *out there,* it was enough to scare them to death. They died of fright."

66

Statistically, you were more apt to get killed during your first sixty days in combat than during the rest of your year's tour. You went through three separate phases. To begin with, there was the FNG phase when you were so green you didn't know what was going on and you were most likely to get creamed; during the middle period, you did your job, did your time, and tried not to think much about anything else; and then came the last phase when you were a short-timer. That was when you got cautious and paranoid. You no longer chuckled over the short-timers making their bids on the private bunker at the volleyball courts; you even thought of making a bid yourself. No one wanted to be the last GI killed in Vietnam, especially for the hazy principles of a war that everybody, including politicians, was abandoning.

I saw Captain Beatty, Mr. Miles, Shaky, Mississippi, and the others transition from the go-get-'em middle stages to near-paranoia, even though they tried to hide it. Pressure started to build up about ninety days or so before DEROS, then grew into a big head of steam when you were down to about thirty days. Guys woke up in the middle of the night with nightmares, screaming.

Bird Dog in the White Platoon had been one of the biggest jokers in the Headhunters. He was, as Mighty Morris put it, "First in mischief, first in grabass, and first to fart in a helicopter." He was a happy-go-lucky kid from Idaho and remained that way through three times being shot down in his Loach. But then he became a short-timer with sixty days left before his DEROS. He started getting shaky. He came in from a mission and the first thing he did, even if he hadn't been shot at that day, was head for the O Club. His entire attitude changed. He became a withdrawn loner drinking by himself in the club, starting at every little sound, gazing out into space with that thousand-yard stare that said, psychologically, you were about to break. Apache Troop CO Major Powdrill asked me to take him into lifts for ass-and-trash missions and to transfer one of my middle-phasers over to Loaches. Meeker took his place in Whites.

Ass-and-trash—maintenance flights to Cu Chi, beer runs to Vung Tau, and the like—was looked upon as a turning point in your personal war and signified that it was all over except for the hail-and-farewell bash. Whenever I could, I pulled my men out of combat when they were down to within thirty days of going home and assigned them nothing but ass-and-trash. That meant the rest of us doubled up on the hairy missions, but nobody complained. We had our own short-timer grace period to look forward to.

But until that final month, you had to pull your own cultivator, as Farmer Farmer put it. We always had more combat missions to run than I had men or machines to run them with. Of the eight helicopters assigned to my platoon, two or three were almost always down for maintenance or combat damage. Of my sixteen pilots, I couldn't afford to have more than two or three down for combat damage themselves.

"Whew! I made it again. One more day," Mighty Morris exclaimed each time he returned from *out there,* our hunting grounds.

He faithfully maintained his short-timer countdown calendar. By the time he was down to forty-nine days, he became concerned over why his rotation orders had not come. Normally, you received them about sixty days in advance.

"Them hillbillies in Army Personnel have done lost your orders," Farmer Farmer ribbed him. "The Pentagon wants you to do another tour 'cause you done cleaned so many gooks' plows this time over."

"Damnit, Farmer, stop being country," Rouse scolded. "How do you clean a gook's plow when all he's got is a rice stick and a buffalo and a wife to pull it?"

"See what you can do, Cap'n *Mini-Man,*" Mr. Morris pleaded, taking me aside. "I'm having my mother contact our senator about it. They *have* forgot me and lost my orders."

The more beers Mighty Morris drank, the more mournful his song at the O Club.

> *"If I die in ol' Vietnam,*
> *Please write a letter to my mom;*
> *Tell her I died with a grin,*
> *Bringing smoke on Ho Chi Minh. . . ."*

Farmer Farmer and Swede and a couple of other jocks pulled chairs around a table into which a couple of generations of pilots had carved pithy sayings such as *Fuck Charles*. At first, there were the usual rowdy exchange of stories. Swede had shot up a "VC truck," which was his term for water buffalo, and chased its owner across a rice field. Conrad and Bijorian buzzed a bunch of nude Vietnamese girls bathing in the river and shot at a VC peeping tom hiding in the bushes ogling the girls. They used their handguns, getting in some target practice, leaning out the Huey's windows and banging away at the crazy scared gook until he reached the jungle.

"We missed that cocksucker every round," Conrad said, laughing. "It was his lucky day."

Somewhere during the evening, the conversation turned more weighty. It began when Mighty Morris laid aside his guitar and joined us at the table.

"The VC are still winning because we're losing," he said. As a short-timer, he wasn't nearly as much fun as he used to be.

Big Swede glared at him. "What the fuck you talking about, Morris?"

"Oh, we're kicking ass on the VC and NVA all right, but the people are taking the beating. That's why we're losing. These poor dinks are born, grow up, and die in the same cruddy little ville."

"Something like Farmer Farmer," Gerard said to lighten the mood. It didn't work.

Mighty Morris continued. "Hell, they don't own nothing except a grass or rock hut, a couple of pigs, a dog, a water buffalo, some chickens and geese, a vegetable garden and a rice field—"

"Look around," Gerard challenged, still trying. "It's more than *we* own."

"—They see us flying over, us Americans up there with all our God-like power. So we come down from time to time and *smite* their water buffalo, tramp through their vegetable gardens, scare their daughters and blow up their hooches. We're really winning hearts and minds, aren't we?"

"Ol' Charlie does worse than that," Swede pointed out. "VC come in and butcher their chickens and take half their crops for taxes. They hang the village chief up by his heels and cut out his guts as an example not to cooperate with the Americans."

"True. But Charlie is one of *them* and not a foreigner. Besides, they're politicians who do that and everybody knows politicians are scumbags. You *expect* them to take your rice and butcher your geese. That's what politicians do."

Swede shook his head and gazed into his beer. Gerard got up for another suds. Farmer Farmer, who hadn't fucked up a helicopter in more than a month, said, "Morris, you're getting a short-timer's attitude."

"I ain't *getting*. I already *got*." He looked around the table. "The best thing could happen to any of us," he said, "is the same thing that happened to shitbird Captain Williams from West Point. Remember him? The best thing could happen to any of us is a minor bone wound."

Conrad winced. "Fuck. I heard he lost his whole fucking leg. Maybe they'll call off the war first for lack of interest."

"I'm serious as a dead pilot," Morris went on. "Tell 'em, Cap'n. You're our next short-timer."

Swede snorted. "*Mini-Man* has always been a *short* timer. When are you leaving, Cap'n? When's your DEROS?"

"They'll have to run me out of Vietnam," I joked. "I eat this shit up."

"Think about it, Cap'n Alexander," Mighty Morris persisted. "You can't keep doing what you're doing and not finally get hit. It's gonna happen sooner or later. Best thing for you when it happens is you get a bone wound in the hand or foot or arm. You're out of here *just like that*." He snapped his fingers.

I was already getting paranoid over this *charmed* shit anyhow. I even took the C-4 out from underneath my seat and started eating my C-rats cold. One thing you didn't need in a helicopter was an ejection seat if a round happened to hit the explosives. I still stood my rotation like everyone else, ran more missions than I asked of any of my men, but I also thought things through more carefully than I had before.

The law of averages was bound to catch up to *Mini-Man* one of these days. Sooner or later I was going to take a round that would dump me in the jungle with Charlie and the snakes. Lately, I had started having more and more nightmares. Sometimes when it rained at night I sat up suddenly so soaked with anxiety sweat that I thought the roof was leaking. It was astounding for me at this phase to think that I had once, in the middle phase, considered extending my tour. That I had actually enjoyed being hero of the oppressed and champion of truth, justice, and the American Way.

I lay in my bunk later that night and stared up into the darkness, thinking about the different changes I had gone through. Mighty Morris was twisting and flopping in bed, having nightmares. A barrage of H&I artillery shuddered the bunkhouse. Big parachute flares with a lot of candlepower lit up the entire world. The barracks screens glowed like dying fluorescent bulbs, casting shadows. Shadows oozed through the room like hooded ghouls, tiptoeing over sleeping men and appearing, disappearing, and reappearing like dark ghosts in a graveyard. Jesus, was I flipping out or what?

After nearly a year listening to artillery, sleeping as we were right next to it, I had long ago learned to distinguish between incoming and outgoing rounds. I heard a high-pitched whine that grew rapidly louder until I thought I would explode first. I sprang out of bed.

"Incoming-g-g-g-g-g!"

Mighty Morris heard it in his sleep. He had recently come to believe the enemy was out to get him personally. He was the first out the door and into the bomb shelter pipe. He crouched in the very dark center of it. I hunkered next to him while a few mortar rounds *crumped!* and *cracked!* around the base. The enemy's version of H&I.

There was something about cowering in the darkness like a rat in a sewer that bred all kinds of negative thoughts and feelings. It occurred to me suddenly and inexplicably that sometime between now and my DEROS in February, I was going to get it. Shot down *out there* and tortured to death, or perhaps a mortar shell or a rocket landing in my bunk, or maybe a stray bullet through my *Mini-Man* helmet... Charlie was out there every day like we were, hunting heads of his own, putting tick marks on his version of the Vulture Board. B-I-L-B-Y.

67

LRRPs were commonly inserted just before dark to give them time to set up and camouflage in a listening post before the lights went out and cockroaches started scurrying about. They pegged Claymores around their hide in case they needed to set them off to delay bad guys while they pulled an E&E to the nearest PZ. Then they hunkered alongside the trail counting feet and dividing by two.

When they went out, they often went deep and they stayed deep. That made extraction hell when you had to get them out. It seemed when they *did* run into shit, they ran into it in the middle of the night.

Stockton and I scrambled Three-Seven around midnight when the TOC alarm went off. A single blast—ground troops in contact. Mighty Morris and Rouse flew wing, while Swede and a Red Platoon FNG took up a pair of guns for support and cover. While we were en route, TOC explained that we had a team of five LRRPs in jungle surrounded by a pissed-off company of NVA. As far as the LRRPs knew, there wasn't a suitable PZ within five hundred meters. We were going to have to jerk them up through the trees with McGuire rigs.

It didn't take long once we were over station to determine that this was a chopper pilot's absolute worst nightmare scenario. The jungle was triple canopy, down inside which gunfire and explosions flashed and flickered. NVA soldiers were closing in on our guys. And, sure enough, there wasn't a PZ within five hundred meters.

I raised the terrified LRRPs on FM and explained what I intended to do—come down on top of the trees and drop lines for them. Flying at such low altitudes, in the dark, with the lives of nine guys—five on the ground, four in my chopper—riding on how much balls I had and how good I was at the controls demanded total concentration. I knew when I choppered down toward the forest and the firefight blazing inside it that I was going to be tested in ways I had only had nightmares about. I hoped I could pull it off.

The backup slick with Mr. Morris at the stick rode high, temporarily out of the action, waiting for me to start the ops. His red-and-green position lights blinked rhythmically against a sky full of stars but without a moon. I radioed him with instructions.

"Apache Three-Two?" I felt the edge in my voice, felt it cracking and rough in my throat. "I'm going to drop three lines and pull three of 'em out." Three lines were all I had aboard. "I want you right on me, coming in low and slow. I'll inform you when I'm through. You come in to the same place and drop your lines for the other two. Roger that, Apache Three-Two?"

"Roger that, Mini-Man."

The other slick shifted in the sky. Its lights floated swiftly down and toward me from the rear. In the darkness, I eased the chopper toward the forest roof above the firefight. Red tracers told me where our troopers were dug in on the defense.

I tried not to think about how the night snapped and cracked with rifle and machine-gun fire and how green tracers streaked silently past as I tapped the Huey's skids on the black forest's leafy roof. It required cooperation and concentration—and luck—from everybody if we hoped to yank our guys' asses out of there before the bad guys overran them. I looked out over the black ledge of the instrument panel or peered intently down through the chin bubble at my feet where foliage swirled dimly violent in the glow of my position lights. Sweat rolled from underneath my helmet and streamed down my face.

My gunner and crew chief, O'Brien and Renko, each took an open doorway and dropped down on his belly to act as observer, helmeted head stuck out into the darkness. I instructed them to drop the McGuire rigs. The two supporting Snakes rolled into racetrack mode, one behind the other, their miniguns sparkling and laying streams of red eating into the trees as they dived to the attack.

"Four-One, the lines are down," I reported to the ground patrol leader. "Get on."

"We can't!" The voice was strident, accusing, desperate, threatening, and terror-stricken. All at the same time. *"They're too short! The ropes are about ten feet above us. You gotta get lower."*

Lower? How? I already had the chopper nesting in leaves and limbs. Frantic thoughts raced through my mind. Options, Plan B.

There was only one way. One chance. Maybe.

"I'm coming down and under the trees," I radioed. "Throw a trip flare out in front of me so I can see."

68

Rotor tips whirred back illumination from the flare. Ahead of the helicopter and down through the trees toward the flare appeared a tunnel-like opening whose leafy walls were in turbulent motion from rotor wash. Staring through the chin bubble at my feet, I fixed the flare as my goal. I had to concentrate totally on one thing—getting us down inside the trees, inside the tunnel, by another ten feet. It didn't sound like much, but that was the height of a one-story building.

I eased cyclic forward and nudged the collective. As intended, the chopper responded slowly, inching through the explosive air and descending in a careful hover. Tree silhouettes rose on all sides, blocking out the horizon and stars except for those directly above. It was like floating on a dark sea while you gradually sank.

Mr. Stockton remained frozen. I wasn't sure he was even breathing. He undoubtedly wished he were somewhere else. He sat, as instructed, with his hands clasping his thighs and his feet pulled back from the pedals. I couldn't take the chance of four hands on the controls. One slip on the cyclic, a little too much rudder, an instinctive unintended grasping of the collective or throttle, and we faced the worst kind of fiery disaster. It was a one-man job where there was no room for error.

My legs felt iced in position on the rudder pedals, heels necessarily off the deck because my legs were so short. Even with the seat pushed all the way forward and the pedals extended, I was unable to brace my elbows on my knees for needed support. I was free-flying. I tried not to think of how a few inadvertent inches moving the helicopter one way or the other meant we were all goners. The four of us in the chopper and probably the five LRRPs directly below. Had I more strength in my hand and arm, I might have crushed the cyclic handle out of my intensity.

It was impossible to completely ignore enemy tracers bouncing all around inside the tunnel. Pilots who had been hit before said you heard this loud *tick!* when a bullet penetrated an aircraft's skin. So far, I hadn't heard it during my months of combat flying with the Headhunters. Tonight, I thought, would determine whether or not I really was charmed.

I sat in my own sweat and flew where a helicopter had never flown before. I let the bird slowly settle. The machine seemed alive and nervous at being trapped inside the wind tunnel. I eased forward until my blades were *underneath* the sprawling branches of a jungle giant directly in front. I settled bit by bit, inch by inch, and the noise of it all roared in my ears with the rush and pounding of my blood.

We were actually flying *inside* the forest.

O'Brien kept breathless watch out one cargo door, Renko out the other. I was almost disappointed that Shaky had left and missed this one.

Renko's voice whispered hoarsely through the intercom, as though a louder tone might startle me into catastrophe. "Don't bring your tail to the right," he warned.

"Why not?" My own voice sounded equally hoarse.

"There's a tree about six inches from the tail rotor."

"Don't go left," O'Brien put in. "Your tail boom is about a foot from a tree on this side."

Holy Jesus! I had brought the tail boom down between two trees. For an instant, for just that instant, I almost panicked. I thought my heart was going to leap out of my chest and take off. It was nasty, nerve-wracking business. A single slip of judgment and the aircraft beat itself to death, spraying pieces of metal and human flesh for a hundred yards in all directions.

The instant passed. I found myself once again in that strangely detached auto mode in which I performed mechanically while seemingly out of my body and watching from a distance. I knew I had a good chance of pulling this thing off if I could stay in that state of mind.

My entire world of the moment composed itself around me

inside that tunnel: engine sounds magnified in the close confines to deafening proportions; near total blackness softened only by my position lights and the flare burning dimly below; blades reflecting back the flare's sputtering light; green streaking tracers; dim tunnel leading down into eternity . . .

My aircrew continued providing guidance through the intercom. "Easy, easy, you can go down a little more, but don't wobble the tail boom. . . . We're cutting limbs on the left with the rotor! . . . *Mini-Man,* you got a foot or so on this side. . . . We've got limbs sticking through the chopper door. . . ."

Tree limbs and leaves and bark filled the air, banging and swirling frenetically, as in a storm.

"I'm gonna return fire!" O'Brien barked.

"Have at it," I said.

The dinks knew where we were anyhow from all the noise, the flare, and my position lights. I couldn't believe the bastards hadn't already shot us down.

O'Brien raked the jungle in the direction from which most of the green basketballs originated. The machine gun banged clapping against my ear drums. I heard O'Brien yelp with sudden insight.

His spray of bullets worked almost like a machete in clearing out foliage around us. He gave up on the enemy and concentrated instead on cutting jungle with the M60, enlarging the tunnel.

"Smart boy," I complimented him.

"Mr. Morris is gonna owe me a beer," he said over the rapid-clapping of his machine gun turned machete.

The worst part of this entire maneuver was that we had to do it *twice.* Even if I succeeded in reaching the LRRPs, there was no chance of pulling all five men up through the trees in one trip. Not from a vertical climbing hover. Far too much weight. Besides, I only carried three McGuire rigs. For the grunts, it was a lottery situation. Two of them had to remain behind. Their lives depended on Mighty Morris and Rouse duplicating my effort. O'Brien's discovery that he could enlarge

the tunnel contributed significantly to Three-Two's chances of
a repeat success. The odds against two choppers descending into
the jungle like this in one night decreased from impossible to
only improbable.

I came to a stationary hover. Any lower into the second,
thicker canopy meant certain suicide. Were we low enough? I
gave the order to drop the McGuires.

The radio almost exploded with shouts of exultation. *"We
got 'em! We got the ropes!"*

They suddenly realized there were only *three* lines.

"Mini-Man, *there's five of us!*"

I calmly explained that a second chopper was right behind
me ready to pick up the remaining two men. Captain Beatty
had once encountered a similar situation involving panicked
Vietnamese ARVN. They all wanted out on the same ship.
They damned near pulled down the helicopter with everyone
trying to crawl up the same ropes. The crew chief cut the lines
to avoid crashing.

Americans were different. It always astonished and humbled
me how self-sacrificing American GIs could be. Guys really *did*
throw themselves onto grenades to save their buddies.

"Okay, Mini-Man . . . *We're rigging up . . . Go! Get us out of
here!"*

The extraction had to be accomplished swiftly. Enemy soldiers attempting to move in on the remaining two LRRPs
banged away, filling the forest with their deadly insane fireflies
and basketballs. The withdrawal with recon men dangling on
the ropes, swaying the chopper, proved almost as stressful as
the approach. Renko guided me out while O'Brien resumed
clearing timber with his machine gun.

I talked myself through it. "I'm backing up . . . Watch me . . .
Watch the trees . . . Okay, hang on. I'm clear . . ."

We were above the forest suddenly, out of the tunnel. Stars
appeared astonishingly bright compared to from where we
had just surfaced. I continued up and forward, dragging the
poor LRRPs through the canopy. They swung wildly on their

tethers, bouncing off tree branches until they were suddenly jerked into open air, bursting out of the leaves and branches. It was a rough ride but a welcome discomfort compared to what the enemy had in store for them.

"Mini-Man, *I'm coming in on your tail!*" Mighty Morris radioed.

Although O'Brien had blown down a bunch of branches, making the tunnel larger again by half, it was still no LZ in there. Apache Three-Two showed no hesitation in taking over the nest as soon as I vacated it. I was so damned proud of Mr. Morris. Here he was, a short-timer, but still doing his job. There were still two guys in there—and the Headhunters left no one behind.

I swerved off to the west away from the firing and clawed for the safety of altitude while three grateful although battered GIs dangled below. I don't think I breathed for the next two or three minutes while I waited on word from Mighty Morris.

Then it came. "Mini-Man, *head for home plate. We have a home run.*"

I was so damned proud not only of Mighty Morris but also simply to be a part of such men. We let the LRRPs down at nearby FSB Barber; we had all earned our wooden nickels tonight.

My muscles were so tight I could hardly move my arms and legs now that everything was over. Stockton flew the chopper back to Tay Ninh while I slouched in my seat, spent. O'Brien checked for bullet holes as soon as we landed.

"None!" he declared.

Three-Two had several holes. Mighty Morris shook his head. I was still outrunning the law of averages. Don't look a gift horse in the mouth lest his teeth fall out.

69

DECEMBER 1969–FEBRUARY 1970

DECEMBER 15—President Nixon ordered the withdrawal of an additional 50,000 troops from Vietnam, bringing the total reduction to 115,000.

DECEMBER 20—Henry Cabot Lodge resigned as head negotiator in the Paris Peace Talks, citing complete deadlock in negotiations.

DECEMBER 31—The number of U.S. troops killed in Vietnam now totaled 40,024.

JANUARY 2—The VC New Year's truce ended.

JANUARY 17—VC ordered a massive guerilla campaign intended to destroy "Vietnamization" efforts.

JANUARY 31—Over one hundred bases were assaulted by Communist missile fire in the worst series of attacks since mid-1969.

FEBRUARY 2—U.S. B-52 bombers carried out heavy air strikes on the Ho Chi Minh Trail in response to increases in enemy activity.

FEBRUARY 12—NVA began a major offensive in Laos. U.S. aircraft began bombing in support of the Laotian government.

FEBRUARY 20—National Security Adviser Henry Kissinger began secret peace talks in Paris.

70

Major Powdrill recommended me for the DFC, Distinguished Flying Cross, for the "going down through the trees" episode. The very next day I was recommended for another Army Commendation with "V" for valor when Roff set his wounded bird down in a clearing and I went in and got him out. I figured that since the war wasn't going well, neither in Vietnam nor back home, the brass were looking to make heroes out of us that remained behind following troop withdrawals all over the country.

"Flying into the trees" was one thing—I probably deserved a medal—but the Roff crash had become more or less routine by this time. I really believed that it was my reputation that was attracting both attention and medals. The commander said flyers and troops all over the division were talking about *Mini-Man,* who flew into all the shit in the world and came out smelling as fresh as a rose. It made me increasingly nervous, everybody talking about it and my being *charmed* and all that. I was getting to be a short-timer; I didn't want to be jinxed so near the end of my tour.

I was flying lift in a Purple Team with Roff in White and Swede in Red when the scout pilot received fire. His tail jerked up the way the Loaches did when they were shot at. He took off skimming over the trees, fleeing. Swede made a gun run and I dropped down to direct Roff into a nearby clearing I had already located. His observer was wounded and his metal detector light had come on. Helicopters had an instrument that detected metal in the oil system. He was losing power fast.

O'Brien, my crew chief, and gunner Autberto Palma crowded into the one door on the enemy's side and hammered out a duet with their machine guns. I flew right on Roff's tail as we succeeded in clearing enemy positions and sliding into a clearing about two hundred meters away.

The observer wasn't hit bad. The crew grabbed their weapons and ammo. I lifted all three flyers back to Tay Ninh. Not a big deal—unless, of course, you were the one in the crash and needed out of there. Things like this happened all the time. They continued to happen, and I continued through some miracle to avoid gunfire.

Mighty Morris's orders came in a few days after Thanksgiving. We were supposed to have turkey for Thanksgiving, which we did, even though it came out of cans. I happened to be at the TOC when a Caribou from division headquarters at Phuoc Vinh arrived to deliver a satchel of mail and other papers. Morris's rotation orders were included. I took them and beelined for the O Club. It was after hours and most of the pilots not on standby were beginning a night of flying beer cans. The mongooses Pepe and Sam were running up and down the bar after a successful bout with a cobra, for which they were being justly rewarded with treats, and Mr. Morris had broken out his guitar.

> "Hooch maid on the green line sending spot reports,
> Calling in those rockets and mortars, of course;
> Here in Tay Ninh your life ain't worth five P,
> 'Cause you cannot get a transfer—
> Just another D-F-C. . . ."

"Then I guess you don't want this transfer," I shouted, brandishing his orders.

"What? *What?*"

He grabbed them out of my hand. He stared at them, transfixed. Other guys slapped him on the back in congratulations. He finally looked up at me. He sounded stunned, disbelieving.

"My God. My God," he croaked. "I've actually made it out of here. I survived it, *Mini-Man.* I survived."

71

Mini-Man, Blue Platoon's "Captain Blue," was feeling blue as the Christmas season approached. The mess cooks had prevailed upon the boonirats to bring back from the field a little evergreen-looking tree, like a cypress, which they decorated with lights and tinsel in the chow hall. One of the FNGs—to me, *everybody* in the troop was now an FNG with the exception of Farmer Farmer and Swede—decorated our bunk hooch with a wreath his mom sent him from Indiana. This was all intended to bring a little of home to us, but what it did instead was emphasize how pitiful were our attempts at alleviating homesickness.

I had always been a gregarious guy, a "party mouse" as Sandy put it, but lately as my DEROS approached I found myself pulling a Bird Dog or a Mighty Morris and sticking more and more to myself. If Mighty Morris had bequeathed me his guitar when he left, and if I could have played it, I would have been singing sad songs in the O Club at nights and drinking beer.

About all the "old guys" were gone. Most of them had DEROS'd stateside after their normal tours of duty expired. Others, like Ryberg, Jamison, Bleeker, a number of aircrew and even more of our boonirats, had gone home in body bags. You tried not to think about them because it underlined your own mortality. You almost forgot their names until you became a short-timer yourself. Then you started to think about what had happened and what could happen.

If Charlie had his way, there would be many more of us going home in body bags and silver coffins over Tet, the Vietnamese New Year's season. A lot of rumors, sometimes disguised as "intel," floated around about how the enemy planned a Christmas and New Year's present for us. Everybody in our AO expected massive attacks along the line of the 1968 Tet. Something was definitely happening out there. All through

December we encountered more enemy traffic than during any month since the summer. Bicycles, motorbikes, those little goofy French-looking trucks that could almost travel on footpaths, and people. Trails were beaten down. We found more rice caches. It appeared Charlie was forwarding supplies so he could make another deep surge toward Saigon.

If I weren't platoon leader with the responsibilities that entailed, I might have let down and looked forward to my thirty days of ass-and-trash beginning in January. As it was, however, I continued to take on many of the most hazardous missions myself. I couldn't let my men get killed while I watched from the sidelines.

In November, Major Powdrill had summoned me to headquarters to introduce me to a stocky lieutenant FNG with a rusty crewcut and deep lines around his mouth. He looked to be about twenty-five, a little older than many new pilots, but still fresh and innocent-looking and scared and naked with his bare upper lip.

"Captain Alexander, this is Lieutenant Joe Douglas," the major said. "I'm assigning him to your platoon. Take care of him."

Other than me, Douglas was the only commissioned officer in the platoon. All the other pilots were warrants. That meant one thing: this guy was my replacement, provided he proved himself capable. I took him under my wing like, in the homespun argot of Farmer Farmer, a fat duck on a pond with a new duckling. Like Captain Beatty had done for me.

"I'm not *asking* you not to let me down, Douglas," I said. "I'm *ordering* you not to let me down. And, Douglas, you're in the cavalry now. Grow a mustache."

Lieutenant Douglas was coming along. Major Powdrill took me aside for some one-on-one counseling.

"Ease off on yourself, Captain Alexander," he advised. "You've done more shit than most. You've got medals you can't even carry home. Don't you think it's about time you abandoned the *Mini-Man* character?"

I had been in-country ten months. *Mini-Man* still hadn't been hit. He had served me well. If I survived two more months, I was out of here and going home. That was when *Mini-Man* retired.

72

Former Blue lift pilot Meeker, whom I had sent to Loaches in exchange for Bird Dog when Bird Dog started getting shaky at the end of his tour, got shot out of the sky up near the Cambodian border. It was his second time being gunned down. Neither he nor his crew were injured. The extraction was more or less routine. We were all used to the procedure by this time.

Lieutenant Douglas flew my right seat. He had yet to come under fire. Consequently, none of this was more or less routine to *him*. We dropped off Meeker and his bunch at Tay Ninh, where we picked up three more lift ships and our platoon of Blue infantry to provide security while maintenance hooked up to the crashed Loach and pulled it out. Charlie prowled the area and I wanted to make sure we had sufficient firepower to keep him back. The maintenance Huey hovering over the Loach during the extraction provided a juicy target.

Meeker had gone down at one end of a large clearing. Maintenance guys hooked up to the Loach, slung it underneath, and tugged it swinging into the sky. Just then, at the other end of the clearing, boonirats on security encountered a concentration of NVA forces on its way to the scene. By the sustained crackling of the firelight, it was obvious the force was of some size.

Of course, we couldn't hear the shooting from altitude, but we saw the stabbing blinking of muzzle flashes, smoke and tracers. Our guys, overwhelmed by the odds, retreated across the open field, running like a football team after the kickoff. They dug in their heels in the opposite treeline, whereupon the fight resumed with the gooks in one treeline and our guys in the other, exchanging fire across the clearing. There was so much spiderwebbing of green and red across the meadow that a dragonfly would have avoided it. Our Blues wanted out of there in the worst possible way.

Douglas looked as though he could pull his helmet down to

about his knees and crawl into it. I remembered my own first missions. It was obvious he feared we might try to land in all that garbage. He needn't have worried. Even in my reckless early days I wouldn't have attempted to place a chopper directly in a crossfire.

"Mini-Man, *is there any place you can pick us up?*" the ground platoon leader asked. His name was Lieutenant Sorenson, also an FNG with that strident FNG first-time-under-fire voice.

"Four-Six?" I replied, looking over the terrain from two thousand feet above. "There's a small clearing less than two hundred meters directly behind you. If you can get your men through the trees to it, I think we can pick you up there."

"Roger that, Mini-Man."

Lieutenant Douglas's posture relaxed slightly. He looked relieved.

Several Cobras from our neighbor, Blue Max of the 2/20th, were in the air. We coordinated our resources and quickly planned tactics. I asked Blue Max if they could keep the bad guys pinned down and out of the large clearing long enough for our Blues to scurry back to the second clearing and be picked up.

"*It's Christmastime for Charlie,* Mini-Man," Blue Max leader said. "*We got lots of presents for the little suckers.*"

With that, the Cobras formed a racetrack and rolled in on the enemy positions one behind the other. I pitied the poor dinks when all that shit started falling on them. Talk about unfair logging practices when an entire strip of forest could be eradicated within minutes and turned to smoke and fire and kindling. One of the pilots sang while he worked.

> "*Here comes Santa Claus,*
> *Here comes Santa Claus,*
> *Right down Santa Claus Lane. . . .*"

"Jesus God, what's *wrong* with him?" Lieutenant Douglas cried over the intercom. "That lunatic is *singing.*"

"He enjoys his job."

"What kind of men *are* these . . . ?"

I didn't have time to explain it to him. He would understand soon enough.

I went down to fly over the second clearing for a quick look-see. It looked bigger from the air than actual size. Not only that, it was a daisy cutter opening. The Air Force sometimes dropped "daisy cutters," which were bombs on a stick, in order to clear forest. The sticks stuck in the ground and the bombs exploded about three feet above the surface, blasting down the surrounding forest but leaving snags and stumps. Hueys couldn't land here because of them. We would have to McGuire the platoon out.

Murphy's Law. Anything that could go wrong, would.

Boonirats were already bursting into the opening. When you were as spooked as they were, there was no such thing as being delayed by wait-a-minute vines. These guys were coming through the jungle like little bulldozers.

Palma, my crew chief, was already getting the McGuires ready. There was enough room over the clear-cut for two choppers to hover at the same time. I circled high and picked up my wing mate, Rouse. Mosby and Bijorian hovered at altitude, waiting to come in on second shift. Each of us, because of the ample size of the clearing, could hoist out four or five troopers. They traveled much lighter than LRRPs.

Rouse and I flew in low and side-by-side above the jungle. There was one brief span of time when we offered ourselves as targets to Charlie in the distant trees. Green tracers streaked past and between us, arcing as though lobbed. Once we reached the clearing, we dropped below the line of fire while we McGuire'd troops out of the field.

We were again vulnerable when we lifted out with boonirats strung on lines below us like fish. We had to come out slowly, affording even more tempting targets. The only thing that saved us was the long range. Even though Cobras were pounding the enemy, Charlie still spun tracer webs in the air. I understood how flies in an old haunted house must feel. Lieutenant Douglas *looked* like a fly about to be captured.

If we were scared, imagine the boonirats hanging exposed in the middle of the air with all that lead and steel flying. Several had to be pried from the ropes when we landed at the nearest FSB to bring them aboard. They were white-faced and speechless. One guy fell to his knees and threw up.

Douglas's hands trembled. So did mine, but I had become adept at concealing my fears. Even now, when I was a short-timer and my fears were magnified.

I threw Douglas's words back at him: "What kind of men *are* these? They are guys who'll go anywhere they have to in order to get you out. They're Headhunters. Look around you, Lieutenant. Soon, this will be all yours."

73

The most expensive small piece of real estate at Tay Ninh, perhaps in all of Vietnam, had to be the private bunker next to the volleyball court. No one presently on post knew the bunker's complete history, as it was now into its sixth or seventh generation of tenants. However, it was easy to see that it had started off essentially as a small hooch copied after the larger barracks. It had had screens from halfway up the walls and a tin roof. The only difference was that the lower half-walls were built of heavy mortar-stopping timbers the original architect had scrounged from somewhere.

Each resident thereafter had improved upon it according to the intensity of his short-timer paranoia, which could be considerable as I was discovering toward the end of my own tour. The timber walls rose to six feet in height, reinforced and landscaped on the exterior with sandbags. A roof was added of the same timbers, on top of which was laid heavy black plastic sheeting to weatherproof the little building. Rocket boxes filled with sand were stacked on top of the plastic, then a layer of sandbags, followed by pieces of heavy metal culvert cut in half lengthwise and laid with the curved sides facing upward to deflect incoming mortar rounds or rockets.

The screen door faced toward the center of the compound and had the added protection of opening next to the back of the supply hooch. Everyone agreed the bunker's fortunate owner was the safest man at Tay Ninh.

The original owner had simply abandoned it when he DE-ROS'd. Subsequent occupants recognized the little gold mine they controlled. The second guy sold it for ten dollars when he left. Like real estate everywhere to which improvements are made, it appreciated from owner to owner. The current resident reportedly paid fifty dollars for it.

On a relatively quiet Sunday afternoon while the ongoing

volleyball game raged, while Farmer Farmer was hunting for bamboo rats to shoot with his pistol and while some of the Blue boonirats were cheering on Yosemite Sam and Pepe LePhew in a fresh contest with a snake, I happened to notice a sign on the front of the bunker. Its current deed holder, a redheaded guy who flew Loaches, had received his orders. The sign said: FOR SALE. SEALED BIDS. ALL OFFERS CONSIDERED.

I looked it over like any young husband back in the States about to purchase a starter home for his family. I pointed out defects, such as poor lighting and a dirt floor. The scout nodded agreement. He had been sunbathing in shorts when I walked up. He leaned back in his chair against the outside wall and lit a cigarette while pretending interest in the volleyball game.

"A year or so ago," he began contemplatively, "there was a pilot here named Peters. See that barracks over there? That's where he stayed. He was like you, *Mini-Man*—had all the luck in the world. He made it right down to his DEROS date without so much as a hangnail. The night before he flew out of here to catch the Freedom Bird home, Charlie mortared the base. One of the rounds hit his barracks. Peters went home in a body bag."

He paused to draw on his cigarette. He looked at me with a grave expression and lifted one brow.

"You're a short-timer, *Mini-Man*. How many days do you have left?"

I immediately jotted down my bid on a scrap of paper and sealed it in an envelope. *One hundred dollars*. It was the highest bid. As soon as the scout moved out to go home, I moved in and started my own renovations.

The first thing I did was build a hardwood floor from rocket boxes. I paneled the walls likewise. I moved in my bunk with the mosquito netting around it, ran electricity from a generator, then added the little amenities that made a house a home—a reading lamp above the head of my bed; an electric fan; a tiny refrigerator; tape recorder; radio; TV; a little desk and chair in one corner; and my short-timer's calendar. My home was the envy of the post. I could probably sell it for two hundred dollars when I left.

The next time Charlie mortared the base, I awoke with a start as the *Crump! Crump! Cra-a-a-ck!* stomped around the flight line. My first reaction was to make a run for the culvert. Then I remembered where I was. I merely yawned and turned over in bed to go back to sleep.

"Goodnight, Sandy. I'll be home soon."

74

The American withdrawal from Vietnam escalated sharply after the summer of 1970. The 1st Cavalry Division, assigned to fill in the gap left by redeploying U.S. units, spread out even farther in an immense region of 4,536 square miles east of Saigon. The Cav's AO now spanned the width of the entire country from the Cambodian border through War Zone D all the way south to the South China Sea.

Beginning in February 1971, Vietnamese territorial forces gradually assumed guardianship of the AO's roads and hamlets while ARVN forces occupied former Cav fire support bases and LZs. Even though the division was scheduled to be withdrawn in April, it remained in constant combat until the last day. The First Battalion of the 5th Cavalry fought fifteen skirmishes against NVA units during its last week in the field.

On April 29, 1971, the 1st Cavalry Division (Airmobile) furled its flags and departed Vietnam for Fort Hood, Texas, leaving behind only the 3d Brigade "Gary Owen" Task Force. The 3d continued ops as a "mini-division" until June 26, 1972, when it was also redeployed from South Vietnam to relink with the rest of the division at Fort Hood.

The 1st Cavalry Division had sustained almost constant combat from September 18, 1965, until the last of the 3d Brigade left South Vietnam on June 26, 1972, more than six and a half years later. General James Gavin's vision of modern aerial cavalry had been tested—and proved in Vietnam's Helicopter War.

AFTERWORD

U.S. Army Captain Ron Alexander, call sign *Mini-Man*, rotated out of Vietnam on February 20, 1970. He returned to the United States as one of the most highly decorated helicopter pilots of the Vietnam War, having been awarded more than forty medals. Yet during twelve months of combat, not a helicopter he flew in action was so much as touched by enemy fire. It was a remarkable record, only short of being miraculous. He truly flew *charmed*. Not before or since has a pilot flown warplanes so extensively in action without being hit at least once.

Captain Alexander remained in the U.S. Army Reserves to become a member of the elite U.S. Army Special Forces (the Green Berets), where he served, among other assignments, as a company commander and as a group staff officer. He retired from the military in 1998 with the rank of lieutenant colonel.

He currently lives with his wife, Sandy, in Tulsa, Oklahoma, where he teaches high school math in the public school system.